BestMasters

Mit **„BestMasters“** zeichnet Springer die besten Masterarbeiten aus, die an renommierten Hochschulen in Deutschland, Österreich und der Schweiz entstanden sind. Die mit Höchstnote ausgezeichneten Arbeiten wurden durch Gutachter zur Veröffentlichung empfohlen und behandeln aktuelle Themen aus unterschiedlichen Fachgebieten der Naturwissenschaften, Psychologie, Sozialwissenschaften, Technik und Wirtschaftswissenschaften. Die Reihe wendet sich an Praktiker und Wissenschaftler gleichermaßen und soll insbesondere auch Nachwuchswissenschaftlern Orientierung geben.

Springer awards **“BestMasters”** to the best master’s theses which have been completed at renowned Universities in Germany, Austria, and Switzerland. The studies received highest marks and were recommended for publication by supervisors. They address current issues from various fields of research in natural sciences, psychology, social sciences, technology, and economics. The series addresses practitioners as well as scientists and, in particular, offers guidance for early stage researchers.

Milena Hake

Shopping in Virtual Stores

An Empirical Analysis of Customer Experience and Gen Z's Intention to Use Virtual Stores

Springer Gabler

Milena Hake
Hochschule Niederrhein University
of Applied Sciences
Krefeld, Germany

ISSN 2625-3577 ISSN 2625-3615 (electronic)
BestMasters
ISBN 978-3-658-48633-4 ISBN 978-3-658-48634-1 (eBook)
https://doi.org/10.1007/978-3-658-48634-1

This Springer Gabler imprint is published by the registered company Springer Fachmedien Wiesbaden GmbH, part of Springer Nature.
The registered company address is: Abraham-Lincoln-Str. 46, 65189 Wiesbaden, Germany

Danksagung

An dieser Stelle möchte ich mich bei meiner Betreuerin, Frau Prof. Dr. Silvia Zaharia, bedanken. Ihre wertvolle Unterstützung, ihre fachlichen Impulse und ihr offenes Ohr haben mich während der gesamten Entstehung dieser Arbeit begleitet. Besonders schätze ich, dass sie jederzeit erreichbar war und mir selbst in kritischen Momenten mit Rat und Tat zur Seite stand. Ihr Vertrauen in mich, ihre Geduld und ihr unermüdlicher Support haben mich immer wieder motiviert und bestärkt.

Mein Studium an der Hochschule Niederrhein war eine prägende und bereichernde Zeit, die mich sowohl fachlich als auch persönlich wachsen ließ. Die praxisnahe Lehre, die vielfältigen Entwicklungsmöglichkeiten und das inspirierende Umfeld haben diesen Weg besonders gemacht. Besonders Sie, liebe Professorin Silvia Zaharia, haben mir gezeigt, was es bedeutet, Studierende nicht nur zu lehren, sondern sie aktiv zu fördern und in ihrem Vorhaben zu bestärken. Sie sind zu einem meiner größten Female Role Models geworden. Eines Tages möchte ich all das, was Sie mir mit auf den Weg gegeben haben, weitergeben – jemanden pushen, unermüdlich supporten und so inspirieren, wie Sie es bei mir getan haben.

Ich danke Ihnen von ganzem Herzen für alles und freue mich auf alles, was noch kommt!

Ein ebenso großes Dankeschön gilt meiner Familie und meinen Freund:innen, vor allem Sophie und Kimberly, die immer an mich geglaubt und mich in jeder Phase unterstützt haben. Ohne euch wäre diese Arbeit in dieser Form nicht möglich gewesen.

Milena Hake

Abstract

This Master's thesis investigated shopping in virtual stores in virtual reality and aimed to find out whether the customer experience (CX) has an influence on Generation Z's intention to use virtual stores in the future and whether there are differences between people who are more inclined to use virtual stores in a virtual environment such as the metaverse. Understanding virtual stores as a new shopping channel is crucial to creating future online shopping experiences and engaging Generation Z as a brand. Firstly, 95 existing virtual stores were analyzed and characteristics and features of virtual stores were derived and compared with those of brick-and-mortar and e-commerce stores. The characteristics of virtual stores were then matched with the dimensions of the customer experience. An online survey was conducted with online shopper of Generation Z in Germany (N = 302). The evaluation was carried out using partial least squares structural equation modeling and multigroup analysis (MGA). The results show that sensory, social and immersive experiences are particularly important to Gen Z in virtual stores and have a significant influence on the customer experience in virtual stores. The emotional and cognitive dimensions have no significant influence on customer experience. The customer experience has a comparably weak influence on the behavioral intention to use virtual stores, so did the general customer experience. The evaluation of the characteristics using MGA showed that introverts have a higher intention to use virtual stores than extraverts, VR-inexperienced people than VR-experienced and non-gamers than gamers. In addition, the majority of Generation Z prefer a realistic virtual store design with features from both brick-and-mortar and e-commerce stores. These include product configuration, gamification, search function and history. This study contributes to research into consumer behavior and the future of online shopping in virtual stores. The findings have implications for both management and research with regard to the design of virtual stores and the creation of customer experiences using several store features.

Keywords: Consumer Behavior · Customer Experience · Immersive Experiences · Features of Virtual Stores · Generation Z · Intention to Use · Marketing · Metaverse · Retail · Virtual Commerce · Virtual Reality · Virtual Shopping · Virtual Stores · VR Glasses

Zusammenfassung

Diese Masterarbeit untersuchte das Einkaufen in virtuellen Läden in der virtuellen Realität und zielte darauf ab, herauszufinden, ob die Customer Experience einen Einfluss auf die Absicht der Generation Z hat, virtuelle Läden zukünftig zu nutzen, und ob es Unterschiede zwischen Personen gibt, die eher geneigt sind, virtuelle Läden zu nutzen. Das Verständnis für virtuelle Läden als neuen Einkaufskanal ist entscheidend, um als Marke oder Händler in Zukunft fesselnde Online-Einkaufserlebnisse für Konsumenten zu schaffen und die Generation Z als Marke zu gewinnen. Zunächst wurden 95 bestehende virtuelle Läden analysiert und die Eigenschaften und Merkmale (Features) virtueller Läden abgeleitet und mit denen von stationären Läden und Online-Shops verglichen. Die Features virtueller Läden wurden dann mit den Dimensionen der Customer Experience verknüpft. Es wurde eine Online-Befragung mit Online-Shoppern der Generation Z in Deutschland durchgeführt (N = 302). Die Auswertung erfolgte mittels Strukturgleichungsmodellierung (PLS-SEM) und Multigruppenanalyse (MGA). Die Ergebnisse zeigen, dass sensorische, soziale und immersive Erlebnisse für die Generation Z in virtuellen Läden besonders wichtig sind und einen signifikanten Einfluss auf die Customer Experience in virtuellen Läden haben. Die emotionalen und kognitiven Dimensionen haben keinen signifikanten Einfluss auf die Customer Experience. Die Customer Experience hat wiederum einen vergleichsweise schwachen Einfluss auf die Absicht der Generation Z, virtuelle Läden zu nutzen, ebenso wie die allgemeine Customer Experience. Die Auswertung der Merkmale mittels MGA zeigt, dass Introvertierte eine höhere Nutzungsabsicht für virtuelle Läden haben als Extravertierte, VR-unerfahrene Personen als

VR-erfahrene und Non-Gamer als Gamer. Für Gaming und vorherige Erfahrungen mit VR konnten keine signifikanten Einflüsse festgestellt werden. Darüber hinaus bevorzugt die Mehrheit der Generation Z ein realistisches Ladendesign mit Features von stationären Läden wie auch von Online-Shops. Dazu gehören Produktkonfiguration, Gamification, Suchfunktion und Suchhistorie. Die Masterarbeit trägt zur Erforschung des Verbraucherverhaltens und der Zukunft des Online-Shoppings und der Customer Experience in virtuellen Läden bei. Die Ergebnisse haben Auswirkungen sowohl auf das Management als auch auf die Forschung im Hinblick auf die Gestaltung virtueller Läden und die Schaffung von Einkaufserlebnissen mittels präferierter Features.

Schlüsselwörter: Einzelhandel · Generation Z · Immersive Erlebnisse · Konsumentenverhalten · Kundenerlebnis · Marketing · Merkmale virtueller Läden · Metaverse · Nutzungsabsicht · Virtual Commerce · Virtuelles Einkaufen · Virtuelle Läden · Virtuelle Realität · VR-Brillen

Contents

Abbreviations

3D	Three-Dimensional
ADQ	Additional Question
AI	Artificial Intelligence
API	Application Programming Interface
AR	Augmented Reality
AV	Augmented Virtuality
AVE	Average Variance Extracted
BI	Behavioral Intention to Use
C&F	Characteristics and Features
CAGR	Compound Annual Growth Rate
CB-SEM	Covariance-based Structural Equation Modeling
CEM	Customer Experience Management
CFI	Confidence Interval
COD	Cognitive Dimension
CTA-PLS	Confirmatory Tetrad Analysis
CX	Customer Experience
DAU	Daily Active User
DV	Discriminant Validity
EE	Enjoyment Experience
EMD	Emotional Dimension
FL	Fornell-Larcker Criterion
GAME	Gaming
GCX	General Customer Experience
Gen Z	Generation Z

GSCA	Generalized Structure Component Analysis
HCM	Hierarchical-Component Model
HMD	Head-Mounted Display
HOC	Higher-Order Construct, Higher-Order Component
HTMT	Heterotrait-Monotrait Ratio
IMD	Immersive Dimension
IQR	Interquartile Range Rule
IRV	Intra-individual Response Variability
KPI	Key Performance Indicator
LM	Linear Regression Model
LOC	Lower-Order Construct, Lower-Order Component
LVS	Latent Variable Score
MAMAA	Meta, Apple, Microsoft, Amazon, and Alphabet
Meta Commerce	Metaverse Commerce
MR	Mixed Reality
NFT	Non-Fungible Token
NYC	New York City
OLS	Ordinary Least Squares
PERS	Personality
PLS-SEM	Partial Least Squares Structural Equation Modeling
p_{min}	Minimum Path Coefficient
POS	Point-of-Sale
RV	Reality-Virtuality
SED	Sensory Dimension
SEM	Structural Equation Modeling
SOD	Social Dimension
SOR	Stimuli-Organism-Response
SRMR	Standardized Root Mean Square Residual
UGC	User-Generated Content
USD	United States Dollar
UTAUT	Unified Theory of Acceptance and Use of Technology
UTAUT2	Unified Theory of Acceptance and Use of Technology 2
VB2B	Virtual Business-to-Business
VB2C	Virtual Business-to-Consumer
V-Commerce	Virtual Commerce
VIF	Variance Inflation Factor
VR	Virtual Reality
VREX	VR Experience
XR	Extended Reality

List of Figures

List of Tables

Introduction 1

1.1 Into the Future of Shopping

"In the metaverse, online shopping becomes newly interactive, more fun and extremely engaging. Customers can try on anything virtually, from a new shade of lipstick to a new pair of boots, and see how they'd look in the real world. Engaging with products in a playful way takes consumers beyond a typical e-commerce transaction; it shapes a one-of-a-kind personalized, inclusive interaction that cultivates a deeper affinity for the brand." (Dogadkina, 2022)

The future of shopping is virtual. As the above quote from Olga Dogadkina, co-founder and CEO of Emperia, in an online article from Forbes Magazine suggests, this does not refer to traditional online shopping in e-commerce stores via the internet browser, but to completely new virtual reality (VR) shopping experiences in three-dimensional (3D) environments such as the metaverse (Ball, 2020a; Dogadkina, 2022; McDowell, 2020). Fueled by the increasing trend towards experience orientation on the part of the shopper (Ahlert, Kenning, & Brock, 2020a, p. 141).

On October 28, 2021, Mark Zuckerberg unveiled his vision of the metaverse at Meta Connect 2021 and postulated the metaverse as the successor to the mobile internet. He emphasized the almost infinite possibilities that this new metaverse era will bring and once again demonstrated the influence of the MAMAA (Meta, Apple, Microsoft, Amazon, and Alphabet)[1] on the market and all its participants (Meta Platforms, Inc., 2021a). Ever since, the metaverse has been referred to as

[1] Formerly known under the acronym FAANG (Facebook, Amazon, Apple, Netflix, Google) (Fernando, Boyle, and Rathburn, 2021).

M. Hake, *Shopping in Virtual Stores*, BestMasters,
https://doi.org/10.1007/978-3-658-48634-1_1

the next evolution stage of e-commerce and the next big thing since the internet (Barrera & Shah, 2023, p. 8; Byrnes, 2022). In the famous "Hype Cycle for Emerging Tech 2022", the metaverse was considered as one of the emerging technologies for 2022 (Perri, 2022a). There, the evolution as well as the expansion of immersive experiences are one of the three main topics covered by the 2022 technologies such as the metaverse. Moreover, the metaverse was indicated as the "Gartner Top Strategic Technology Trend for 2023" (Perri, 2022b).

Furthermore, the global market size of the metaverse is expected to reach USD 936.57 billion by 2030 and the metaverse market is expected to register a CAGR of 41.6% from 2023 to 2030[2], owing to increasing demand from end-use industries according to a new report by Grand View Research, Inc. (Grand View Research, 2021, 2023b). An analysis by McKinsey & Company (2022a, p. 1) shows that the metaverse has the potential to reach a value of up to five trillion US dollars by 2030, with e-commerce as the largest economic driver (USD 2.6 trillion). There are also many prominent actors who are already present in the metaverse and are working flat out to create this new era of immersive experiences, e.g., MAMMA, Epic Games, Nvidia, Roblox, and Unity (Arnoldy, Witt, Lütjen, & Kopankiewicz, 2022, p. 6; Grand View Research, 2023b).

This all sounds very promising, but why does e-commerce actually need a new experience? How are these virtual shopping experiences created and what role does the metaverse play in this? During the COVID-19 pandemic in 2020, the lockdown led to the closure of local retail stores[3], resulting in a significant shift in consumer behavior from offline to online shopping and the increasing use of e-commerce stores by consumers around the world (Chazan, 2020). When shopping online, consumers missed one thing in particular: the shopping experience from brick-and-mortar stores. They complained that it is not possible to touch and test products (e.g., size or color) and that the online customer service is not as good as in brick-and-mortar stores (PFSweb, Inc., 2021). With the advent of so-called virtual stores, the problem initially seemed to be solved. Compared to traditional, grid-based e-commerce stores, virtual stores created unique, immersive, virtual shopping experiences through e.g., augmented reality (AR) try-ons, product customization, chatbots, or video online shopping appointments with experts (McDowell, 2020). As Applin (2020) aptly described it: "A joyful

[2] Compared to the e-commerce expected global market size by 2023 of USD 6.3 trillion and a CAGR of 15.0% from 2023 to 2030, the expected global market size of the metaverse is already very large and its CAGR more than twice as high, emphasizing its potential (Baluch & Main, 2023; Grand View Research, 2023a). At first glance, the opportunities for this market, which has neither a clear name nor a uniform definition, appear to be good.

[3] Hereinafter referred to as brick-and-mortar stores.

twist on e-commerce" (Applin, 2020). The fun of shopping seemed to return (McDowell, 2020). But then, in 2021, the renaming of Facebook into Meta and the increasing attention for the metaverse catapulted this idea of virtual stores to the next level.

Although such virtual stores have been around for some time, as eBay and Myer had already jointly launched their first VR shopping experience together in 2016, this campaign by a MAMAA company attracted particularly attention (Matovina, Johns, Ward, & Dalton, 2016).

Hence today, virtual stores are more interesting than ever before, especially for brands. Why is this so? Well, without giving too much away: In line with the previous quote from Dogadkina (2022), in a virtual environment such as the metaverse, a network of 3D virtual worlds in which consumers can interact with their environment and everything and everyone in it in real time via their individual avatars, shopping experiences in virtual stores, especially via VR, take on a whole new meaning. For brands in particular, virtual stores can serve as the starting point for entering the metaverse (Obsess, 2021b).

To understand the growing interest in virtual stores, it is worth taking a brief trip back in time. The idea of a metaverse emerged much earlier. Exactly 32 years ago, science fiction author Neal Stephenson wrote about the metaverse, "a computer-generated universe", in his novel "Snow Crash" and put his idea of an immersive virtual world on paper, which seemed to replace the Internet with the help of VR glasses (Stephenson, 1992, p. 21). In 1995, W&V reported that "Freeport", the first virtual city in cyberspace, went online, where visitors could walk the streets of the city and go shopping in virtual retail stores (Lassak, 1995).[4] On June 23, 2003, the virtual world "Second Life" went online. Over the years, this platform lost relevance. The technology was probably not yet ready (Linden Research, Inc., 2023). Virtual shopping, as it was predicted at that time, initially remained an illusion.

However, with the emergence and establishment of new technologies such as the Meta Quest or the Apple Vision Pro, this vision of the future of shopping seemed to be becoming more and more of a reality. According to MacRumors, Apple has sold over 200,000 Apple Vision Pro headsets in just ten days as part of their very first sale in the United States (Clover, 2024). This clearly shows the great interest and demand for this technology on the part of consumers. At

[4] According to Lassak (1995), entering the cyber world by joining the Hamburg World Wide Web server with the help of the Hamburg agency Multiversum Media Lab would have cost DM 1,500 at the time. Additional pages would have cost 150 marks per page (up to a data volume of 50 kilobytes). In comparison, according to SAP (2024), a company today pays an annual fee of USD 200,000 for a virtual store from Obsess.

the same time, once again it signals the influence of a MAMAA company on the assertiveness, establishment and adoption of new technologies (J. Pfeiffer, 2023, p. 17). Moreover, this vision of the future of shopping is being driven by the emergence and increasing establishment of virtual worlds such as Roblox and Decentraland. Collaborations between companies such as Obsess or Emperia with companies such as Meta and Apple, which are jointly designing virtual store shopping experiences for well-known brands such as Lacoste, Alo Yoga or Mytheresa.com, are also making the vision of a metaverse a reality (Namogoo, 2022).

Since then, such collaborations have been running at full speed and the list of use cases is getting longer and longer. This development is likely to be of particular interest to brands when it comes to appealing to and winning over Generation Z (Gen Z) in the future. A study from the ECC Cologne and Salesforce.com (2022, p. 11), found out that especially young consumers (aged between 18 to 29 years) are optimistic and see virtual commerce (v-commerce) as a relevant development for online shopping in the future. Above all, brands should make targeted use of the potential for virtual stores in virtual worlds such as Roblox. In Q4 2023 alone, Roblox had around 71.5 million daily active users (DAUs) with a year-over-year growth of 22%, of which 29.3% were under 13 years old and 41.4% over 13 years old which promises significant brand reach on this platform (Roblox Corporation, 2024b, p. 22). In particular, it is Gen Z that spends most of its time in these virtual worlds with its community (Auxier & Arbanas, 2023; Roblox Corporation, 2023, p. 4).

But what exactly should such virtual shopping experiences look like? How can they be created with the help of virtual stores and how can Gen Z be inspired to ultimately use virtual stores?

Currently, virtual stores are still in their infancy. The concept will certainly continue to evolve with the establishment of technologies and the metaverse. However, it is already worth taking a closer look at how the new shopping channel "virtual stores" can be used in a meaningful and successful way for the benefit of both companies and consumers compared to traditional shopping channels such as brick-and-mortar and e-commerce stores. This automatically leads to the next chapter.

1.2 Problem Statement and Research Objectives

In mid-2023, it was said that the metaverse hype was over and that the future belonged to artificial intelligence (AI), especially generative AI (GenAI) (Zitron, 2023).[5] Suddenly, the metaverse was no longer part of "Gartner's Hype Cycle for New Technologies" (Willemsen, 2023). But at the end of 2023, Apple Inc. (2023a) presented its Apple Vision Pro. Only this time not under the term metaverse, as was the case with Meta in 2021, but everything under the umbrella term "Spatial Computing" (Apple Inc., 2023a; Meta Platforms, Inc., 2021a). The world suddenly began to turn around again. The event triggered a renewed wave of enthusiasm for what was once again prophesied to be a new era (Solis, 2024).

Consumers in particular seemed to show great interest in this technology and could hardly wait for this device to be launched on the market, which at the same time promised an increase in the acceptance of this new technology (Gurman, 2024). Gartner also suddenly took up the topic again in its Impact Radar for 2024 (Perri, 2024). Solis (2024), a Forbe's contributor, agrees that spatial computing is a further step towards the establishment of a metaverse.

This shows once again how unpredictable and fast-moving this topic is. At the same time, however, it also underlines the need for research in this area, particularly with regard to consumer behavior. Some authors have already taken up the topic and are pursuing a similar objective (see Chap. 3). It is therefore time to take up and examine this topic, especially in research on consumer behavior. Only in this way the topic create sustainable added value and at the same time establish a uniform understanding. The aim of this work is therefore to find a generally acceptable definition of the metaverse and to provide a comprehensive overview of shopping experiences in virtual stores in the metaverse. In order not to be so dependent on the fast moving nature of this area, the entire work uses the latest developments on the one hand and traditional elements that have proven themselves in terms of consumer behavior in the past and continue to do so today on the other. As this topic is so new and difficult to grasp, companies do not know where to start and how to create such experiences. This in turn makes it difficult to scale (see Sect. 2.4.2). The great uncertainty surrounding platforms such as Meta Horizon Worlds, Roblox, etc. in terms of their assertiveness also means that companies are not necessarily exploiting their full potential. The effect of customer experiences (CX) on these platforms and in the metaverse in general has also hardly been researched. Some companies are already experimenting with

[5] Fun fact: One requires the other, and GenAI is increasingly being used to create virtual stores (Flora, 2023).

this, but the costs are often very high (Repp, Horvat, Michel, & Maier, 2023). In order to counteract this and demonstrate the potential of virtual stores and increase their attractiveness for companies, this work aims to provide initial starting points to encourage companies to use virtual stores. The involvement of Gen Z is particularly important. After all, what benefit is there if virtual stores are not used? Hence, another aim is to develop a timeless model that can be used in the future by researchers as well as companies and brands to design virtual stores.

But what does it take for virtual stores to create a shopping experience and convince consumers to use them in the future? The trend towards experience orientation has long been known from stationary retail in terms of point-of-sale (POS) marketing (e.g., Ahlert, Kenning, & Brock, 2020b; Gröppel-Klein, 1991, 2012; Haeusel, 2012). E-Commerce is also increasingly interested in designing shopping experiences (e.g., Heinemann, 2022; Kollmann, 2019).

This is particularly fueled by the increasing experience orientation on the part of consumers (Ahlert et al., 2020a, p. 141). Virtual stores are similar in their design to brick-and-mortar stores. At the same time, they have characteristics and features (C&F) that are familiar from e-commerce stores, such as 24/7 accessibility, convenient shopping from home and personalization (DuBoff, 2021). It is interesting to find out which C&F of the experience that are familiar from both, brick-and-mortar as well as e-commerce stores, also apply to virtual stores from the consumer's perspective.

The following research questions arise in order to ultimately pave the way for companies to enter the metaverse in terms of establishing virtual stores, as well as to successfully exploit the potential of virtual stores and offer consumers a unique shopping experience in order to stand out from the competition and successfully position themselves in the market in the long term:

Research Question 1.

What influence does the customer experience have on Generation Z's intention to use virtual stores and what are the determinants of the customer experience?

Research Question 2.

Is the effect of customer experience and general customer experience on behavioral intention significantly different depending on different consumer characteristics?

Research Question 3.

> *What should virtual stores look like in virtual environments such as the metaverse (including virtual store design, features and characteristics / stand-alone virtual stores, shopping centers, malls, or cities / physical products or NFTs)?*

The research objectives are therefore (1) to find a generally acceptable definition of the metaverse and to provide a comprehensive overview of shopping experiences in virtual stores in the metaverse, (2) to find out whether the CX has an influence on Gen Z's intention to use virtual stores in the future and (3) if there are differences between people who are more inclined to use virtual stores. Beyond that, (4) to provide initial starting points to encourage companies to use virtual stores, (5) to develop a timeless model that can be used in the future by researchers as well as by companies and brands to design virtual stores, (6) to find out which elements of the experience that are known from both brick-and-mortar and e-commerce stores also apply to virtual stores from the consumer's point of view and which other features can be used in virtual stores.

The release of the Apple Vision Pro and Apple's drive to establish use cases with it, shows that there is huge hidden potential in this topic. When it comes to new technologies, it is more important than anything to investigate consumer behavior and willingness to adapt and use this new technology. Hence, their feedback is a valuable contribution to its success. Based on this, the following work aims to not only investigate the shopping in virtual stores but particularly to investigate the opinion of consumers to this topic and to find out, what virtual stores need according to them, to create experiences in virtual stores.

1.3 Structure of the Thesis

The work is divided into two main parts: a theoretical and an empirical part. The theoretical part will first lay the definitional foundations in order to obtain a uniform picture of shopping in virtual stores in virtual environments such as the metaverse (see Chap. 2). This is because there is currently neither a uniformly used term nor a collective understanding of it. This is followed by an in-depth look at virtual stores as a new shopping channel. Various types of virtual stores are presented, their characteristics and features, and how they differ from or are similar to other shopping channels in terms of their characteristics and features. For this purpose, a list is created containing the characteristics and features identified for each channel—brick-and-mortar stores, e-commerce stores and virtual stores. In addition, the advantages and disadvantages of virtual stores are examined from both a consumer and a company perspective. Chap. 3 builds on the findings from the second chapter. First, the concept of CX and its dimensions are introduced. Then, based on the findings from the previous chapters and a literature review, those dimensions are identified that suit the intended research project and the novelty of the topic. In addition, findings from a qualitative preliminary study on metaverse commerce (meta commerce) conducted by the author and his fellow students together with Prof. Dr. Zaharia in the winter semester 2022/23 are used, which are also incorporated into the research context. The aim is to examine the shopping experience in virtual stores more closely and to pair the previously identified characteristics and features of virtual stores with the dimensions of the CX. The research questions and objectives on which the work is based are then derived.

This is followed by the empirical part, introduced by Chap. 4. The chapter is structured according to the previously derived research questions and objectives.

The theoretical explanatory model is developed, potentially discriminatory consumer characteristics are discussed, the need for further findings on virtual stores is emphasized and corresponding hypotheses are formulated. Chap. 5 is dedicated to the methodology and operationalization of the study. This is followed by the data analysis in Chap. 6. Chapter 7 forms the final part of the thesis and consists of (1) a summary of the core results to answer the research questions posed, (2) the derivation of strategic implications and (3) the discussion of limitations of the thesis as well as the identification of starting points for further research projects.

2 Shopping in Virtual Stores

2.1 Terminology

The metaverse is a network of various virtual worlds creating an immersive 3D virtual environment that exists alongside the real world (Sect. 2.1.1). It can be accessed via several devices such as head-mounted displays (HMD), e.g., VR glasses (Sects. 2.1.1 and 2.1.2). With the help of avatars, people can interact with other people or other virtual representatives, like shopping assistants, as well as with objects, e.g., products (Sect. 2.1.5). Meta, a company once known as Facebook, sees the metaverse as "[…] the next evolution of social connection and the successor to the mobile internet" (Meta Platforms, Inc., 2023b). Therefore, Vishal Shah, Vice President at Meta, says that "commerce is going to be a big part of that Metaverse" (Shah & Aina, 2023; Weiß, 2023). However, before exploring how the metaverse will revolutionize the way consumers shop and unprecedented experiences will be created (Sect. 2.1.3 and 2.1.4), it is important to first explain the key terms. This will be done in the following chapters.

2.1.1 Metaverse

Metaverse, a portmanteau of the prefix "meta" (meaning beyond) and the word "universe" (L.-H. Lee et al., 2021, p. 1). First of all, it is very important and fundamental to understand what exactly the metaverse is. Unlike the internet,

Supplementary Information The online version contains supplementary material available at https://doi.org/10.1007/978-3-658-48634-1_2.

M. Hake, *Shopping in Virtual Stores*, BestMasters,
https://doi.org/10.1007/978-3-658-48634-1_2

there is neither a standardized metaverse nor a well-established definition of it. One reason for this is certainly its novel appearance.

Hardly anyone currently knows exactly what the metaverse is, but there are many ideas and visions about what it could and will be. Among these, there are also some definitions that are already widely accepted. A few of them are discussed later. First of all, it is interesting to find out where the metaverse originally came from.

The Origin of the Metaverse

The idea of a metaverse is actually not all that new. It first came up around 1984 in William Gibson's science fiction novel "Neuromancer" in which Gibson created "Cyber Space", a synonym for the emerging internet (Gibson, 1994). The term "metaverse" itself was first coined by Neal Stephenson in June 1992, when he published his science fiction novel "Snow Crash" (Stephenson, 1992). In his novel, Stephenson sees the metaverse as an "imaginary, […] computer-generated universe [that the computer of protagonist Hiro projects] onto his VR glasses" (Stephenson, 2022, p. 28). In both novels, "Cyber Space" and "Metaverse" metaphorically stand for a dystopian 3D internet (Songuer, 2022).

When the books were published, the now standardized World Wide Web was just in its infancy. So, narratives about the 3D internet and virtual environments like these seemed very visionary and very far from becoming reality.[1] Thus, both "Neuromancer" and "Snow Crash" were originally created not to make predictions about the future, but as commercial entertainment pieces. However, with the advent of advanced technologies, the latter no longer seems so unrealistic, and it seems that both books have greatly influenced the language and thinking about what digital worlds might look like in the future (J. Pfeiffer, 2023, p. 11; Songuer, 2022).

In 2011, Ernest Cline expanded on the metaverse concept in his novel "Ready Player One" with "Oasis", a VR platform, that requires VR glasses and a haptic input device to access. Cline (2011, p. 170) also mentions the use of more complex technologies such as haptic full-body suits in combination with treadmills. Steven Spielberg, Hollywood's most famous director according to IMDb, adapted Cline's novel into a movie in 2018 under the same name (IMDb, 2024a, 2024b). At the same time, the technology was getting better and better. The metaverse no longer seemed so far away and the authors' earlier visions seemed to become

[1] In an interview in Kevin Scott's podcast "Behind The Tech", Neal Stephenson himself commented on his novel Snow Crash and the current state of the metaverse: "Metaverse is kinda a catch-all term for stuff that people want you to buy a few years from now. And by process of elimination t's got to be something beyond screens" (starting at min. 21:30; Scott (2022).

tangible. But it was the act of a MAMAA company that brought the metaverse to the fore: renaming Facebook into Meta.

In 2021, Meta announced the renaming of Facebook into Meta at its annual developer conference "Connect" and used Stephenson's term "metaverse" to introduce the world to the company's new vision and, at the same time, its vision of the internet of the future (Velazco, 2021). Out of nowhere, the metaverse suddenly began to attract a lot of attention. Indirectly, Meta declared itself the inventor and pioneer of the emerging metaverse, even though, as already pointed out, the term had already existed for 30 years. This once again underlines the importance of these companies' activities and their impact on awareness and mass adoption of new technologies. It remains exciting to see how things will develop.

Definition of the Metaverse

Nevertheless, the first ideas about a metaverse came from science fiction. Since then, many different definitions of the metaverse occurred and it seemed that everyone dealing with this topic, tried to find a comprehensive and widely accepted definition of it (e.g., Davis, Murphy, Owens, Khazanchi, & Zigurs, 2009; L.-H. Lee et al., 2021; Park & Kim, 2022). So did Ball (2020a). Matthew Ball, CEO of Venture Capital and advisory firm Epyllion Industries, has stepped up to the plate in 2020 to share his understanding and interpretation of the metaverse based on these previously developed fictional ideas (Ball, 2020b). Two years later in 2022, he published his book "The Metaverse and How It Will Revolutionize Everything", in which he depicts the metaverse and anything related to it (Ball, 2022). The Economist (2022) reviewed his book, saying, "Mr. Ball's summary of the history of virtual worlds, both in fiction and in computer science, provides helpful context. But the most valuable contribution of his book may turn out to be his definition of the metaverse… […]". Unlike the other definitions, his definition of the metaverse has received a great deal of attention and acceptance (Haas, 2022). For this reason, Ball's definition of the metaverse also serves as the basis for this work. Ball (2022, p. 29) defines the metaverse as follows:

> *"A massively scaled and interoperable network of real-time rendered 3D virtual worlds that can be experienced synchronously and persistently by an effectively unlimited number of users with an individual sense of presence, and with continuity of data, such as identity, history, entitlements, objects, communications, and payments."* (p. 29)

In his opinion, the metaverse is based on virtual worlds that are originally known from video games or movies.

Therefore, in addition to his definition of the metaverse, his definition of virtual worlds must also be taken into account in this work. Ball (2022, p. 30) defines virtual worlds as follows:

> *"Virtual Worlds refer to any computer-generated simulated environment. These environments can be in immersive 3D, 2.5D (also known as isometric 3D), 2D, layered atop the "real world" via augmented reality, or purely text-based, as in the game-like MUDs [multi-user dungeons] and non-game like MUSHs [multi-user shared hallucinations] of the 1970s. These worlds can have no individual user [...]. In other cases, they might be limited to a single user [...]. These users might affect and be affected by this virtual world through any number of devices, such as keyboard, motion sensor, or even a camera that tracks their motion."* (p. 30)

According to Ball (2022), virtual worlds can be an exact replica of the real world which are also referred to as "digital twins". Furthermore, virtual worlds can be a "fictionalized version" of the real world or a completely fictional reality in which, unlike in the real world, anything seems possible. Virtual worlds can be game-like or non-game-like. Game-like means that a goal is pursued, such as winning, scoring or defeating, whereas non-game-like includes, e.g., commerce, socializing, fitness and more (Ball, 2022, p. 30).[2] Hence, the following work focuses on non-game-like virtual worlds, more precisely on commerce (Sects. 2.1.3 and 2.1.4). Another apt definition of virtual worlds stems from I. G. Krasonikolakis, Vrechopoulos, and Pouloudi (2011). They define virtual worlds as "[3D] environments where users engage in numerous activities through their in-world representatives, the so-called avatars" (I. G. Krasonikolakis et al., 2011, p. 59). Next to his definition, Matthew Ball also highlights characteristics of virtual worlds in his book. These include: 3D, real-time rendering, interoperability, massive scaling, persistence, and synchronicity (Ball, 2022, pp. 33–57). Well-known platforms that are often referred to as virtual worlds and have almost all the aforementioned characteristics established by Ball (2022) include Fortnite, Roblox, Decentraland, Spatial, Meta Horizon Worlds, The Sandbox, Sim City and Second Life. One platform in particular has attracted a lot of interest recently: *Roblox*. Why is that?

This will become clear in the next chapters. In addition, there are numerous other definitions of the metaverse, which essentially almost always address

[2] The analysis of virtual stores in Sect. 2.2 has shown that virtual worlds cannot be clearly divided into game-like and non-game-like virtual worlds, as defined by Ball (2020, p. 30). This is because there are virtual worlds such as Roblox, which according to Ball's definition represent game-like virtual worlds, but also contain commerce, which Ball defines as non-game-like virtual worlds.

the same definitional aspects of the metaverse (e.g., Bundesverband Digitale Wirtschaft [BVDW], 2023; Capgemini Research Institute, 2022; Guibert, 2023; Hackl, 2021, 2023; Zuckerberg, 2021):

- The metaverse is a massively scaled,
- three-dimensional,
- real-time-rendered,
- decentralized,
- virtual environment,
- which is interoperable, and
- perpetual, i.e., does not disappear, and
- which can be visited by avatars,
- unlimited in the number of simultaneous users.

Nevertheless, both scientists and economists lack a common understanding of the metaverse and at present, everyone still has a slightly different understanding of it. One reason for this could be that the metaverse is still more of an idea than a reality (Hackl, 2023, p. 7). Furthermore, its understanding is constantly changing with the advent of new and improved technologies and their accessibility, e.g., the launch and availability of the Apple Vision Pro (Apple Inc., 2024b; McKinsey & Company, 2022a, p. 1). In the context of this work, these definitions provide a necessary foundation to understand the world in which unprecedented shopping experiences could take place in the future and in which consumers may spend much of their time (Meta Platforms, Inc., 2023b).

At its core, the metaverse is seen as a virtual environment consisting of a multitude of virtual worlds that exist alongside the real world and can be accessed in different ways for different purposes, for example via VR devices or conventional screens. Moreover, in business contexts, a distinction is made between three different types or sectors of metaverses: The Enterprise Metaverse, the Industrial Metaverse, and the Consumer Metaverse (MIT Technology Review Insights & Siemens, 2023, p. 6; Whiting, 2023; World Economic Forum & Accenture, 2023, p. 5). Within the Enterprise Metaverse it is investigated how the future of work could look like. This involves investigating technologies that can enable immersive collaboration in companies, including productivity tools and virtual workspaces (MIT Technology Review Insights & Siemens, 2023, p. 6).

A famous example, which also gained several "Drum Awards" recently, is "EYVerse", established by EY's Metaverse Lab. It incorporates not only the Enterprise Metaverse sector but especially the Industry Metaverse. Within EYVerse, several use cases are investigated, not only about the future of work, but also on Internet of Things (IoT) and digital twins, which are examples for the Industrial Metaverse (The Drum Awards, 2023). The Industrial Metaverse explores what the future of industry could look like. This includes technologies such as simulated factories, machines, logistics, networks and other highly complex systems that can map and help solve real-life problems in industry and manufacturing (MIT Technology Review Insights & Siemens, 2023, p. 6). The following work concentrates entirely on the Consumer Metaverse, which is concerned with exploring virtual worlds and immersive shopping, gaming, socializing and entertainment experiences (MIT Technology Review Insights & Siemens, 2023, p. 6). A study by McKinsey & Company (2022a, p. 2) found that metaverse consumers are enthusiastic about moving their lives to the metaverse, with nearly six in ten of these consumers preferring at least one experience in the metaverse over its physical alternative. Shopping for physical or virtual goods is the most popular activity for consumers in the metaverse (79%) (McKinsey & Company, 2022a, p. 2). The focus of this work lies on exactly this: shopping in virtual worlds and the creation of immersive experiences. So what could these virtual shopping experiences in virtual worlds look like in the metaverse? The next section is dedicated to answering this question.

But first it needs to be clarified how we get there. Because so far it has been briefly mentioned, but not dealt with in detail: What is needed to realize a metaverse? The so-called building blocks of the metaverse are essential for its realization. According to Hackl (2023, pp. 11–20) there are eight in total, including: Spatial Computing[3], AI, Blockchain, NFTs and Virtual Assets, Gaming, VR and AR, 5G and advanced networks as well as Social Media. L.-H. Lee et al. (2021, pp. 1–3) speak of "the Metaverse enabling technologies" that are extended reality (XR), user interactivity (HCI), AI, blockchain, computer vision, IoT and robotics, edge and cloud computing. Moreover, they summarize six factors of user centricity, including avatars, content creation, virtual economy, social acceptability, security and privacy, trust and accountability (L.-H. Lee et al., 2021, pp. 1–3).

VR as a building block of the metaverse is important in the context of this study, as it represents the underlying technology that will be used to enter virtual

[3] According to ByondXR (2023), spatial computing actually arises from the combination of three technologies that are mentioned by Hackl (2023), but not in connection with spatial computing. These include AR, VR and MR. In addition to these, 3D modelling and visualization as well as photogrammetry and 3D scanning are also included. With VR, spatial computing also includes the technology that plays a significant role in the development of virtual stores.

stores in the future. Hence, VR is explained in more detail in the following section.

2.1.2 Virtual Reality

As already discussed in Sect. 2.1.1, the metaverse includes environments that can be in AR, VR, and mixed reality (MR). The differences between these are explained below using the revised reality-virtuality continuum by Skarbez, Smith, and Whitton (2021). Furthermore, the one technology that is the focus of this work is highlighted: VR. VR is an abbreviation for the English term "virtual reality". To give a lexical definition of it first, the Oxford Learner's Dictionaries (2024) defines it as "made to appear to exist by the use of computer software, [e.g.,] on the internet".

In 1994, Milgram and Kishino established the so-called reality-virtuality (RV) continuum, which defines the different technologies such as AR, VR and MR and how they can be differentiated from one another (Milgram, Takemura, Utsumi, & Kishino, 1994, p. 283). In addition, they established a 3D taxonomic framework that can be used to further categorize MR displays (Milgram et al., 1994, p. 291). Since then, it has been used and continuously adapted for the research and development of VR and AR.

In 2021, Skarbez et al. (2021) claimed that the original RV continuum by Milgram and Kishino (1994) is not contemporary anymore, particularly due to the acceleration of technological progress in recent years (Skarbez et al., 2021, p. 1). Therefore, the authors presented a revised RV continuum and made several arguments as to why the original version of Milgram and Kishino's RV continuum is outdated. First, Skarbez et al. (2021) criticize the fact that Milgram and Kishino's RV continuum only takes into account visual displays and display hardware neglecting others, such as haptic or sound devices. Secondly, they point out that the original version would only consider "observers / users" with past life experiences and the visual sense of sight, but other senses like hearing, smell, touch and taste would have been totally neglected. Furthermore, they criticize the fact that the overall experience is not considered further. In their opinion, it is important to take a holistic view of the technology used, the content provided and the resulting user experience.

Finally, they argue that the existence of a perfect, complete VR, as proposed by Milgram and Kishino (1994), is unrealistic as they believe it cannot be achieved (Skarbez et al., 2021, pp. 2–3). Since this work focuses on VR technologies such as VR glasses and the resulting CX, which includes the appeal to nearly all senses, the revision by Skarbez et al. seems more suitable than the original by Milgram and Kishino (1994).

The revised RV continuum by Skarbez et al. (2021) is illustrated in Fig. 2.1. Similar to the original version, it consists of two ends, with the left end being the "real environment" that contains only real objects, while the right end is not the "external virtual environment" as it was in the original version, traditionally referred to as VR, but a "matrix-like virtual environment" that they added right after the "external virtual environment". Both, the real environment as well as the external virtual environment are subordinates of MR environments, meaning that they are part of the MR spectrum. Between the real environment and the external virtual environment, there is AR and augmented virtuality (AV). AR describes MR environments enhanced with virtual content, and AV those MR environments in which the content is mainly virtual. Skarbez et al. (2021, p. 3) argue that, unlike the real and external virtual environments, the matrix-like environment would be the only environment capable of existing outside the spectrum of MR (Skarbez et al., 2021, p. 3).

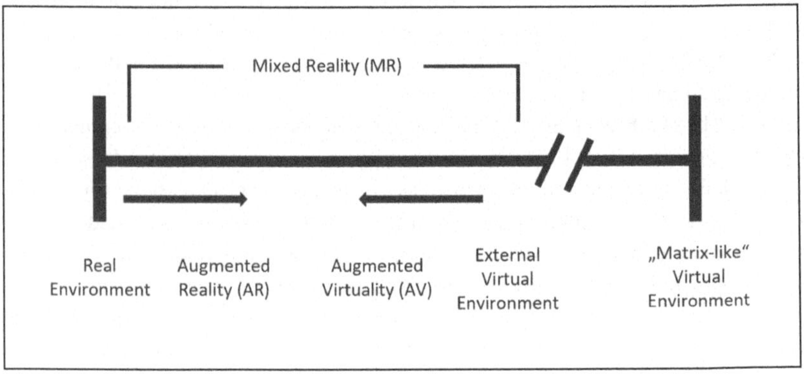

Fig. 2.1 Revised Reality-Virtuality Continuum. (*Note.* Adapted from *Revisiting Milgram and Kishino's Reality-Virtuality Continuum* (p. 3), by Skarbez et al. (2021))

Skarbez et al. (2021) unify several definitions of MR that were developed after the appearance of Milgram and Kishino's original MR definition by slightly but fundamentally adapting the original definition.

They propose the following MR definition:

> *"A mixed reality (MR) environment is one in which real world and virtual objects and stimuli are presented together within a single precept. That is, when a user simultaneously perceives both real and virtual content, including across different senses, that user is experiencing mixed reality[4]" (Skarbez et al., 2021, p. 4).*

The authors agree with the original definition in that they also subsume AR under MR. However, unlike Milgram and Kishino (1994), the authors are of the opinion that external virtual environments are also included, but are not understood as the other endpoint. This is because in the context of external virtual environments, not only virtual content is perceived with the senses during the VR experience, but in their opinion, real content can also be perceived by other senses at the same time. When experiencing both, virtual and matrix-like environments, Skarbez et al. (2021) distinguish between exteroceptive and interoceptive senses. Exteroceptive senses relate to those senses that come "from outside the body", i.e., the basic senses such as sight, hearing, touch, smell and taste, while interoceptive senses are senses that "monitor the body's internal state", like the proprioceptive and vestibular senses. Exteroceptive senses can nowadays be addressed and influenced relatively easily by computer-generated stimuli, which makes them very easy to control too, unlike the interoceptive senses, which are non-manipulable. Skarbez et al. (2021) also speak of a "sensory conflict" (Skarbez et al., 2021, p. 3). According to the authors, this sensory conflict can only be resolved in a matrix-like environment. Here, the authors refer to the science fiction film "Matrix" from 1999, in which "a person's sensory organs are in some way disconnected from their brain such that both interoceptive (e.g., proprioception) and exteroceptive (e.g., sight) senses are stimulated by technology" (Skarbez et al., 2021, p. 3).

In their opinion, external virtual environments can only be experienced through exteroceptive senses, thus interoceptive senses cannot be manipulated by external virtual environments. To return to the above: For them, perfect VR, as described by Milgram and Kishino (1994), is only possible if all senses—exteroceptive as well as interoceptive—can be fully manipulated by computer-generated content, and this, can only be the case in Matrix-like environments, as mentioned earlier (Skarbez et al., 2021, p. 4). VR is a digital, artificially created world that is created and experienced with the help of special, so-called immersive technology, including both, software and hardware. Users gain access to it via HEMs

[4] Xi and Hamari (2021) also emphasize that VR should not only be defined on the basis of its technology, but based on its effect that VR "substitutes the current reality we perceive" (p. 47). "VR is related to substituting any and all of our senses, and therefore it logically follows that VR has to be "sense-agnostic" in its definition" (Xi & Hamari, 2021, p. 47).

such as VR glasses (Suh & Prophet, 2018, p. 79). In order to be able to interact with the virtual world, controllers are usually used in addition to VR glasses.[5]

If users put on such VR glasses (and take the corresponding controllers in their hands), they can fully immerse themselves in the 3D virtual world and explore it in a 360-degree view (= all-round view). It then can feel to them as if they were actually there, in a completely different world (Regt & Barnes, 2019, p. 20; Suh & Prophet, 2018, p. 79; Xi & Hamari, 2021, p. 38). Javornik (2016) defines virtuality as the ability of a device, e.g., VR glasses, to simulate a virtual world or virtual elements with the help of computer graphics and to give the user the feeling of being immersed in the simulated virtual world and actually being there (Javornik, 2016, p. 255). Javornik (2016) differentiates between virtuality and AR and concludes that the main distinction between those two is that while AR is embedded into physical reality, VR is totally separated from it. This definition is also followed by several other authors.

Xi and Hamari (2021) define VR as "technologies for substituting the perceived reality" and underline the special feature of VR compared to AR: With VR devices such as head-mounted displays or CAVE headsets, users no longer just look at a screen, but are part of it, have full control over their movements and navigation in 3D virtual worlds and feel as if they are actually there (Xi & Hamari, 2021, p. 38). In line with Whyte (2002), VR can be primarily defined by its four main characteristics: immersion, interactivity, 3D, and real-time response to action (Whyte, 2002, p. 3; also see Skarbez et al., 2021, p. 7 or McKinsey & Company, 2022b, p. 11).

In their latest report "Total immersion" about immersive experiences, the Capgemini Research Institute (2022, p. 5) also distinguishes between AR, MR and VR, while XR forms the umbrella term for all three technologies.

Moreover, Capgemini highlights that the metaverse forms just such an environment where immersive experiences can be offered through various forms of interfaces. These interfaces can be separated in three different main categories: (1) Flat User Interface (2D), (2) Natural and Spatial Interfaces and (3) Extended Reality (3D). The third category, the one on which the following Master's thesis focusses on, is best suited to create fully immersive experiences (Capgemini Research Institute, 2022, p. 6).

As the focus of this thesis is on how these immersive shopping experiences can be created in virtual stores and what influence these might have on Gen Z's intention to use virtual stores, and what characteristics and features (C&F) virtual

[5] There are now even VR glasses that work completely without controllers, the Apple Vision Pro which was released on February 2, 2024 in the United States (Apple Inc. (2024a, 2024b).

stores should offer to create exactly these immersive experiences, virtual stores and immersive experiences will be discussed further.

2.1.3 Virtual Commerce

With all this background information on VR, virtual worlds, VR glasses etc., it is not yet entirely clarified how the metaverse can transform the way consumers shop. The following chapter provides an answer to this question.

In scientific and business context, the shopping of consumers in a virtual environment such as the metaverse is called virtual 3D commerce (also referred to as v-commerce, VR-commerce or meta commerce) (Hackl, 2022; Regt & Barnes, 2019, p. 18; Trier & Steiger, 2023, p. 204). Regt and Barnes (2019) define v-commerce as "electronically mediated commercial transactions that originate from an alternate reality technological platform and involve either digitally-generated or real-world products and services" (Regt & Barnes, 2019, p. 18). Experts, like e.g., Regt and Barnes (2019), DuBoff (2021) or Hackl (2021), are currently discussing possible use cases for v-commerce and new retail models, particularly in light of the general development of retail from traditional brick-and-mortar stores, e-commerce, over mobile, voice, live, social, quick and finally v-commerce (Boer, Momani, & Federowski, 2022; DuBoff, 2021; ECC Koeln & Salesforce.com, 2022, p. 9; Hackl, 2022; Heinemann, 2022, p. 292; Regt & Barnes, 2019, p. 19). In a Forbes online article, Hackl (2022) writes about new commerce models that will emerge as the metaverse becomes increasingly present. She emphasizes their impact on how customers will make choices and future purchasing decisions.

According to Hackl (2022), aside from commerce models such as physical-to-physical, digital-to-physical and virtual-to-virtual (which all have been known for a long time now), new commerce models will be virtual-to-physical and physical-to-virtual (Hackl, 2022). The first, virtual-to-physical mainly relates to the purchasing of physical goods in virtual worlds, meaning the customer buys a product in virtual worlds such as Roblox and will receive it at home in the real world. In contrast, physical-to-virtual can be referred to the receipt of a digital good after a purchase in a brick-and-mortar store, e.g., a digital twin of the purchased physical garment that can be worn by the customer's avatar on Roblox (Hackl, 2022). At their annual Investor Days 2023, Roblox announced that they will release a new feature called "Real-World Commerce" on their platform that will actually make the former possible (Wootton, 2023). Another recent development with regard to the realization of such novel commerce models is the release of "Apple Vision Pro Shopping Apps". Apple collaborated with Obsess and designed virtual shopping apps for each of the four brands: Mytheresa, Alo Yoga, J.Crew and e.l.f. Cosmetics (Obsess, 2024c). This once again underlines the rapid pace of this development, as Apple has only recently released its spatial hardware and is already offering the first use cases (Apple Inc., 2024a; Obsess, 2024c).

Rori DuBoff (2021), who is a digital strategist and was Managing Director at Accenture Song, appeals to the merging of the above-mentioned online and offline channels, which would result in a seamless, unprecedented, immersive experience for the customer. To this end, she provides an overview of the previously discussed development of commerce and explains how such immersive and seamless experiences can be realized (DuBoff, 2021). DuBoff (2021) essentially refers to what the following work is all about: the shopping in so-called virtual stores that can lead to immersive experiences for the customer, especially when they are linked to other channels in the sense of omnichannel (DuBoff, 2021). The questions now arise as to what exactly is meant by virtual stores and how consumers will be able to shop there in the future. This question along with the question of how to integrate virtual stores into the customer journey will be addressed in the following chapters.

2.1.4 Virtual Stores

As the term "virtual stores" (also referred to as VR stores) is still at a very early stage, it can be defined in different ways (Chittaro & Ration, 2000, p. 87).

In the past, e-commerce stores were often referred to as virtual stores (L.-D. Chen & Tan, 2004, p. 74; Sousa & Voss, 2006, p. 358). Tesco also used the term virtual (grocery) stores in 2012 in the form of an electronic billboard that showed shelves filled with products and an integrated QR code that customers could use to order the respective products to their homes (Steadman, 2012).

Today, a completely different understanding of virtual stores prevails (Gröppel-Klein, 2012, p. 662). In the search for a definition of virtual stores, it has become apparent that virtual stores are often defined by their superiority over other channels such as e-commerce and brick-and-mortar stores. For instance, Neha Singh, CEO of Obsess, one of the leading experiential e-commerce platforms and a leader in virtual store creation, defines virtual stores as "web-based, shoppable 3D environments that transform the traditional flat e-commerce thumbnail grid into something that is highly visual, contextual and customized to a brand's unique story" (Singh, 2023, p. 86). Singh (2023, p. 86) adds that virtual stores would contain "digitized versions of physical products" that would serve as an ideal endpoint for 3D assets such as non-fungible tokens (NFTs) or skins[6]. Thus, she emphasizes the experiential benefits that virtual stores can create, which traditional e-commerce stores lack (see Sect. 1.1).

Another very apt definition of virtual stores, which highlights the superiority of virtual stores not only over e-commerce but also over brick-and-mortar stores, comes from DuBoff (2021). DuBoff (2021) describes virtual stores as digital 3D environments that allow the marketing and sale of products and services (DuBoff, 2021). Accordingly, brands should combine "the tangible and sensory aspects of a brick-and-mortar store with the interactivity, accessibility, and scale" of digital channels to create shopping experiences that offer the best of both worlds, physical as digital (DuBoff, 2021). That is exactly what virtual stores do.

Virtual stores are currently either integrated on a brand's e-commerce website, are part of virtual worlds in the metaverse, such as Roblox, Decentraland or Spatial, or in app stores (Obsess, 2023b). These virtual stores can be easily accessed via desktop or mobile devices such as laptops, tablets or smartphones, but also via devices such as VR glasses (Wiggers, 2023). The latter promises a much more immersive experience with a much higher level of engagement and immersion (Obsess, 2021b, 2021c; Xi & Hamari, 2021, p. 38). The following work focuses on virtual shopping experiences in virtual stores that are accessible via VR glasses.

In recent years, a number of companies emerged that have developed platforms through which they have already successfully created and launched virtual stores and immersive experiences for renowned brands and retailers, to name just a few of them: Byondxr, Demodern, Emperia, Obsess, Spatial or Unity. Taking Obsess as an example, they create different types of virtual stores, from virtual stores that are a digital replica of existing brick-and-mortar stores like virtual retail stores to flagship stores (also see Sect. 2.2). They already did it for brands like Fendi, Dior, Ralph Lauren and many others (Obsess, 2023a, 2023h). Moreover, Obsess designs and launches virtual pop-up stores that only exist for a limited time, or themed stores, like virtual holiday stores, e.g., Crocs (A. Lee, 2022; Obsess, 2022c). These are not always just real-life stores that also exist in the real world (also referred to as digital replica), but also fictional virtual stores that do not exist in the real world. Obsess was even recognized by Interbrand as "Breakthrough Brand" in 2023 (Interbrand, 2023). Alongside Obsess, Emperia is the other leading platform for virtual stores (Pan, 2023). In 2023, Emperia launched several types of virtual stores. For instance, a cross-platform shopping

[6] Skins are also known from the gaming industry (UK Safer Internet Centre (UK SIC), 2022).

experience was created for Tommy Hilfiger on Decentraland, Roblox, Spatial, DressX and Ready Player Me in parallel with Metaverse Fashion Week (MVFW) 2023 (Emperia, 2023e; MVFW, 2023; Spatial, 2023).

Nevertheless, it is reported that the first ever virtual store as defined in this work was the eBay x Mayer VR department store, which could be experienced via an app. Shoppers could browse around 12,500 Myer products which they could select and add to their shopping cart via the "ebay Sight Search" feature. The VR department store was connected to eBay.com.au's existing application programming interface (API), enabling real-time updates to Myer's product assortment, pricing and inventory information. The idea behind this was to give tech enthusiasts and shoppers who do not live near a department store and can easily shop there, the opportunity to do so from the comfort of their own home through virtual shopping (Matovina et al., 2016). Sect. 2.2 deals with the different types of virtual stores in more detail and provides further examples.

The above definitions of virtual stores underline the new opportunities that virtual stores offer in terms of creating immersive shopping experiences for customers (see also Sect. 2.4). Accordingly, it is assumed that these experiences are primarily created by combining traditional C&F of physical and e-commerce stores with new ones. What characteristics and features these could be is examined in more detail below (particularly in Sect. 2.3). First of all, the second, previously posed question of how consumers can shop in virtual stores will be addressed.

2.1.5 Avatars

The answer is: avatars. Virtual stores are usually visited by users as avatars. Apple has indeed recently shown with its virtual shopping apps that it is also possible to go shopping in virtual stores as a real person. Consumers can then meet with sales advisors, for example, and they can see each other (Obsess, 2024c). However, the following work focuses on shopping with avatars, as this has been the most established way so far, especially in virtual worlds such as Roblox.

In addition, Roblox Corporation (2023) found that in 2022 many of its users, who belong to Gen Z, were already finding it more important to express themselves as avatars in the digital world than in the physical world (Roblox Corporation, 2023, p. 4). The latter underlines once again that, with regard to Gen Z, shopping in virtual stores as avatars seems more realistic than as real persons.

An avatar is a graphical, digital representation of a real person (Boehm, Esser, & Seidel, 2022, p. 12). Avatars are used in social media, communities, on websites and also in virtual worlds as character images (Roblox Corporation, 2023, p. 4). They can be a realistic, 3D representation of a human being (the avatar looks the same like the user), or the user can get creative and design his or her avatar according to his or her preferences (much like a made-up character from a computer or video game) (Nokia & Ipsos, 2022, p. 31).

There are several platforms like Ready Player Me, Bitmoji or Obess that have their own avatar configurator. For instance on Ready Player Me, which describes itself as "an avatar system for games, apps, and VR/AR experiences", allows users to create their own avatar and update it at any time (Ready Player Me, 2023b). Updating means giving their avatar a new hair style, dressing or even a completely new look (author's own experience on https://readyplayer.me/). Brands or retailers can cooperate with Ready Player Me and launch virtual versions of their products such as garments or accessories. Typically, all apps and games that use avatars from Ready Player Me are compatible with these virtual products, e.g., Spatial, VRChat, or HiberWorld (Ready Player Me, 2024). Hence, Ready Player Me avatars cannot only be used on a single platform but on several platforms and applications. This is very important in the context of interoperability, as previously mentioned in Sect. 2.1.1. Several brands and retailers have already successfully experimented with Ready Player Me.

Tommy Hilfiger partnered with Ready Player Me as part of the "Look great anywhere" campaign to launch digital clothing items for the metaverse based on physical products that were sold online, on their website, as well as in Tommy Hilfiger stores, and at several retailers (Ready Player Me, 2022). The digital avatars outfit collection could be previewed by consumers on pre-created Ready Player Me avatars. These avatars as well as the digital clothing items were also freely available on https://readyplayer.me/. However, only for a limited time, so Tommy Hilfiger customers had to be quick to get their hands on one of these (Tate, 2022). Once users have clothed their Ready Player Me avatars with the limited digital collector's item, the avatar clothed with exactly this digital clothing item remained in their Ready Player Me Hub (author's own experience on https://readyplayer.me/). Moreover, when purchasing a physical garment, customers had the option of receiving a digital twin of their physically purchased garment, which can then be worn by their Ready Player Me avatars. According to Ready Player Me (2022), over 1,200 avatars were dressed in Tommy Hilfiger outfits, and over 400 outfits were created in more than 56 countries (Ready Player Me, 2022).

Recently, ALDI SÜD cooperated with Ready Player Me and launched their very first digital fashion collection as a digital twin to their physical unisex summer collection “ALDImania”. Whereas the physical collection was only available from 31.07.2023, customers were already able to try on all items in the collection digitally on their Ready Player Me avatars from 27.07.2023 (Leipe, 2023).

While Ready Player Me avatars can be used across platforms and applications, the “Branded Avatars” avatar creator from Obsess is a feature that is integrated in the virtual store or on the website of the respective brand or retailer and can only be used there by the customer. The brand or retailer pre-creates a set of avatars, and customers then are able to personalize these pre-created, branded avatars, e.g., the body shape, their skin tone, or hair style/color and many more (Obsess, 2023c). “Magic Charlotte”, the avatar created by Obsess for Charlotte Tilbury’s virtual store, is an example of this (Obsess, 2021c). Companies such as Meta and Apple also have their own avatar creation tools. Meta calls it “Meta avatars”. It can be used across all of Meta’s platforms, e.g., on their social media channels Facebook, Instagram, and WhatsApp. High of interest within the context of the Metaverse, those Meta Avatars can also be used on Meta Quest, in Meta Horizon Worlds, and in Meta Horizon Workrooms (Meta Platforms, Inc., 2024). Meta also partnered with Naomi Osaka, tennis player and fashion and design enthusiast, and brought a collection to the Meta Avatars Store (Meta Platforms, Inc., 2023a).

Meta announced that there will be more features within Meta Avatars to come (Meta Platforms, Inc., 2024). Apple has its own avatar creator for its Apple product users as well. It is called “Memoji”. Currently, it works more like a sticker, but Apple users can also send voice messages or do FaceTime calls with it. The user’s memoji is then put over his or her face like a filter (Apple Inc., 2023b). All avatar creators have in common that users can create avatars and use it for different purposes. What makes Ready Player Me special and what sets them apart of the others is that it is the only one that does not require users to create an account to try out their avatar creator. In addition, Ready Player Me can be used on different platforms and applications, making it more accessible for the user, brand or retailer (especially in terms of the use of virtual stores). As introduced in this chapter, Roblox’ findings on avatars show that avatars are crucial for shopping in virtual stores. Nokia and Ipsos (2022) also discovered that avatars are most commonly used by Gen Z to express their identity and play an important role for them, especially in terms of the first impression they make on other avatars (Nokia & Ipsos, 2022, p. 18). In a consumer survey on the metaverse, Deloitte found that 60% of respondents in Germany were open to the use of digital avatars.

As many as 25% were already using an avatar (Boehm et al., 2022, p. 12). This shows once again that avatars are very important when it comes to virtual stores. Hence, avatars can be seen as a doorway for brands into the metaverse.

Now that it has been explained how consumers can visit virtual stores, it is interesting to learn what distinct types of virtual stores consumers can visit (with their avatars).

2.2 Virtual Store Types

In order to find out what different types of virtual stores exist, a comprehensive analysis of a total of 95 existing virtual stores was carried out. From this, a list of analyzed use cases[7] was created based on author's own experience with these virtual stores. The list[8] can be provided upon request and also forms the basis for Sect. 2.3, which deals with the characteristics and features of virtual stores.

Eleven different types of virtual stores could be identified: (1) Virtual Retail Stores, (2), Virtual Flagship Stores, (3) Virtual Store-in-Stores, (4) Virtual Designer Outlets, (5) Virtual Shopping Malls, (6) Virtual Pop-up Stores, (7) Virtual Holiday Stores, (8) Virtual Showrooms, (9) Virtual Platform Stores, (10) Virtual Store Shopping Apps, and (11) Virtual Product Configurators.[9] In general, virtual stores can be created for a various of industries. The virtual stores

[7] At this point, it is emphasized that the current use cases are mainly visited via mobile or desktop, given that VR glasses are not yet so well established. Nevertheless, they represent realistic use cases of what shopping in virtual stores via VR glasses could look like in the future.

[8] During the analysis, it was particularly noticeable that most of the use cases currently available come from luxury brands, e.g., Fendi, J.Crew, or Gucci. This could be related to the fact that luxury brands in particular have more marketing budget available and that people with higher incomes in particular are more likely to own VR glasses, as the price of VR glasses is currently still quite high compared to what consumers are willing to spend on VR glasses (ECC Koeln, 2022, p. 26).

[9] I. Krasonikolakis, Vrechopoulos, Pouloudi, and Dimitriadis (2018, p. 1229) identified five different store layout types of virtual stores that can already be found in 3D online environments. These are: Avantgarde Stores, Warehouse Stores, Pragmatic Stores, Boutique Stores and Department Stores. However, these types are based exclusively on the characteristic "store layout", while the virtual store types identified by the author consider both the meta- and micro-level, and also take other characteristics and features into account (I. Krasonikolakis et al. (2018, p. 1229)).

examined are mainly from the fashion, retail, beauty, consumer electronics, automotive, food and furniture industry. Virtual stores differ not only in their type, but also in their style (i.e., realistic[10], minimalistic, futuristic, abstract).

In line with Ball's definition of virtual worlds in Sect. 2.1.1, virtual stores cannot only be real virtual stores that also exist in the real world (also known as digital replicas), but also fictitious virtual stores that do not exist in the real world. Furthermore, virtual stores can either be individual and independent of other virtual stores (also referred to as "stand-alone virtual stores"), but they can also be part of virtual shopping malls or cities (Gandzeichuk, 2022; Obsess, 2021b). The types of virtual stores and corresponding examples are presented below.

2.2.1 Virtual Retail Stores

The first type of virtual store is the virtual retail store. The virtual retail store is very similar to the regular physical retail store that is known from real life. It can either be a virtualized retail store, which is a digital replica of a real brick-and-mortar store (also known as photorealistic), or a fictitious store. In addition, the virtual store can be a mix of both, e.g., a realistic virtual retail store with fictitious elements or vice versa. Usually, this type of virtual store is permanently, i.e., that it can be visited not only for a limited time. An example of a fictitious virtual retail store with a realistic store design is the "Alo Immersive Store" (Alo Yoga, 2023). It was created by Obsess and can be discovered via desktop, mobile, or the Meta Quest 2 headset.

In contrast, Ralph Lauren's "The 888 House" is an example for a realistic designed virtual retail store with fictitious elements that is not existing in real life. It was part of Ralph Lauren's campaign to launch their new handbag collection "RL 888" (Ralph Lauren, 2023b). Figure 2.2 is a collage of "The 888 House" showing various areas of it, e.g., the front (first row, first image) or the entry with a quote of designer Ralph Lauren on the wall (first row, second image).

An example of a purely fictitious virtual retail store is Lululemon's virtual store created by Emperia and available on the brand's e-commerce website. In addition to in-store and e-commerce activations, it was part of the product launch of the new chargefeel 2 women's shoes (Emperia, 2023c).

[10] Along with realistic design, the term skeuomorphism (also called "affordances") often occurs, which refers to a design style that mimics real-life objects through the use of realistic textures and details. This is in contrast to flat design, which uses bright colors and little to no realistic textures and shadows (Interaction Design Foundation (IxDF), 2016a).

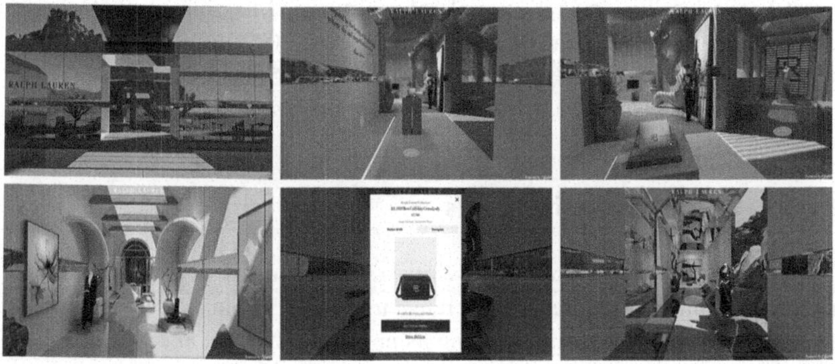

Fig. 2.2 Virtual Retail Store from Ralph Lauren. (*Note.* This collage shows the virtual retail store "The 888 House" from Ralph Lauren. *Source.* Author's own illustration based on Ralph Lauren (2023a))

2.2.2 Virtual Flagship Stores

Another type of virtual store is the virtual flagship store. Virtual flagship stores differ from virtual retail stores in that they are often a pure digital replica of real-life flagship stores, which are characterized in particular by their size, assortment (presentation) and location, as they are often located in metropolitan areas like NYC (Zentes, Morschett, & Schramm-Klein, 2017, p. 118). Usually this type of virtual store is permanently accessible, not only for a limited time.

A recent example of such a virtual flagship store is the immersive 3D virtual replica of Crate&Barrel's NYC Flatiron Flagship at historic 881 Broadway which was created by Obsess (Crate & Barrel, 2025; Obsess, 2023f). Sebastian Brauer, Senior VP of Product Design at Crate&Barrel, posted it on social media platform LinkedIn and wrote: " [...] so that we could welcome anybody, anywhere, any-time to explore, shop and experience [the virtual flagship store]" (Brauer, 2023). Moreover Brauer (2023) announced that the virtual flagship store would incorporate over 1,000 virtually modeled products as well as interactive animations, content and more that will be updated frequently. Figure 2.3 shows a bird's eye view of the Crate&Barrel virtual flagship store and provides further insights into its store interior. Another example is the Fendi 57th Street Virtual Flagship Store, which is also located in NYC. Like Crate&Barrel's, it also exists in real life and was created by Obsess (Fendi, 2022, 2024). Figure 2.4 below shows Fendi's 57th Street Virtual Flagship Store on the right side. Burberry's virtual store "Regent

Street Experience" is another example of a virtualized flagship retail store, created by Capgemini AIE and Matterport (Burberry, 2022). It is a photorealistic replication of the real Burberry retail store on Regent Street in London. All three examples can be visited via desktop or mobile, but also with VR glasses.

2.2.3 Virtual Store-in-Stores

The third type of virtual store is the virtual store-in-store. It is similar to department stores familiar from real life. It refers to a space within a larger retailer and is often designated to a brand featuring its products (Ahlert et al., 2020a, p. 127). There are also such store-in-stores in the virtual world. One example of this is Bloomingdale's.

Fig. 2.3 Virtual Flagship Store from Crate&Barrel. (*Note.* This collage shows the "Crate&Barrel NYC Flatiron Flagship at 881 Broadway". *Source.* Author's own illustration based on Crate & Barrel (2025))

Together with Emperia, Bloomingdale's has launched three different virtual experiences in which virtual store-in-stores in a virtual retail store of Bloomingdale's can be experienced by users via desktop, mobile and VR glasses. All three virtual experiences are fictitious but with realistic as well as futuristic elements. The first virtual experience was created to celebrate Bloomingdale's 150th anniversary in 2022 (Bloomingdale's, 2022). This virtual experience can still be experienced and consists of several futuristic virtual store-in-stores, e.g., a virtual store-in-store of frozen yoghurt brand Forty Carrots (author's own experience on https://emperiavr.com/project/bloomingdales/#demo). Visitors can also explore the anniversary collection of Bloomingdale's. In another Bloomingdale's virtual experience, which was also launched in their 150th anniversary year in 2022, there are virtual store-in-stores, e.g., from Ralph Lauren (located in a cozy chalet) and Chanel (placed on the moon) (Emperia, 2022a, 2022d). This experience can also be subsumed under the virtual store type "virtual holiday stores" which will be discussed in Sect. 2.2.7 as it was originally created for the Christmas shopping and gifting season (Emperia, 2023d).

2.2.4 Virtual Outlet Stores

As the name suggests, virtual outlet stores which form the fourth type of virtual stores, are similar to (designer) outlets from real life.

One example is the real-life Bicester Village, which was recreated virtually by Emperia along with their other eleven villages across Europe and China, including "Ingolstadt Village" or "La Vallee Village". This virtual experience is intended to offer visitors the opportunity to virtually explore the surroundings of the individual villages and to prepare virtually for their next in-person shopping trip to the local designer outlets (Emperia, 2023a).

2.2.5 Virtual Shopping Malls

Virtual shopping malls or centers are the virtual counterpart of real-life shopping centers. These typically include different types of stores, e.g., retail stores, specialist stores but also restaurants (Ahlert et al., 2020a, p. 130). For this type of virtual store could only be found two exemplary use cases. However, according to Gandzeichuk (2022), there could be two different types of virtual shopping malls. The first type represents the virtualization of real-life shopping malls such as the German Westfield CentrO, located in Oberhausen, containing different types of stores that can be visited by desktop or with VR glasses. The second type refers to virtual shopping malls that are either fully artificial or similar to real-life shopping malls but contain artificial elements, including "different degrees of realism" (Gandzeichuk, 2022). McMillen (2023) uses the term "Avamall" and defines it as "a cyber community of various 3D virtual stores operated by retailers" which consumers can access without the need for VR headsets and shop as they would in real life. An example of such a virtual shopping mall could be the coming "Outfit Shopping Mall" on Roblox (also see Sect. 2.2.9).

2.2.6 Virtual Pop-up Stores

Virtual pop-up stores are similar to real life pop-up stores (e.g., Miss Dior pop-up store in 2022) that are usually only available for a limited period of time and often are part of new product launches, limited editions, new store openings, or anniversaries. An example of a virtual pop-up store is J.Crew's "Virtual Beach House" from 2023, which was launched to celebrate J.Crew's 40th anniversary. Together with Obsess, J.Crew created its first virtual store to give customers from all over the world the opportunity to celebrate with them (Obsess, 2023g, 2024b).

This would have been impossible with physical pop-up stores, as they are location-bound and therefore cannot be visited by everyone (Fonrouge, 2023). The virtual pop-up store cannot be visited anymore.

Another example is the virtual pop-up store "The World of Olympia", which was created by Emperia in collaboration with Burberry and Harrods to introduce the new Burberry "Olympia" signature bag. As with J.Crew, the virtual pop-up of Burberry was also intended to complement the official premiere at the Burberry department store in London as well as a series of real pop-up installations worldwide (Emperia, 2021b). Along with the two mentioned, there are many more use cases of virtual pop-up stores. The list can be provided upon request.

2.2.7 Virtual Holiday Stores

Virtual holiday stores are somewhat different from virtual pop-ups. They are similar to virtual pop-ups in that they are usually only available for a limited period of time. Unlike virtual pop-ups, they are launched as part of specific shopping or gifting seasons, for example around Christmas season (Emperia, 2022b). An example is the virtual holiday store of Taylor Swift. Together with Obsess, she created this virtual store during last year's Christmas season, in which fans could shop merchandise in a gamified and festive way. This virtual holiday store was only available during Christmas season, but it can still be visited via the UK URL, as the author found out herself (Taylor Nation LLC, 2023).

In November 2023, Emperia launched a virtual holiday store for L'Occitane called "L'Occitane Christmas". This virtual holiday store was set in a festive, realistic Christmas winter wonderland in the French Alps, integrated into their e-commerce store and could be visited via mobile, desktop and VR glasses (Emperia, 2023b). Emperia also created a virtual summer holiday store for Lacoste at the start of the summer season which was launched in 2023 and is still available on their e-commerce website in 2024 (Lacoste, 2023). A possible reason for this could be that they still sell the collection items in their e-commerce store, and therefore continue to offer these items for sale in their virtual holiday store until they are sold out. These and many others can be categorized as virtual holiday stores.

2.2.8 Virtual Showrooms

The next type of virtual stores are virtual showrooms. Two forms of virtual showrooms can be distinguished: virtual business-to-business (VB2B) and business-to-consumer (VB2C) showrooms.

A VB2B showroom usually addresses the business clients of a brand (from wholesale), not the direct customers or consumers. The brand can present its new collections or products in a virtual environment. This makes it easier for everyone involved, as they no longer have to be on site, but can do so from the comfort of their location. Examples are the virtual showroom of Falke "FALKE Virtual Experience"[11], created by Zreality (see Fig. 2.4), or the "Yamaha Virtual Showroom" which was created by Virtuloc (Falke KGaA, 2023; Virtuloc, 2022). Another example is the virtual showroom of H&M, created by DEPT. agency (Gutkuhn, 2022). An example of a VB2C showroom is the BOSS Immersive Experience on Spatial, which was part of the Metaverse Fashion Week (MVFW) in 2023 (Hugo Boss, 2023). Shoppers were able to explore the new BOSS collection presented at Spring/Summer 2023 Fashion Show in Miami. The virtual showroom acted as a digital extension (Hugo Boss, 2023). There are also fifteen other examples of virtual showrooms which can be provided upon request.

2.2.9 Virtual Platform Stores

Virtual platform stores are virtual stores on (gaming) platforms such as Roblox, Minecraft, Fortnite, Meta Horizon Worlds or Decentraland (Morris, 2022). As these platforms are often referred to as virtual worlds, or even metaverses, they can also be referred to as "virtual world stores" (Marr, 2022). These are usually creative and fictitious virtual stores, or even brand worlds that are designed in line with the brand and the corresponding game or platform (Thomaset, 2023, p. 118).

[11] The FALKE Virtual Experience can be visited even by both B2B and B2C customers (Falke KGaA, 2023).

Adidas launched a series of virtual pop-up stores on Roblox in late 2023 in which they offered officially licensed digital clothing and customized outfit items known on Roblox as user-generated content (UGCs). These included the famous Adidas design garments and accessories, exclusive limited-edition collections that can be worn by Roblox avatars (Adidas AG, 2023).

Next to Adidas, there are also several other brands that experiment with virtual stores on Roblox, e.g., Vans, Mango, Alo Yoga, Ralph Lauren, Givenchy and Amika (Givenchy, 2022; Mango, 2024; Obsess, 2024d; Roblox Corporation, 2024a; Roblox Corporation & Ralph Lauren, 2021; Vans & Roblox Corporation, 2021).

Fig. 2.4 Virtual Showroom from Falke. (*Note.* This collage shows the virtual showroom from FALKE. *Source.* Author's own illustration based on Falke KGaA (2023))

For instance, in Vans' virtual platform store called "Vans World", users can design and create their own skateboards and sneakers (Thomaset, 2023, p. 117). Mango will also be part of a so-called "Outfit Shopping Mall", which can be imagined as a large shopping center on Roblox, in which various brands will have their virtual stores and where users can visit together with their fellow players and enjoy various experiences (Mango, 2024). Recently, on their Investor Days 2023, Roblox announced a new feature called "Real-world Commerce", which will make it possible to purchase not only digital but also physical items that the consumer receives at home in real life (Dypiangco, 2023; Wootton, 2023). Another example for a virtual platform store is Alo Yoga's "Alo Sanctuary" which was released in 2022 on Roblox (Alo Yoga, 2022). There are more than twenty-two examples of virtual platform stores.

2.2.10 Virtual Store Shopping Apps

There are also so-called virtual store shopping apps. Shoppers can usually visit them through their VR headset, e.g., Apple Vision Pro or Meta Quest, and shop products or do other activities, such as meditation, or gaming (Ludmir, 2024; Obsess, 2024c). Just recently, Apple has developed four such apps for the brands J.Crew, Mytheresa, Alo Yoga, and e.l.f. Cosmetics in collaboration with Obsess for its recently launched headset, the Apple Vision Pro (see Sect. 1.1). However, this kind of virtual store is not so new. eBay already created the first shopping app together with Mayer in 2016 (Matovina et al., 2016). Dyson together with Meta already had the Dyson VR demo as a virtual store for their hairstyling products in 2021 (Meta Platforms, Inc., 2021b). Shoppers can experience Dyson products by interacting with them or even buy them (Dyson Limited, 2021).

2.2.11 Virtual Product Configurators

The last type of virtual store is the virtual product configurator. Technically, this is not a type of virtual store, as the focus is on configuring products and services rather than visiting a virtual store. Visitors can configure products such as cars or their own (living) rooms. Examples include the "Mazda VR Car Configurator" or the "Ikea Virtual Reality Showroom", both created by *Demodern* (Demodern, 2017a, 2017b).

The analysis has shown that the classification of types of virtual stores, especially virtual holiday and pop-up stores, is not always clear, as there are virtual stores that can be classified as one type of virtual store or another, e.g., Lacoste's Virtual Store (Emperia, 2022c). This virtual store was launched as a virtual holiday store, as is usual with this type of virtual store, was only available for a limited period of time. In fact, it can no longer be found on Lacoste's e-commerce website. Unlike Lacoste's second virtual holiday store, which opened in 2023 and can still be found on the e-commerce website in 2024, making it more of a permanent virtual retail store than a temporary virtual holiday store (Lacoste, 2023).

Furthermore, the analysis has shown that—contrary to Ball's definition of virtual worlds from Sect. 2.1.1—virtual stores, which Ball categorizes as purely non-game-like virtual worlds with the term "commerce", can also be game-like, especially virtual stores such as virtual platform stores on Roblox (see Sect. 2.2.9).

Now that a comprehensive overview of virtual store types has been given, the next chapter will take a closer look at the characteristics and features of virtual stores.

2.3 Store Characteristics and Features

Just like brick-and-mortar stores and e-commerce stores, virtual stores can have different store characteristics and features[12] (C&F), depending on the purpose of the brand or company that is being pursued with a virtual store (author's own finding). As outlined in the previous chapters, the aim is to find those that serve to create shopping experiences for customers. To find these, a comprehensive analysis of the C&F of existing virtual stores was carried out. In addition, the C&F of traditional brick-and-mortar stores and e-commerce stores were also examined because, as already stated in Sect. 2.1.4, virtual stores combine the best of both channels. Therefore, the C&F of these stores that could be integrated into virtual stores should also be identified. For this purpose, the C&F of virtual stores from the list of use cases were analyzed and relevant literature[13] was reviewed. The analysis of C&F of brick-and-mortar and e-commerce stores can be found in Appendix A. An overview of the C&F of virtual stores, including references to the list of use cases from Sect. 2.2, is at the end of this section.

First of all, it is necessary to define what is meant by store C&F. Store C&F include all aspects that contribute to the design of a store and its environment, whether it is a virtual store, a brick-and-mortar store or an e-commerce store. Characteristics can also be referred to as instruments, attributes or activation parameters, e.g., by Gröppel-Klein (2012, p. 647), Schwertfeger (2012, p. 50) or Ahlert et al. (2020a, p. 296). Whereas features can be referred to as elements (Schmitt, 2011, p. 75). In this work, features are defined as relevant components

[12] I. Krasonikolakis, Vrechopoulos, and Pouloudi (2014) also refer to "features" of virtual stores.

[13] The focus was on German literature. In addition, international studies were also reviewed.

of the specific characteristic, while characteristics is the umbrella term of corresponding features, e.g., characteristic is store design and its features are visual elements such as colors, lighting.

2.3.1 Characteristics and Features of Brick-and-Mortar Stores

According to Gröppel-Klein (2012, p. 654), the store design of brick-and-mortar stores is understood as the process of designing the sales area. This also includes the store front and window (Fließ, Hogreve, & Nonnenmacher, 2005, p. 29; Gröppel-Klein, 2012, p. 654). Part of store design is the presentation of goods (Zentes et al., 2017, p. 327). It implies the distribution, arrangement and decoration of the products in the store. The store design and the presentation of goods create the store atmosphere (sometimes equated with store environment), which has an effect on customer behavior in the store and triggers both emotional and cognitive processes inside the customer (Julia Baker, Levy, & Grewal, 1992, pp. 446–447).

The design of brick-and-mortar stores is also referred to as POS marketing or in-store marketing (Gröppel-Klein, 2012, p. 645; Zentes et al., 2017, p. 327). Thereby, Gröppel-Klein (2012, p. 647) distinguishes between information-related and communication-related marketing instruments that can be used in the design of brick-and-mortar stores. This includes all measures relating to the structure and arrangement of the store layout, the qualitative and quantitative division of the store space, the presentation of goods, window dressing as well as the store atmosphere (Zentes, Swoboda, & Foscht, 2012, 522ff.). Under these instruments, further instruments can be subordinated, e.g., Gröppel-Klein (2012, p. 655) further specifies within the presentation of goods between decoration, color design and design of the room environment (in relation to atmospheric environmental elements such as music or fragrances). Ahlert et al. (2020a, p. 296) subsume the store layout, the presentation and placement of goods and the store atmosphere as store design areas under presentation policy. However, they deal with the same content under the respective terms. Schwertfeger (2012, p. 50) differentiates between controllable versus uncontrollable and, on the other hand, object-related versus subject-related attributes that can be used by retail companies to generate shopping experiences in brick-and-mortar stores. The C&F mentioned above can be allocated to controllable and object-related attributes. But, there are also other attributes that will be considered further, controllable, subject-related attributes, e.g., the perception of sales assistants and, more specifically, their behavior in the context of interaction with the customer (professional and social skills) (Gröppel-Klein, 2012, p. 645; Schwertfeger, 2012, p. 50).

All emphasize the influence of the shopping atmosphere on consumer behavior and advocate creating a pleasant and exciting shopping environment (Ahlert et al., 2020b, p. 304; Gröppel-Klein, 2012, p. 650).

According to Ahlert et al. (2020b, p. 304), the main aim of the store design is to provide users with a pleasant and appealing shopping atmosphere. Therefore, he highlights the action parameters for designing the shopping atmosphere. In particular, these are the interior design, store fittings, color scheme, decoration, lighting and the room environment (e.g., music, room temperature, scents) (Ahlert et al., 2020b, p. 304). According to Gröppel-Klein (2012, p. 650), customers expect a store atmosphere that is unique and differs from other stores and would generate excitement. Visitors would also expect the store atmosphere to trigger activation, pleasure and dominance in them. It should encourage browsing and strolling and should address all senses. It should also show the customer a lifestyle which is aspired by him or her (Gröppel-Klein, 2012, p. 650). Zentes et al. (2017, p. 333) emphasize that the store atmosphere plays a particularly important role when it comes to creating exceptional CXs in brick-and-mortar stores (also referred to as experiential retailing). Ahlert et al. (2020b, p. 305) and Gröppel-Klein (2012, p. 650) also underline the positive influence of store design and store atmosphere on the shopping experience. Furthermore, Ahlert et al. (2020b, p. 298) emphasize that in the overall store design of a brick-and-mortar store, it is important to ensure that the design, store type and brand concept (corporate design, brand philosophy for a uniform brand presence) harmonize. This would create a positive shopping atmosphere and at the same time pursue the goal of providing users with a pleasant environment that encourages them to shop (Ahlert et al., 2020b, p. 304). In general, companies also worked and collaborated with artists, designers or other brands to enhance shopping experiences in brick-and-mortar stores, e.g., Douglas collaborated with the Berlin studio Mary Lennox and George Tyebcho for floral shop window installations in 2022 (Fließ et al., 2005; Kirst, 2022).

2.3.2 Characteristics and Features of E-Commerce Stores

Following Zentes et al. (2017, p. 336), the fundamentals of store design (e.g., store layout and grouping of products), and store atmosphere (e. g., use of colors) can be also applied to e-commerce stores. In addition, the trend towards experiential shopping and the emotionalization of shopping can also be observed in e-commerce (Haeusel, 2012; Heinemann, 2022, p. 276). In e-commerce, this means above all the staging of so-called worlds of experience[14] (Heinemann, 2022, p. 279).

Nevertheless, based on their findings, Vrechopoulos, O'Keefe, Doukidis, and Siomkos (2004, p. 20) concluded that observed preferences for certain store layouts in brick-and-mortar stores are not easily transferable to e-commerce stores, due to different shopping motives of consumers. Similarly, Dwivedi et al. (2022, p. 25) found that hedonically driven customers are more likely to shop in VR stores than utilitarian driven customers who would rather prefer shopping in e-commerce stores. Furthermore, as with brick-and-mortar stores, the store design highly depends on the strategic positioning of the e-commerce store (GS1 Germany, 2018, p. 35). In general, there are several C&Fs that are used in the design of e-commerce stores. These include, e.g., various multimedia components such as text, images, graphics, sound, video or animation. In addition, interactive elements or 360-degree product views are becoming increasingly common (Heinemann, 2022, p. 279; Petereit, 2024). E-commerce stores are characterized in particular by the interplay of multimedia presentation, detailed information offers, search functions, configuration functions, dialogue elements (e.g., chatbots, live chats) and interactive entertainment elements (e.g., gamification, size finder) (Heinemann, 2022, p. 274; Kollmann, 2019, p. 337). Wish lists and the creation of user accounts are also important features in e-commerce stores (Kollmann, 2019, p. 269). The structure and navigation are particularly important with regard to the store layout so that visitors can find their way around the store quickly and easily, e.g., using a navigation bar (Kollmann, 2019, p. 268). Various types of interactions are also becoming increasingly important in e-commerce stores, e.g., the implementation of chatbots (Petereit, 2024). The same applies to the development of communities in the form of online discussion forums or the integration of customer feedback via product reviews (e.g., product ratings) or experience reports (Heinemann, 2022, p. 280; Mull, 2023; Zentes et al., 2017, 77f., 336). In addition, the integration of corporate social media accounts or the collaboration with influencers is particularly important, especially with regard to social proof for building trust (Mull, 2023).

[14] "Erlebniswelten" in German language.

2.3.3 Characteristics and Features of Virtual Stores

After analyzing the virtual stores, the statements made by the experts (including DuBoff, Singh, Hackl, etc.) described in the previous chapters can be confirmed. This is because the analysis has shown that virtual stores have C&F and both brick-and-mortar and e-commerce stores. The main ones are discussed below, starting with the C&F known from brick-and-mortar stores.

In general, the basic principles of brick-and-mortar stores in terms of store design, store layout and store atmosphere can also be applied to virtual stores. This is because virtual stores are structured like brick-and-mortar stores, except that much more is possible in terms of the store design of virtual stores (author's own experience). In November 2023, Emperia (2023d) launched a virtual holiday store for Bloomingdale's called "Bloomingdale's Holidays". This virtual store was a creative, fictitious store that offers everything that is almost impossible to realize in real life, e.g., Willi Wonka's chocolate factory paying homage to the new Wonka movie (Emperia, 2023d; Lockwood, 2023). For instance, in terms of store layout, the store areas of a virtual store can be divided qualitatively into item-oriented store areas, just like in brick-and-mortar stores. However, unlike in brick-and-mortar stores, there is no limitation of space in virtual stores. The "L'Occitane En Provence" holiday store by L'Occitane, for example, is divided into four worlds inspired by the key ingredients of their four collections: Lavender, Strawflower, Almond and Shea Butter. While the creation of four completely different worlds is difficult to realize in real-life stores.

In addition, virtual stores can be fully explored in real-time and 360-degree view, recreating the shopping experience in brick-and-mortar stores, which is impossible in e-commerce stores (Whyte, 2002, p. 3). This also creates a higher level of telepresence for visitors, i.e., the feeling of really being there in the virtual store, than in e-commerce stores (J. V. Chen, Ha, & Vu, 2022, p. 5; Kim, Kim, Park, & Yoo, 2023, p. 4). J. Pfeiffer (2023, p. 14) confirm that the feeling of telepresence also leads to more fun for the consumer, above all through the real-feeling interactions with the product that are possible in virtual stores. Consumers can try out the products or even configure them according to their preferences (e.g., Dyson VR demo, Mazda car configurator). Moreover, consumers can better estimate the size relations of products (J. Pfeiffer, 2023, p. 14). In addition, the products in virtual stores look more realistic and lifelike (also known as vividness) than in e-commerce stores. In the virtual store shopping app of J.Crew, Vision Pro users can create life-size outfit combinations for different occasions interactively. With intuitive hand and eye movements, customers can configure different products and looks. Through the integration of Apple Pay, all looks can be seamlessly added to the shopping cart and purchased directly in the app (Obsess, 2024b). This shows how C&F of brick-and-mortar and e-commerce stores are combined in virtual stores, i.e., the interaction with the environment and products from brick-and-mortar stores and the seamless integration of the payment process through Apple Pay from e-commerce stores.

Apart from interacting with products, consumers also have the opportunity to interact socially with other people such as friends, acquaintances or sales assistants in virtual stores, which is also known as social presence in the VR context (Trier & Steiger, 2023, p. 205). Disney's virtual store in collaboration with Charlotte Tilbury, called "Virtual Disney 100 × Charlotte Tilbury Beauty Wonderland", has a "Shop with Friends" feature that allows consumers to shop together and discover products as they would in the real world. They can give each other real-time opinions via audio or video, exchange looks and explore the virtual store together (Hanson, 2021). J. Pfeiffer (2023, p. 14) also tested sales assistants who may appear or be activated when consumers need help, either in the form of a human-controlled sales avatar or a algorithmically controlled avatar.

Like e-commerce stores, virtual stores cannot appeal to all the senses like brick-and-mortar stores do. The sense of sight and hearing can be addressed easily and even much better via the VR headset than in e-commerce stores when consumers only look at a flat display. Other senses such as touch, taste and smell require more hardware, e.g., haptic devices, which is not affordable for the average consumer (Fang, Zhang, Şensoy, & Magnenat-Thalmann, 2014, p. 412; T. Pfeiffer, 2023, 37; J. Pfeiffer, 2023, p. 14).

Conversely, virtual stores can also have C&F that are known from e-commerce stores and that brick-and-mortar stores cannot have. One example of this is personalization (J. Pfeiffer, 2023, p. 14; Xi & Hamari, 2021, p. 47). In the Crocs Jibbitz™ experience, visitors can create their own Crocs. In the Alo Yoga virtual store shopping app, users can personalize the environment, e.g., by changing the background scene.

Another example is social proof. Although there have also been use cases in brick-and-mortar stores such as *Thalia*. For a while, Thalia placed short reviews written by employees on the top books in the stationary store (author's own experience). However, it is not possible in the brick-and-mortar store to the same extent as in the e-commerce store or now also in the virtual store. Just like community building and events, which are much easier to realize in an e-commerce store or virtual store than in a brick-and-mortar store. The availability of information, educational as well as user-generated content, which is particularly present in e-commerce, can also be integrated into virtual stores (e.g., Clinique Virtual Lab).

In Fendi's virtual store, the 57th Street Flagship NY, there is a wish list, similar to those found in e-commerce stores, which offers visitors an alternative to the "Add to cart" button if they do not want to buy a product directly but would like to remember it for a potential future purchase.

Most virtual stores have gamified elements, such as scavenger hunts or quizzes. In the example above, Bloomingdale's has integrated a "chocolate treasure hunt" (also referred to as scavenger hunt) within the Wonka area of their virtual store, which encourages the visitor to collect all five chocolate bars to receive a special surprise (Fonrouge, 2023). These special surprises can be discounts, but also access to exclusive areas in the virtual store or exclusive content (for example see Emperia, 2023b; Lacoste, 2023).

In addition, there are brands that have collaborated with artists, not only in the design of their virtual stores (e.g., Steven Wilson for the L'Occitane Christmas Virtual Store), but also for events such as concerts (e.g., Coldplay in BMW Joytopia or Lil Dre for Vert Metamorph Experience by Diesel and Fossil).

On their blog, Obsess (2023e) presented the five most important features for 2023 that encourage engagement in virtual stores. These were (1) gamification, (2) branded avatars, (3) shop with friends, (4) welcome tutorial, and (5) store maps. Gamified elements led to a ten times higher probability of clicking on "Add to cart". Branded avatars increased the likelihood of proceeding to checkout by 183%. Shopping with friends led to a 104% increase in time spent in the virtual store. A welcome tutorial led to 72% more visits to virtual store pages. Finally, store maps increased the likelihood (3.8 times higher completion rate) of consumers completing a virtual store once (Obsess, 2023e). This could be due to the fact that maps enable more intuitive navigation (see "wayfinding", Appendix A, Tab A-1).

In 2014, I. Krasonikolakis et al. (2014) also investigated potential features of virtual stores and those that consumers would use to select or visit a virtual store and how these would influence the choice of visiting a virtual store (I. Krasonikolakis et al., 2014, p. 10). They could identify four types of features that highly influenced the choice: (1) core store features, (2) peripheral store features, (3) security and privacy, and lastly, (5) social and promotional impulsion (I. Krasonikolakis et al., 2014, p. 31). The first, core store features included the "variety of products", quick access", "easy walking through the store", as well as the "prices". The second, peripheral store features, comprised of the "quality of the products", "store reputation", "value added services" and "customer support". Security and privacy protection were subsumed under security and privacy. Social and promotional impulsion incorporated the following features: "my friends visit the particular store", "quality of advertising and exhibitions" and "entertaining activities within the store" (I. Krasonikolakis et al., 2014, p. 16).

To conclude, the advantages of brick-and-mortar stores especially lie in their multi-sensory staging of the store and the goods as well as the possibility of social interactions, including personal and individual advice from store assistants or other visitors. Moreover, a brick-and-mortar store can transfer emotions directly to the consumer, e.g., through the feeling of actually being there (Haeusel, 2012, p. 631). On the other hand, the advantage of e-commerce stores lies in their convenience, accessibility and availability of information (Rohleder, 2021, p. 7, 2022, p. 11). Virtual stores seem to combine both and in this way they gain a superiority over the other channels. The C&F used highly depend on the virtual store type, similar to the basic strategic emotional positioning in the form of shopping worlds in brick-and-mortar stores and the strategic positioning in e-commerce (GS1 Germany, 2018; Haeusel, 2012, p. 635). Table 2.1 below summarizes the characteristics and features of virtual stores (based on both literature and author's own analysis of virtual stores).

2.4 Advantages and Disadvantages of Virtual Stores

This section concludes Chap. 2 with a comparison of the advantages and disadvantages of virtual stores from both the customer's (see Sect. 2.4.1) and the company's point of view (see Sect. 2.4.2).

2.4.1 Consumer Perspective

From the customer's point of view, virtual stores offer several advantages. According to Regt and Barnes (2019, p. 20), virtual stores would create "a more personalized, immersive and interactive experience". Moreover, for the first time, people have the opportunity to visit in-real life existing stores from all around the world since virtual stores can be visited by everyone and they are not limited to their location as is the case with brick-and-mortar stores (Obsess, 2023h). Furthermore, virtual stores provide a convenient alternative to visiting brick-and-mortar stores as people can visit them around the clock from the comfort of their homes (Emperia, 2024; Obsess, 2020). Besides, J. Pfeiffer (2023, p. 16) pointed out that customers would have more fun through telepresence and the possibility

Table 2.1 Store Characteristics and Features / Virtual Stores

Characteristics	Features		Reference to Use Case List [No.][a]	Sources
Store Design / Store Atmosphere	Depends on type of virtual store (Virtual Retail Stores, Virtual Flagship Stores, Virtual Store-in-Store, Virtual Designer Outlets, Virtual Shopping Malls, Virtual Pop-up Stores, Virtual Holiday Stores, Virtual Showrooms, Virtual Platform Stores, Virtual Store Shopping Apps, and Virtual Product Configurators; also see section 2.2)			
	Storytelling	E.g., entry ride in a car	[06], [09], [10]	Fuchs, 2023; Regt et al., 2019, p. 20.
	Place / Background Scenes / Ambience	Beach (house)	[03], [12]	
		Cinema	[20]	
		House	[10], [70]	
		Light House	[12]	
		Boat House	[12]	
		Skyscraper	[32], [43]	
		Chalet	[06], [20], [58]	
		City	[09], [15], [32], [43], [45]	
		Golf Course	[87]	
		Crocodile	[11]	
		Snow Lodge	[06]	
		Winter Wonderland	[06], [47], [58], [89]	
		North Pole	[48]	
		Ski Mountains	[22]	
		Forest	[65]	
		Desert	[10]	
		Sky	[49]	
		Night	[09]	
		Moon	[48; Chanel's Space]	

(continued)

Table 2.1 (continued)

Characteristics		Features	Reference to Use Case List [No.]	Sources
Store Design / Store Atmosphere	Theme	E.g., classic, festive, spiritual, urban, self-expression, movie, energetic	[06], [09], [12], [13], [17], [41], [42], [47] [56], [57], [62], [74], [85]	
	Style	Realistic / skeuomorphism	[02], [12], [15], [17], [24], [30], [32], [33], [52], [53], [68], [93]	
		Futuristic	[49]	
		Fictional	[08], [14], [16], [19], [46]	
		Mixed	[10], [45], [62], [66], [74]	
	Color Scheme	Warm	[08], [10], [45]	
		Cold	[48]	
		Earthy	[10], [14]	
		Clean	[17], [32], [61]	
		Bright	[14]	
		Corporate Identity	[12], [17], [66]	
		Fluorescent	[09], [16], [30], [49]	
	Fonts		All	
	Shapes and forms	E, g., brand logo	[10], [16], [28]	
	Decoration	E.g., wardrobe, sculptures, mannequins, buildings, balloons, plants, flowers, tree	Almost all, e.g., [09], [10], [15], [30], [32], [45]	
	Quotes		[09], [10]	
	Window Dressing	Fantasy window (theme oriented), poster window, stacking window, overview window, installations	[32], [33], [40], [41], [43], [45]	
	Entrance	Welcome	All	
		Help and usage instructions		
		FAQ		

(continued)

Table 2.1 (continued)

Characteristics	Features		Reference to Use Case List [No.]	Sources
Store Design / Store Atmosphere	Orientation, Wayfinding, Direction	Maps	[06], [09], [14]	
		Floor plan	[32]	
		Signs	Almost all	
		Info points	Almost all, e.g., [42], [62]	
	Attention Points		Almost all, e.g., [62]	
	Favorites / Wishlist		[32], [35]	
	Presentation of Goods	3D product visualizations	All	
		Product details (e.g., name, price, size)	Almost all [06]	
		Product descriptions	[11]	
		Product images	Almost all, e.g., [2], [32]	
		Basic collection	[17], [32]	
		Bestseller collection	[62]	
		Latest / seasonal collections	[01], [11], [12], [15], [19], [20], [57], [58]	
		Product range	[33]	
		True-to-life product displays	Almost all, e.g., [13], [32]	
	Lighting	Lighting (intensity, brightness, brighter or dimmed lighting)	[83]	Lau / Lee, 2019, p. 260.
		Lighting installations	Almost all [32], [41]	
	Senses / Sensory Feedback	Sight, sound, (touch)	Almost all	Lau / Lee, 2019, p. 256; Krasonikolakis et al., 2011, p. 65.

(continued)

Table 2.1 (continued)

Characteristics	Features		Reference to Use Case List [No.]	Sources
Audio	Music	Background music (genre, e.g., blues, bossa nova, classic, fast fashion beat, jazz and mid-fashion beat)	Almost all, e.g., [56], [72]	Lau / Lee, 2019, p. 260
		Jukebox	[11]	
		Spotify playlist	[06]	
	Sounds	Traffic	[45], [32],	
		Crackling fire	[06]	
		Birds		
	Volume control		Also depends on device	Lau / Lee, 2019, p. 260.
Digital Signage, Multimedia and Technologies	Videos	Introduction, products, collections, tutorials, short clips, campaign, advertising, technical features, product design	Almost all, e.g., [06], [15], [32], [42], [45], [66], [76]	
	Images		All, e.g., [10]	
	Illustrations		All	
	Graphics		All	
	Displays		[15], [45]	
	Banner		[45]	
	Animations	E.g., ski lift, butterflies, falling leafs, animated garments	[06], [19], [30], [43], [66]	
	QR-Codes		[72]	

(continued)

Table 2.1 (continued)

Characteristics	Features		Reference to Use Case List [No.]	Sources
Store Layout				
Visual	Qualitative Division of Store	Theme-oriented	[62]	Krasonikolakis, 2018, pp. 1224-1226
		Item-oriented, product-line-oriented	[10], [13], [51], [56], [62]	
		Brand-oriented	[42], [48], [49]	
	Store-within-a-Store	Multi-brand	[42], [48], [49]	
		Floors	[09], [13], [30]	
		Buildings (e.g., chalets)		
		Showroom	[17], [68], [72], [75], [82], [94]	
		VIP rooms	[11]	
		Gallery	[72], Vogue	
		Community Club	[72]	
		Creative Hub	[74]	
		Catwalk	[14], [16], [31]	
		Fireplace Room	[44]	
		Iglo Dance Floor	[57]	
	Guidance system			
	Freedom of movement			
	Crowding and dysfunctional density (prevention)		[76]	Coeper, Hake et al., 2023.
	Menu		[06], [30]	
	Elevator		[11]	
	Escalator		[30]	
	Stairs		[24]	

(continued)

Table 2.1 (continued)

Characteristics	Features		Reference to Use Case List [No.]	Sources
Quality	Resolution / Fidelity / Definition	Visuals, products		
Usability	Ease of use	Maps, tour	[09], [25]	
Information Availability	Usage-related	Instructions		
	Product-related	Product detail pages		
		Product information		
		Product descriptions		
Interactivity	Social Interactions	Video chats	[01], [60]	
		Voice chats	[01]	
		Avatars	[04], [08], [14], [21], [25], [34], [36], [45], [54], [64], [72]	Mango, 2024; Claire's, 2022; Fortnite, 2022.
	AI Chatbot		[19]	
	Product Interactions	Try-ons (e.g., on avatars, on mannequins)	[01], [03], [50], [62], [68]	
		Try-outs	[54], [58], [59], [76]	
		Textures	[01], [58],	
		Zoom	[01], [54]	
		Tap on products	Almost all [30]	
		Rotate / 360-degree-view	Almost all	
		Product configurations, e.g., interactive closet, creation of new looks, colors	[01], [15], [57], [76], [83], [90]	
	Activities	Guided meditations, stretching excercises, yoga, pilates and medations classes	[03], [15], [56],	
	Real-time		All	
	Wishlist	e.g., Santa's wishlist	[10], [58]	
	Gift finder		[68]	

(continued)

Table 2.1 (continued)

Characteristics	Features		Reference to Use Case List [No.]	Sources
Personalization / Customization	Sound (on/off)		All that have integrated sound	
	Background scene		[01], [03]	
	(Interior) Colors		[06]	
	Products		[13], [45], [68]	
	Offers / Promotions			
	Language		[10],	
	Name		[06], [15]	
	Avatars		[14], [60]	
	360-degree-view		All	
Gamification	Levels		[45]	
	Scavenger hunt	E. g., crocodiles, chocolate bars, Christmas elements, ski passes, ingredients	[06], [11], [42], [58], [62]	
	Rewards	E.g., discount, non-fungible token (NFT), digital asset, skin	[11], [45], [58], [74], [80]	
	Quiz		[12], [13]	
	Color by Numbers		[56]	
	Other	Ice skating, treasure hunts, dancing, ski tricks, mini games, car racing	[22], [25], [57], [77], [78], [80], [88]	

(continued)

Table 2.1 (continued)

Characteristics	Features		Reference to Use Case List [No.]	Sources
Loyalty Program			[11]	
Content / Education	Brand history, Brand's heritage	E.g., timeline, lookbooks	[06], [10], [12], [17], [45], [62], e.g., L'Occitane Christmas	
	Story			
	Product	E.g., ingredients, production process, application, usage instructions	[61], [62], [66]	
	Tutorials		[62], [76]	
	How-to Videos			
	Styling Tips	E.g., layering	[06]	
	Behind the Scenes / Making-off			
	Brand's Initiatives / Campaigns	E.g., sustainability	[39], [58]	
Access	VR technology	VR headset, VR glasses		
	Mobile	Smartphone, tablet		
	Desktop	Laptop, PC		
Checkout	Direct	Add-to-cart button Remove from cart Check my cart Checkout Back to store Shopping cart	The minority, e.g., [01], [02], [03], [06], [15], [33], [45], [55], [56], [62]	Lau / Lee, 2019, p. 260.
	Indirect	Link to e-commerce store	Almost all, e.g., [10], [14], [15], [32], [33], [42], [45], [48], [66], [72]	
	Payment Integration	Apple Pay integratiom	[01], [56]	

(continued)

Table 2.1 (continued)

Characteristics	Features		Reference to Use Case List [No.]	Sources
Product Offerings	Physical products		Almost all	
	Digital Product		[04], [22], [29], [57], [71]	JBL, 2024; Mango, 2024.
	Phygital Products		[11], [14], [16], [21], [27], [31]	Wootton, 2023; Fortnite, 2022; McGuire, 2021.
Other	Exclusivity	Store spaces for "members only", exclusive content	[11], [14], [15], [16], [19]	
		Exclusive collections, products	[42], [72]	
		Limited editions	[22]	
	Omnichannel	Linking to social media, e-commerce store, brick-and-mortar store	[04], [14], [15]	Mango, 2024.
	Artists / Designer / Creators	Artist *Steven Wilson*	[58]	Obsess, 2023.
		Roblox creator *SimplyALemon*	[57]	
		Roblox creator *Rush Bogin (Rush X)*	[05]	Adidas AG, 2023.
		Roblox creator *Robuilds*	[71]	
	Developer	Roblox developer, e.g., *Funomena*	[22]	
	Digital service provider	*Spotify*	[06]	
	Avatar creator	*Ready Player Me, Obsess*	[14], [64]	
	Events	Concerts, e.g., *Coldplay, BGYO, Lil Dre*	[08], [25], [81], H&M x BGYO	
	Technology	*Obsess, Emperia, byondxr, Zreality, Matterport*		
	Partnerships	*Wonder Works Studio*	[25]	Claire's, 2022.

Note. These tables show characteristics and features of virtual stores (based on both literature and author's own analysis). It should be noted that, despite careful and detailed research, no guarantee of completeness can be given. In addition, some characteristics and features cannot be clearly assigned to just one characteristic or feature.

[a] The use cases in square brackets are examples of the corresponding features, i.e., not all use cases that have this specific feature are listed. The use case list can be provided upon request by the author.

of interacting with products and people, such as sales assistants. In addition, customers have the opportunity to shop with other people in virtual stores or interact directly with sales assistants, which was previously not possible in e-commerce stores in this form. J. Pfeiffer (2023, p. 14) found out that virtual stores would reduce the cognitive load on consumers. What is also good about virtual stores for customers is that they can personalize their environment on their own preferences, e.g., changing the background scene, lightning, or their avatar (J. Pfeiffer, 2023, p. 16) (also see Table 2.1).

In the winter semester 2022/23, the author and three other fellow students conducted research on the topic of "meta commerce" in the form of qualitative interviews about two VR experiences (including the Dyson VR demo and the Burberry Regent Street virtual flagship store), the participants had previously visited with the Meta Quest 2. In these interviews, the participants were asked to talk about the advantages and disadvantages that a virtual store would entail.

Many participants mentioned as advantages the independence of time and place (e.g., visiting a virtual store in London from Germany), but also the joy and fun of visiting virtual stores compared to e-commerce stores. They also saw social contact via avatars as advantageous, as this would preserve a certain degree of anonymity. They also mentioned the advantage of shopping for themselves, without the stress of overcrowding and sensory overload caused by other people. They also liked the ability to interact with the products in real time and gain a better insight into the product and its dimensions. In this context, the participants also emphasized the superiority of virtual stores over e-commerce stores. Not, however, in comparison to brick-and-mortar stores, as many more senses can be addressed in these, e.g., in terms of haptics and smell. They saw an advantage over brick-and-mortar stores in the size and variety of the product range, which, unlike in brick-and-mortar stores but just like in e-commerce, is independent of the floor space. In addition, the participants imagined that with virtual stores it would be possible to switch or jump from store to store, a phenomenon known in e-commerce as "channel hopping" (Heinemann, 2022, p. 362). The author of this work thus derived a new term in the context of virtual stores, namely "store hopping". What would prove to be a shopping marathon or even unthinkable in real life, when shopping in brick-and-mortar stores, is suddenly very easy in the virtual world: visiting one store or shopping mall after another, across all national borders and time zones. This is called "store hopping".

On the other hand, the participants also mentioned some disadvantages of virtual stores, such as motion sickness (Hake, Coeper, Otschik, Schuhmann, & Zaharia, 2023, p. 45). The risk of motion sickness was also recognized by J. Pfeiffer (2023, p. 12) and Jin, Kim, Moore, and Rothenberg (2021, p. 14).

The participants also criticized the price of the hardware and the lack of use cases that currently make it not affordable to buy VR glasses. Contrary to the researchers' expectations, the majority of participants had no concerns about data protection or payment security. They compared virtual stores with e-commerce stores, which in their eyes were also secure and there was no cause for concern in this respect. Other participants, however, feared system and data security risks, but also risks such as social hatred and body shaming. They also saw a high potential for addiction, which could automatically lead to social distancing or even isolation (Hake et al., 2023, p. 45).

2.4.2 Company Perspective

In addition to the advantages and disadvantages that virtual stores bring for consumers, companies can also benefit or be negatively affected by virtual stores. Virtual stores have been proven to lead to higher brand recall, greater willingness to buy and lower price sensitivity among consumers. Moreover, virtual stores provide the opportunity to present larger product ranges (J. Pfeiffer, 2023, p. 16). In addition, virtual stores just like e-commerce stores or omnichannel services have great potential in terms of tracking customers and generating data, be it first party or second party data (Darbinyan, 2022; Hackl, 2022; J. Pfeiffer, 2023, p. 16).

Emperia has disclosed the performance of some of their created virtual stores in the form of key performance indicators (KPIs). Cyberdog's virtual store, for example, generated an average of 15 clicks per session and 14:02 minutes dwell time and had a total of around 19,121 visitors (Emperia, 2021a). ebay's first virtual store achieved high brand awareness with over 787,980,000 media impressions and USD 45 million generated in earned media, resulting in an ROI of 3.75%. In the first hour after the release, around 20,000 Shopticals[15] were sold (Matovina et al., 2016). Campbell-Gross (2022) found that 70% of people who visited a virtual store ended up buying something. In addition, according to Obsess (2022a), virtual stores would reduce companies' costs by (1) incurring less opening costs compared to brick-and-mortar stores, (2) having faster go-to-market times than brick-and-mortar stores and (3) causing less operating costs compared to brick-and-mortar stores.

[15] Shopticals were specially developed VR viewers to experience eBay's VR department store (Matovina et al., 2016).

In addition, through virtual stores companies can have a greater reach than with their brick-and-mortar stores. As e-commerce stores, but different to brick-and-mortar stores, virtual stores enable shopping remotely through which companies can generate higher sales (Obsess, 2021a). This shows that companies can maximize their KPIs (e.g., brand awareness, number of (unique) visitors, reach, engagement rate, click-through-rate, conversion rate, average time spent etc.) through virtual stores full funnel (I. Krasonikolakis et al., 2014, p. 32; Obsess, 2021a, 2024a). At the same time, it is noticeable that similar KPIs are used to measure performance in virtual stores as in e-commerce stores (Zentes et al., 2017, p. 337). In addition, companies can create a lasting and independent competitive advantage with the help of virtual stores, thus setting themselves apart from the competition (Larson, 2021).

With the help of companies such as Obsess or Emperia, the creation and maintenance of virtual stores is affordable for companies. In 2023, Obsess launched a self-service virtual store builder through which brands are able to build and customize virtual stores as well as 3D e-commerce experiences on their own (Marin-Lopez, 2023). In addition, Obsess offers brands so-called "ready-to-use virtual store templates" which are pre-designed spaces that can be customized by brands according to their preferences or e.g., their corporate guidelines (Obsess, 2023d). Hence, virtual stores are not as static as brick-and-mortar stores and their components can be easily customized, as with e-commerce stores (McDowell, 2020). J. Pfeiffer (2023, p. 14) also emphasizes that the presentation of the 3D environment of virtual stores is easy to adapt, as are the store layout, the shopping atmosphere, and the presentation of information and products (J. Pfeiffer, 2023, p. 14). Moreover, virtual stores can be easily integrated into the e-commerce store (Obsess, 2023b). For instance, Obsess is a member of SAP's curated startup ecosystem which makes their virtual stores easy to integrate into SAP commerce cloud (SAP, 2024). On SAP (2024), it states that virtual stores from provider Obsess would lead to an up to 70% higher conversion rate compared to regular e-commerce stores and generate a 20% higher average order value. Another virtual store provider, ByondXR, also emphasizes that virtual stores would lead to higher retention and conversion rates and longer user engagement compared to e-commerce stores (ByondXR, 2022).

On the other side, J. Pfeiffer (2023, p. 16) also points out the current drawbacks of virtual stores that are: (1) technical challenges, e.g., low graphic resolution and interface problems, (2) high costs for programming the 3D environment, (3) concerns about data security and privacy[16], as well as (4) energy consumption for servers and high performance capacity which can automatically affect the brand's reputation with regard to sustainability[17].

[16] Although this could not be confirmed as part of the research project "Meta-Commerce" by the author and her fellow students (also see Sect. 3.2.2).

[17] Obsess (2022b) published a blog post of how virtual stores can help industries, especially the fashion industry in terms of sustainability. Obsess highlights that virtual stores would imply a more sustainable way to shop. They argue that virtual stores would reduce a brand's carbon footprint, as brick-and-mortar stores would create a larger carbon footprint than virtual stores, especially through in-store displays (also see Larson (2021)). They also emphasize that virtual stores would reduce production waste. While the latter may be true, it is questionable whether virtual stores really cause less carbon emissions than brick-and-mortar stores, as virtual stores require high computing power according to e.g., J. Pfeiffer (2023, p. 16).

3 Customer Experience

3.1 Theoretical Background on Customer Experience

Following the brief introduction into immersive experiences in virtual stores in Sect. 2.1.4, this chapter further deals with all about CX. In particular, a definition of the CX is provided and the development of the CX as a latent, multidimensional construct in scientific research is examined. Moreover, theoretical models of the CX and the current state of research on CX in virtual stores are discussed. Subsequently, the identified C&F of virtual stores from Sect. 2.3 are combined with the dimensions of the CX as part of the conceptualization in Chap. 4.

Even today, there is still no scientific consensus on the definition and concept of CX as it can be viewed from multiple perspectives and in different contexts (De Keyser, Lemon, Klaus, & Keiningham, 2015, 14, 16; Lemon & Verhoef, 2016, p. 70; Schwertfeger, 2012, p. 30). However, there are definitions that have found major acceptance and agreement which are at the same time suitable in the specific context of this work. The following explanations are intended to clarify the concept of CX and contribute to its understanding. It concludes with an independent definition of the CX in this context.

First of all, it is important to point out that CX in this work is used as an experience construct, which is assigned to the research area of experience marketing (Bruhn & Hadwich, 2012, pp. 8–10).

According to Bruhn and Hadwich (2012), there are both economic and behavioral approaches to explaining the CX (Bruhn & Hadwich, 2012, pp. 10–12). This work is based solely on the behavioral science approach, which can be especially traced back to Abbott (1955), Hirschman and Holbrook (1982), Havlena and Holbrook (1986), Gröppel-Klein (1991), Weinberg (1992), Schmitt (1999), Gentile, Spiller, and Noci (2007), as well as Brakus, Schmitt, and Zarantonello (2009).

M. Hake, *Shopping in Virtual Stores*, BestMasters,
https://doi.org/10.1007/978-3-658-48634-1_3

3.1.1 Definition of Customer Experience

In the 1980s, Hirschman and Holbrook laid the foundation for the concept of the "customer experience"[1] and were among the first to discuss and conceptualize it in more detail after Abbott (1955) and Alderson (1967) did. They observed a phenomenon that they themselves referred to as "hedonic consumption" and under which they summarized "facets of consumer behavior that relate to the multi-sensory, fantasy and emotive aspects of product usage experience" (Hirschman & Holbrook, 1982, p. 92). Hirschman and Holbrook's (1982) definition focuses on the customer's experience when using a product. Later, Gröppel-Klein (1991, p. 185) compared experiential shopping with a leisure activity. It was emphasized that experiential shopping is not just about satisfying needs, but about making shopping fun for the customer through new and unusual "things" so that he or she enjoys it. Gröppel-Klein (1991) thus focused on the experience during the product purchase and differed from Hirschman and Holbrook's (1982) definition in that it clearly highlights a different type of experience in a different phase of the purchasing process.

Following Gröppel-Klein's (1991), Weinberg (1992) brought a new perspective to the definition of CX by considering the subjectivity of the CX and referring to the impact of it on the customer's quality of life. In addition, Weinberg (1992, p. 3) referred to it as sensory experiences that are anchored in the consumer's emotional and experiential world and make a real contribution to quality of life.

Later, in 1998, Pine and Gilmore (1998) picked up on this phenomenon and predicted the transition of Western economies from a service economy to an experience economy, in which experiences will form the basis of economic performance in the future, for which the provision of goods and services will only be seen as a tool for the creation of experiences (Pine & Gilmore, 1998). By then, the CX was seen as an important, if not the most important lever for value creation in business, which has led to a variety of interests in this topic (Bruhn & Mayer-Vorfelder, 2011, p. 3).

Shortly afterwards, various opinions and definitions on the concept of CX emerged, to name a few, e.g., Schmitt (1999), Mattila and Wirtz (2001), Berry,

[1] In German literature, there are two different meanings for the term "customer experience". On the one hand, it is translated as "Kundenerfahrung" and on the other hand as "Kundenerlebnis". The following work refers to the second translation, customer experience as "Kundenerlebnis" which is the multidimensional reaction of the customer to the experience environment in the virtual store. The second translation would be therefore in turn the summation of these customer experiences (Bruhn and Hadwich (2012, p. 9); Schwertfeger (2012, p. 33).

Carbone, and Haeckel (2002), Gentile et al. (2007), Meyer and Schwager (2007), Brakus et al. (2009), Verhoef, Lemon, Parasuraman, and Roggeveen (2009), Rose, Hair, and Clark (2011), Bruhn and Hadwich (2012), Schwertfeger (2012), Naser-moadeli, Ling, and Maghnati (2013), De Keyser et al. (2015), Lemon and Verhoef (2016), Brun, Rajaobelina, Ricard, and Berthiaume (2017), Zaharia and Schmitz (2019).

In light of this shift from focusing on "(product) features and benefits" to creating CXs, Schmitt (1999) introduced a new, management-oriented approach that totally stood in contrast to traditional marketing and which he called "experience marketing", also known as the CX management approach (Schmitt, 1999, p. 53). As part of his approach, he emphasized that industries and companies should no longer focus on their products, their functional features and benefits, but on the customer, putting him or her in the spotlight, and create experiences through products, communication and campaigns that he or she can identify with and integrate into their lifestyles (Schmitt, 1999, pp. 55–57). To help industries and companies in achieving this and managing CXs, he provided this strategic framework, consisting of so-called "strategic experience modules" on the one hand, and of so-called "experience providers" on the other hand. Particularly, there are five strategic experience modules in total: 1. Sense, 2. Feel, 3. Think, 4. Act, and 5. Relate. By managing these, various experiences could be created. This can be done by the managers of the industries and companies, e.g., through communication, visual and verbal signage or spatial environments (Schmitt, 1999, pp. 60–62). Thus, Schmitt (1999) defined the term "experience" mainly through his strategic experience modules. Later, he concludes that CX is "any form of customer-focused marketing activity that creates a connection to customers" (Schmitt, 2011, p. 63).

Other researcher such as Meyer and Schwager (2007) developed Schmitt's approach further and defined CX as "the internal and subjective response customers have to any direct or indirect contact with a company" (Meyer & Schwager, 2007, p. 2).

Gentile et al. (2009) defined "[…] CX as an evolution of the concept of relationship between the company and the customer: The CX originates from a set of interactions between a customer and a product, a company, or part of its organization, which provoke a reaction (LaSalle and Britton, 2003; Shaw and Ivens, 2005). This experience is strictly personal and implies the customer's involvement at different levels (rational, emotional, sensorial physical and spiritual) (LaSalle and Britton, 2003; Schmitt, 1999). Its evaluation depends on the comparison between a customer's expectations and the stimuli coming from the interaction with the company and its offering in correspondence of the different moments of contact or touch-points [..]" (Gentile et al., 2007, p. 397).

Brakus et al. (2009, pp. 52–53) rather used the term "brand experience" and distinguished between product experience, shopping and service experience, as well as consumption experience. They define "brand experience" as subjective, internal consumer reactions triggered by brand-related stimuli, such as brand-identifying colors, background design elements and others. Moreover, they differentiate brand experience from other constructs like brand attitudes, brand involvement, brand attachment, customer delight, and brand personality (Brakus et al., 2009, p. 53).

Verhoef et al. (2009) defined CX in terms of its holistic and multidimensional nature, encompassing the cognitive, affective, emotional, social and physical reactions of customers to retailers (Verhoef et al., 2009, p. 32). In 2016, Lemon and Verhoef (2016) modified their definition of CX by eliminating the affective and physical dimensions of the CX and focusing on the behavioral, emotional, cognitive, sensorial and relational dimensions. In addition, they have explicitly addressed the holistic nature of the CX, which runs through the customer's entire purchase journey in terms of any experience gained (Lemon & Verhoef, 2016, p. 71).

Another major contribution to the definition of the CX came from A. Palmer (2010), who distinguished between utilitarian and hedonistic definitions of the CX. In particular, A. Palmer (2010) pointed out the role of hedonistic benefits such as positive emotions on the CX and the resulting behavioral intention.

A. Palmer (2010) decided on the use of the CX definition by Gupta and Vajic (2000) resulting through the "interaction with different elements of a context created by the service provider" and highlighted the need of a diverse range of stimuli, such as cues (Gupta & Vajic, 2000, p. 34; A. Palmer, 2010, pp. 198–200). Sect. 2.3 has already mentioned various types of stimuli or cues, which are referred to in this work as C&F of virtual stores.

Back in 2001, Li, Daugherty, and Biocca (2001) distinguished between direct, indirect and virtual experiences. Basically, they concluded that advertising refers to indirect experiences, customers trying out products themselves to direct experiences and a new type of direct experiences, through which it is possible to try-out products virtually, refers to virtual experiences (Li et al., 2001, 15). Linking to this, the term "immersive experiences" became very common in the context of XR (i.e., AR, MR as well as VR; see Sect. 2.1.2). Immersive experiences are based on the concept of immersion, which is defined as the extent to which virtual systems make users feel absorbed, involved and immersed in virtually simulated stimuli or block out stimuli from their physical, real-world environment (Yim, Chu, & Sauer, 2017, p. 97). Additionally, Wedel, Bigné, and Zhang (2020, p. 446), describe the degree of realism of the simulation of the senses of sight, hearing and touch, which are the senses most frequently simulated to the human brain in virtual environments, as immersion. Thus, it can be concluded that immersion highly depends on the technical features of VR systems and devices (Wedel et al., 2020, p. 446).

In the context of defining the concept of CX, Schwertfeger (2012, p. 30) found that the various definitions, even across scientific fields (marketing, psychology, education, sociology and philosophy), have in common that they are subject-determined (meaning that experiences are perceived and felt differently by customers), and that their focus is particularly on affective and cognitive reactions of the customer. Furthermore, not only positive but also negative shopping experiences can arise (Brun et al., 2017, p. 323). In addition, Schwertfeger (2012) has emphasized that in some definitions experiences are also associated with sensory reactions of the customer. These findings by Schwertfeger (2012, p. 30) can also be confirmed by the author. Moreover, what all these definitions have also in common is that the CX is largely defined by its multidimensionality which also lays the foundation for the concept of the CX in this work (Lemon & Verhoef, 2016, p. 70). The next chapter builds on this and explicitly explores CX models.

3.1.2 Customer Experience Models

As previously mentioned in Sect. 3.1.1, Schmitt (1999) provided a strategic framework for experiential marketing in which he defined a total of five strategic experience modules, involving sensory experiences (sense), affective experiences (feel), creative cognitive experiences (think), physical experiences, behaviors and lifestyles (act), as well as social-identity experiences that result from relating to a reference group or culture (relate) (Schmitt, 1999, pp. 60–62; Brakus et al., 2009, p. 54; Schmitt, 2011, p. 68). His framework is considered one of the most important, fundamental contributions when it comes to determining the dimensions of the CX construct (Bruhn & Hadwich, 2012, p. 12). Apart from Schmitt (1999), there are several other important contributions.

Berry et al. (2002), provided insights into how companies can manage the total CX by recognizing the clues companies are sending to their customers in a first step. Berry et al. (2002, p. 86), differentiate between two categories of "clues": (1) clues that relate to functionality and (2) clues that relate to emotions, including "smells, sounds, sights, tastes and textures of the product or service". The latter category is further subdivided into mechanical (clues emanating from things; also referred to as "mechanics") and human clues (clues emanating from people; also referred to as "humanics") (Berry et al., 2002, p. 86). In their work, Bruhn and Mayer-Vorfelder (2011, p. 5) also investigated the influence of emotional and functional experience drivers on CX.

Gentile et al. (2007) expanded on the work of Schmitt (1999) and identified a total of six dimensions of the CX. They divided the construct of the CX into the following dimensions: sensorial, emotional, cognitive, pragmatic, lifestyle, and relational. In contrast to Schmitt (1999), the authors integrate a new dimension—the "pragmatic dimension"—which stems from the concept of usability. It refers to the communication of physical experiences, ways of interacting, It aims to change the rational behavior and lifestyle of consumers over the entire use and life cycle of a product (Bruhn & Hadwich, 2012, p. 13; Gentile et al., 2007, p. 398).

In 2009, Schmitt, together with Brakus and Zarantonello, revised his framework for CXs and used the term "brand experience", which they conceptualized multidimensionally with the following five dimensions: sensory, affective, intellectual, behavioral and social. The social dimension replaced the relational dimension in a semantically consistent way.

In addition, they identified so-called brand stimuli that can trigger the experience dimensions (Brakus et al., 2009, p. 54). They also examined previous experiences with a brand (Brakus et al., 2009, p. 55). In addition to the brand experience, they examined the overall brand evaluation and customer delight (Brakus et al., 2009, p. 62).

Another influential contribution comes from Verhoef et al. (2009). They also concluded that the construct of CX is holistic in nature and emphasized its multidimensionality, encompassing the cognitive, affective, emotional, social and physical responses of a customer to retailers. Furthermore, they considered different situational moderators, such as "store type", "location", or "the culture of the customer" as well as consumer-related moderators, including "experiential or task oriented goals, socio-demographics, or attitudes of the customer" (Verhoef et al., 2009, pp. 32–34).

In 2011, Rose et al. (2011, p. 29) reviewed literature on the concept of CX in the online context. Later, in 2012, Rose, Clark, Samouel, and Hair (2012, p. 308) followed up on this by investigating the cognitive experiential (including interactive speed, telepresence, challenge, and skill) and affective experiential state (including perceived control with ease-of-use, customization, and connectedness, as subdimensions, as well aesthetics, and perceived benefits) as components of online CX (Rose et al., 2012, p. 310).

De Keyser et al. (2015) also highlighted the multidimensionality of the CX and conceptualized it by considering five CX dimensions in total: the cognitive, emotional, physical, sensorial, and social dimension. According to De Keyser et al. (2015), each dimension comprises various corresponding elements that generate both direct and indirect consumer interactions with market players such as retailers or brands (De Keyser et al., 2015, p. 29).

Following their own studies and several other studies on CX, Lemon and Verhoef (2016) modified their definition and conceptualization of CX in 2016 by eliminating the affective and physical dimensions of the CX and modified their definition and conceptualization of CX in 2016 by eliminating the affective and physical dimensions of CX and focusing on the behavioral, emotional, cognitive, sensory, and relational responses of a customer to company's offerings throughout the entire customer journey (Lemon & Verhoef, 2016, p. 71).

In 2017, Brun et al. (2017, p. 323), investigated two affective dimensions of CX, a positive as well as negative affective dimension. They also included a cognitive, sensory, behavioral and social dimension as well as the moderating effect of channel into their CX model (Brun et al., 2017, p. 327).

Finally, Hoffman and Novak (2018, p. 1188) pointed out that there were five key dimensions that were most frequently mentioned and used in the literature and grouped them under the acronym BASIS which stands for the "behavioral (or physical), affective (feelings: emotional, experiential or hedonic), sensory (or sensations), intellectual (cognitive or rational) and social dimensions of the CX".

Zaharia and Schmitz (2019, p. 2) examined the CX in an e-commerce context and integrated a new dimension of fulfillment alongside the cognitive, affective, sensory, social and general CX.

To conclude, CX is a multidimensional construct that is investigated differently and incorporates different dimensions depending on the context of research. The following dimensions of CX could be identified: Sensory Dimension, (Positive / Negative) Affective / Emotional Dimension, Cognitive Dimension, Social Dimension, Conative / Behavioral / Pragmatic Dimension, Lifestyle Dimension, Fulfillment Dimension.

3.2 State of Research on the Customer Experience in Virtual Stores

3.2.1 Overview of Studies on Shopping Experiences in Virtual Stores

To understand the landscape of existing studies on shopping in virtual stores in virtual environments such as the metaverse and the influence of CX on the behavioral intention to use virtual stores (BI), a review of relevant literature apart from the CX construct was conducted. As there is only little research on this, especially in form of empirical research, similar research fields including v-commerce, consumer behavior and CX were investigated (Wedel et al., 2020, p. 457). In addition, literature from the fields of metaverse and store design was also reviewed. Table 3.1 represents the literature reviewed that directly relate to virtual (shopping) experiences (in virtual stores). The literature review shows that no empirical study has yet been conducted on the topic of shopping in virtual stores in virtual environments such as the metaverse and the influence of the CX as a multidimensional construct on the BI.

In 2000, Chittaro and Ration (2000), analyzed the integration of features of real, physical stores into VR stores and developed a first prototype of a VR store called ADVIRT, which could be personalized by so-called adaptive features.

First of all, they listed the benefits of VR interfaces: "(i) it is closer to the real world shopping experience, and thus more familiar to the customer, (ii) it supports customer's natural shopping actions, (iii) it can satisfy the needs of customers who have an emotional style of buying, by providing a more immersive, interactive, and visually attractive experience, (iv) it can even satisfy social needs, by allowing customers to meet and interact with people (e.g., other customers or salespeople)" (Chittaro & Ration, 2000, p. 86). They emphasized the importance of store design including navigation, usability, interactivity, as well as audio (Chittaro & Ration, 2000, pp. 87, 89, 96). However, it should also appeal to the need of the creation of customer profiles to be able to satisfy social needs (e.g., customers can meet and interact in VR stores) and build a sense of community in VR stores. However, they pointed out that personalized features and the simultaneous visit of several customers would conflict, i.e., the more visitors are in the VR store, the less can it be personalized (Chittaro & Ration, 2000, p. 96).

Li et al. (2001, pp. 27f.) did an exploratory study in form of a protocol analysis (N = 30) on virtual experiences and derived a definition of it. They concluded that a "virtual experience consists of vivid, involving, active, and affective psychological states occurring in an individual interacting with [3D] computer simulations" (Li et al., 2001, p. 27) and that a "virtual experience is closer to direct experience than to indirect experience in terms of effective consumer learning" (Li et al., 2001, p. 28). They found that the presentation of 3D products and interactions in VR are positively associated with pleasure (Li et al., 2001, p. 22).

K. C. Lee and Chung (2008) carried out an empirical analysis of consumer reaction to a VR shopping mall. For this, they developed a prototype of a VR shopping mall using 3D graphics and an avatar and conducted a quantitative analysis with undergraduate and postgraduate students (N = 102) (K. C. Lee & Chung, 2008, p. 93). They compared the VR shopping mall (accessible through VR headset) to a so-called "ordinary shopping mall" (accessible through web browser) and found out that the VR shopping mall (accessible through VR headset) creates a significantly better feeling of virtual presence than the ordinary shopping mall. Moreover, the VR shopping mall led to a stronger influence on customer satisfaction than the ordinary shopping mall. In addition, the VR shopping mall was able to overcome the various shortcomings of the ordinary shopping mall via web browser, such as the lack of a sense of touch and presence. K. C. Lee and Chung (2008, p. 99) also found out that quality assurance and enjoyment would significantly influence the customer satisfaction.

I. G. Krasonikolakis and Vrechopoulos (2009) studied literature and business practices to find out how store atmosphere characteristics (store design, scents, sounds, etc.) influence consumer behavior when shopping in VR environments. They found that VR environments have many characteristics of both physical and web environments (I. G. Krasonikolakis & Vrechopoulos, 2009, p. 1443). They also pointed out that the atmosphere seems to have a significant influence on consumer behavior in VR environments (I. G. Krasonikolakis & Vrechopoulos, 2009, p. 1444). The authors noted that research on VR environments is in its early stages and that defining and exploring the role of store atmospherics in virtual stores as a new shopping channel will help guide how retailers should design their virtual stores to fulfill the needs of customers and create certain feelings and emotions (I. G. Krasonikolakis & Vrechopoulos, 2009, p. 1444).

Later, in 2011, I. G. Krasonikolakis et al. (2011) investigated the store atmosphere in v-commerce empirically in form of a two-parted study design, first in-depth interviews and second, an online survey with 102 participants. They were able to confirm that the social dimension of v-commerce limits the possibilities for customization. In addition, they divided store atmosphere attributes into three categories based on their findings: (1) "Store's Appeal" (including storefront, store theatrics, colors, music and graphics), (2) "Innovative Atmosphere" (encompassing crowding, product display techniques and innovative store atmosphere services), and (3) "Store Layout" (I. G. Krasonikolakis et al., 2011, p. 68).

Pantano and Servidio (2012, p. 281) investigated the relevance of advanced technologies in physical retail stores from the user's perspective to understand their impact (including ease of use and enjoyment) on consumer's store perception and satisfaction in stores. To this end, they conducted a quantitative study in the form of a questionnaire and collected data from 150 undergraduate students (Pantano & Servidio, 2012, p. 282). They found that consumer satisfaction with "the introduction of immersive [technologies] in the traditional points of sale is influenced by three main dimensions: (1) perceived ease of use of the innovative tools, (2) provided enjoyment, and (3) new store perception" (Pantano & Servidio, 2012, p. 283).

Lau and Lee (2018), also focused on shopping in VR and conducted a study on consumers' shopping experience in stereoscopic VR (StereoVR). They designed and built a StereoVR (which belongs to VR) called "FutureShop" to simulate a virtual fashion retail store. They aimed to collect consumer responses for further development of the FutureShop.

Participants (N = 59) were asked to go through "a shopping process from product selection to purchase in [the] FutureShop" (Lau & Lee, 2018, p. 262). They concluded that StereoVR can make a significant contribution to creating more interactive experiences in apparel retail by enhancing consumers' hedonic shopping experiences in StereoVR as hedonic shopping experience enhances the purchase intention, especially through features such as music and lighting compared to Web-based shopping (Lau & Lee, 2018, p. 262). Research lacked in features such as interpersonal communication or virtual try-ons. However, participants described StereoVR experience as "innovative, fun and exciting" and highlighted its potential in outperforming the traditional web-based shopping in e-commerce stores (Lau & Lee, 2018, p. 263).

White Baker, Hubona, and Srite (2019) investigated the impact of virtual world's shopping experiences compared to web-based experiences on consumer purchase attitudes and focused on perceived social presence, telepresence, trust, ease of use, perceived usefulness and enjoyment. Among other things, they found that a higher level of social presence leads to a higher level of perceived usefulness, trust and enjoyment (White Baker et al., 2019, p. 31).

Kang, Shin, and Ponto (2020) wanted to find out how the interface features visual-spatial cues, graphic quality and interactivity influence the perceived level of informativeness and playfulness of stores. In addition, they investigate the roles of informativeness and playfulness in influencing consumers' decision-making process. To understand these relationships, they followed the approach of Coyle and Thorson (2001) and created fictitious virtual shopping interfaces (Kang et al., 2020, p. 74). Kang et al. (2020) were able to generate the following insights from their findings: (1) interactivity (e.g., freely moving and rotating the item) and visual-spatial cues increased the perceived informativeness and playfulness in the virtual store significantly, (2) the graphics quality seemed more critical in 2D than in 3D VR environments, (3) the purchase decision process was influenced by informativeness and playfulness in several ways. In particular, "a playful user interface may increase [the preference of consumers] for hedonic product benefits, [while] informativeness [was found to be] a more important explanatory variable for subsequent purchase intentions" (Kang et al., 2020, p. 79).

Wedel et al. (2020, p. 457) examined literature on VR in consumer marketing and found that the "emerging literature in this field is still relatively sparse, disjoint, and lacking significant overarching research frameworks, consensus measurement instruments, and a body of generalizable and replicable findings". Furthermore, they provided managerial implications according to CX as well as to using VR in the purchase stage in retailing.

Relating to CX, they recommend to "focus on creating multisensory (vision, sound, touch, smell) virtual product / brand experiences that embrace interactive telepresence" (Wedel et al., 2020, p. 458). With regard to VR in the purchase phase, they highlighted the use and creation of so-called stand-alone virtual stores, especially in retailing (Wedel et al., 2020, p. 458). They also emphasized the need to explore "what unique features of virtual stores, ads and brands elicit favorable consumer responses" (Wedel et al., 2020, p. 455).

Xi and Hamari (2021), also did a comprehensive literature review of 72 research papers and investigated the topic "Shopping in VR". They concluded that VR shopping offers new dimensions of experience that need to be explored by corporate, retail and marketing research. In addition, they summarized that virtual stores "can be a representation of a real shopping environment", "could bring more positive outcomes than real shopping" and could create better shopping experiences than physical stores (Xi & Hamari, 2021, p. 44). They also pointed out that "social factors such as the presence of others (e.g., shoppers and sales assistants) and forms of social relationships could influence the VR shopping experience" (Xi & Hamari, 2021, p. 45). However, they emphasized that virtual stores do not appear to have an advantage over brick-and-mortar stores in terms of product search efficiency. Furthermore, they pointed out that "factors such as different product types (hedonic vs. utilitarian, see e.g., Kempf,

1999), shopping tasks (information seeking vs. overall experience) and social aspects (single shopper vs. group shoppers, see e.g., Sommer, Wynes, and Brinkley (1992), might have potential influences on effectiveness in the VR shopping context and that they have not yet been sufficiently addressed in the extant literature" (Xi & Hamari, 2021, p. 53). Xi and Hamari (2021), also highlighted the role of shoppers in VR shopping experiences with regard to their, e.g., personality traits, demographic factors, prior knowledge, familiarity towards VR technology that can influence the shopping experience (Xi & Hamari, 2021, p. 53). They also shared constructs that seem to be rarely investigated in consumer research and VR shopping such as perceived (tele)presence, realism and immersion to finding out "whether VR is able to re-create what [customers] have in physical reality—i.e., being seamlessly present and immersed in our surroundings" (Xi & Hamari, 2021, p. 46).

Schnack, Wright, and Elms (2021), investigated how the shoppers' personality influences their behavior in "immersive virtual store environments" by conducting a pre-survey on the big five personality characteristics and then did an experiment in form of a shopping task with HMD device (Schnack et al., 2021, p. 9). They analyzed behavioral metrics such as product inspection time, number of impulse purchases, basket size, in-store dwell time and dollar amount spent.

In general, they found out that "shopper personality [would] not show any impacts on the investigated purchase behaviors" (Schnack et al., 2021, p. 9). When investigating virtual store shopping behavior in further research, they recommended to include constructs such as telepresence, social presence, co-presence, flow and virtual embodiment (Schnack et al., 2021, p. 9). They summarized that "traditional retailer strategies might not be applicable in modern immersive VR store environments", and highlighted "the need for extensive research in this area" (Schnack et al., 2021, p. 9).

Jin et al. (2021) investigated the effect of consumer store experience through VR on emotional states and perceived store attractiveness compared to website experience with the S-O-R model building the overall research framework. Furthermore, they wanted to find out, whether users, who already had experience with VR, and users, who had not, "were differently aroused and pleased by the VR store experience in this experiment" (Jin et al., 2021, p. 9). They did an experiment with 106 participants who experienced recorded 360-degree-based VR store videos, and 107 participants who experienced the store's website (Jin et al., 2021, p. 10). First, they found that there is no difference between users who had previous VR experience and those who had not (Jin et al., 2021, p. 12). Second, compared to the store's website, the store experience in VR triggered positive emotions in consumers and increased the perceived attractiveness of the store (Jin et al., 2021, p. 13). Third, the moderating effect of store familiarity on the relationship between the two types of store experience and evoked emotions could not be confirmed, meaning that "VR is more effective in eliciting positive [emotions] compared to websites" regardless of consumers' familiarity with a store (Jin et al., 2021, p. 16). Hence, it could be confirmed that consumers felt more positive emotion than negative toward the 360-degree-based VR-video experiences. The experience in the VR store was associated with positive words like "cool", "feel", "actual" and "enjoyed". On the contrary, negative words relating to the quality of VR were "blurry" and user-related, like "dizzy," "sore," "sick," and "headaches" (Jin et al., 2021, pp. 15f.).

Shen, Tan, Guo, Zhao, and Qin (2021) did a comprehensive literature review on the current state of v-commerce, application design and consumer behavior and identified factors that would influence purchase intention, e.g., enjoyment experience (EE; defined as "the joy of shopping stimulated through immersive technology"), and also "preeminent design artifacts" (Shen et al., 2021, 1, 9). Based on their findings, they created a conceptual framework for consumer's EE created during shopping in virtual worlds and its influence on the purchase intention (Shen et al., 2021, p. 11).

Shen et al. (2021, p. 9) included the EE influencing factors such as telepresence, perceived social presence, product discovery, and social as well as product interactions.

J. V. Chen et al. (2022), examined how the characteristics of VR shopping influence the consumers' impulse buying behavior in virtual stores, applying the S-O-R framework. They found that customers' telepresence, perceived diagnosticity and playfulness increased positively when a virtual store offered customers the opportunity to experience virtual products in a highly interactive and lively way. Thus, virtual stores elicited both individual cognitive (i.e., telepresence and perceived diagnosticity) and affective (playfulness) responses, with higher interactivity and vividness significantly leading to stronger perceptions of telepresence, perceived diagnosticity and playfulness. Therefore, J. J. V. Chen et al. (2022), recognized vividness and interactivity as different facets of VR and important determinants of users' virtual experience (J. V. Chen et al., 2022, p. 14).

Kim et al. (2023, p. 3) investigated immersive interactive technologies and virtual shopping experiences to determine whether consumer perceptions differentiate between AR and VR using the S-O-R framework. This involved 116 participants downloading the IKEA AR app and experiencing it via their smartphone, while 146 participants experienced the IKEA app in VR via a VR headset in the form of a laboratory experiment (Kim et al., 2023, p. 7). The main findings were that a sense of presence was a significant mediator of 1) the relationship between vividness and sensory brand app experience and 2) the relationship between interactivity and attitude toward technology for VR, but no such relationship was observed for AR. In addition, the relationships between sensory brand app experience, attitude, and behavioral intention were significant in both AR and VR environments (Kim et al., 2023, pp. 8–10).

Overall, it can be concluded that there is a limited number of existing studies dealing with virtual shopping experiences in virtual environments such as the metaverse, nor is there any study on the factors (in terms of C&F of virtual stores) of CX influencing the intention to use virtual stores in virtual environments such as the metaverse, either internationally or in Germany. In addition, several studies have emphasized that it would be interesting to find out what features virtual stores should have in order for consumers to enjoy online shopping and thus create unique shopping experiences. This implies that the need for more research is high. This is also confirmed by Schnack et al. (2021, p. 9), Xi and Hamari (2021, pp. 46f.), Wedel et al. (2020, p. 457), or Regt and Barnes (2019, p. 22) in particular.

Table 3.1 Literature Review on Shopping Experiences in Virtual Reality

Author	Year	Field / Keywords	Study Design	Key Findings
Kim, J.-H., Kim, M., Park, M., & Yoo, J.	2023	AR; VR; Presence; Sensory brand experience; Behavioral intention	For AR, participants (n = 116) downloaded an app to mobile phones. For VR, participants (n = 146) downloaded a VR app to smartphones attached to a Google Cardboard VR headset	Kim et al. (2023) found that sense of presence was a significant mediator for 1) the relationship between vividness and sensory brand app experience and 2) the relationship between interactivity and attitude towards technology for VR, while no such relationship could be observed with AR. Furthermore, the relationships among sensory brand app experience, attitude, and behavioral intention were significant in both AR and VR settings (see Kim et al., 2023, pp. 8-10).
Chen, J. V., Ha, Q.-A., & Vu, M. T.	2022	VR; AR; XR; Shopping Buying Behaviour	Literature review Full 2x2x2 factorial design experiment was conducted with 227 participants	Chen et al. (2022) found that customers' telepresence, perceived diagnosticity and playfulness increased positively when a VR store offered customers the opportunity to experience virtual products in a highly interactive and lively way. Thus, VR stores elicited both individual cognitive (i.e. telepresence and perceived diagnosticity) and affective (playfulness) responses, with higher interactivity and vividness significantly leading to stronger perceptions of telepresence, perceived diagnosticity and playfulness. Therefore, J. J. V. Chen et al. (2022), recognized vividness and interactivity as different facets of VR and important determinants of users' virtual experience (J. V. Chen et al., 2022, p. 14).
Shen, B., Tan, W., Guo, J., Zhao, L., & Qin, P.	2021	Virtual Commerce; Consumer Behavior; Application Design; Immersive Technology; Metaverse	Literature review	Shen et al. (2021) did a comprehensive literature review on the current state of v-commerce, application design and consumer behavior and identified factors that would influence purchase intention, e.g., enjoyment experience (EE; defined as "the joy of shopping stimulated through immersive technology"), and also "preeminent design artifacts" (Shen et al., 2021, 1, 9). Based on their findings, they created a conceptual framework for consumer's EE created during shopping in virtual worlds and its influence on the purchase intention (Shen et al., 2021, p. 11). Shen et al. (2021, p. 9) included the EE influencing factors such as telepresence, perceived social presence, product discovery, and social as well as product interactions.
Jin, B., Kim, G., Moore, M., & Rothenberg, L.	2021	Virtual Reality; Store Attractiveness; Emotions; Sentiment Analysis; Semantic Network Analysis	Literature review Quantitative survey (106 students in VR vs 107 students on websites)	Jin et al. (2021) found that there is no difference between users who had previous VR experience and those who had not (B. Jin et al., 2021, p. 12). Second, compared to the store's website, the store experience in VR triggered positive emotions in consumers and increased the perceived attractiveness of the store (B. Jin et al., 2021, p. 13). Third, the moderating effect of store familiarity on the relationship between the two store experience types and evoked emotions could not be confirmed, meaning that "VR is more effective in eliciting positive [emotions] compared to websites" regardless of consumers' familiarity with a store (B. Jin et al., 2021, p. 16). Hence, it could be confirmed that consumers felt more positive emotion than negative toward the 360-degree-based VR-video experiences. The experience in the VR store was associated with positive words such as "cool", "feel", "actual" and "enjoyed". On the contrary, negative words relating to VR quality were "blurry" and user-related, such as "dizzy," "sore," "sick," and "headaches" (B. Jin et al., 2021, 15f.).
Schnack, A., Wright, M. J., Elms, J.	2021	Big Five' Personality; Immersive Virtual Reality; Online Retailing; Shopper Behaviour	Experiment with shopping-task in VR with HMD (N = 113; Convenience sampling approach: university staff, students, affiliates)	Schnack, Wright, and Elms (2021) found out that "shopper personality [would] not show any impacts on the investigated purchase behaviors" (Schnack et al., 2021, p. 9). When investigating virtual store shopping behavior in further research, they recommended to include constructs such as telepresence, social presence, co-presence, flow and virtual embodiment (Schnack et al., 2021, p. 9). They summarized that "traditional retailer strategies might not be applicable in modern immersive VR store environments", and highlighted "the need for extensive research in this area" (Schnack et al., 2021, p. 9).
Xi, N., Hamari, J.	2021	VR; XR; AR; Rretail; Commerce; Consumption	Literature Review (72 research papers)	Xi et al. (2021) stated that VR shopping offers new dimensions of experience that need to be explored by corporate, retail and marketing research. They also emphasized that ... VR stores could be a replica of a real shopping environment, ... VR could bring more positive experiences than real shopping in some aspects, ... VR could create better shopping experiences than physical stores (p. 44), ... VR stores do not appear to have an advantage over brick-and-mortar stores in terms of product search efficiency. In addition, factors such as "different product types (hedonic vs. utilitarian), shopping tasks (information search vs. overall experience) and even social aspects" (individual shoppers vs. group shoppers) could have potential influences on effectiveness in the VR shopping context that have not yet been sufficiently considered in the existing literature, the authors said (p. 45). Finally, they emphasized that factors such as personality traits, demographic factors, prior knowledge and shopper familiarity with VR technology would play a major role in VR shopping experiences (p. 53).

(continued)

Table 3.1 (continued)

Author	Year	Field / Keywords	Study Design	Key Findings
Wedel, M., Bigné, E., & Zhang, J.	2020	VR; AR; Consumer Experience; Customer Journey; VR/AR Effectiveness	Literature Review	Wedel et al (2020) found that "emerging literature on VR in marketing is still relatively sparse, disconnected, and lacking significant overarching research frameworks, consensus measurement instruments, and a body of generalizable and replicable findings" (p. 457). They identified opportunities for advancing consumer marketing research on VR, e.g., existing opportunities to create stand-alone virtual stores. Moreover, they emphasized that "companies should focus on creating multisensory (vision, sound, touch, smell) virtual product/brand experiences that embrace interactive telepresence." Besides, they pointed out that it would be interesting to find out, "what unique features of virtual stores, ads, and brands elicit favorable consumer responses?" (p. 455).
Kang, H. J., Shin, J., & Ponto, K.	2020	N/A	2D website vs. 3D virtual store; Online Survey (N = 218)	Kang et al. (2019) gained the following insights from their findings: (1) interactivity and visual-spatial cues significantly increase perceived informativeness and playfulness in the virtual store, (2) the role of graphics quality proved to be more critical in 2D displays than in 3D VR environments, (3) informativeness and playfulness influence the purchase decision process in different ways. More specifically, a playful user interface may increase consumers' preference for hedonic product benefits (e.g., a sleek and attractive design), while informativeness emerged as a more important explanatory variable for subsequent purchase intentions (p. 79).
White Baker, E., Hubona, G. S., & Srite, M.	2019	e-Shopping; Virtual Worlds; Social Presence; Telepresence; Trust; Enjoyment; Consumer Attitude	Online Survey (N = 474)	White et al. (2019) found that the influence of trust on attitudes towards shopping is stronger in the virtual world than in the web-based environment. Factors such as presence would have a positive impact on attitudes towards online shopping. They also found that telepresence had no significant direct influence on perceived usefulness. Moreover, they figured out that the effect of telepresence on trust and enjoyment was mediated by perceived social presence. Therefore, increased levels of social presence would lead to increased levels of perceived usefulness, trust and enjoyment. In addition, an increased sense of telepresence would indirectly affect two of these constructs, as mediated by perceived social presence (p. 31).
Lau, K. W., & Lee, P. Y.	2018	Virtual reality; Stereoscopic Displays; Consumer Research; Retailing; Shopping Experiences	Qualitative research with self-designed VR store called "FutureShop, in which participants were asked to complete a shopping process from product selection to purchase (N = 59)	Lau et al. (2018) concluded that "StereoVR can make a significant contribution in creating more interactive experiences for apparel retailing by enhancing consumers' hedonic shopping experiences in the StereoVR" (p. 255).
Algharabata, R., Alalwanb, A. A., Ranac, N. P., Dwivedic, Y. K.	2017	3D Virtual; Product Experience; 3D-Quality; Attitude Toward Product; Attitude Toward Website; Satisfaction; Jordan	Creation of hypothetical online retailer website presenting 3D products (N = 410; non-student sample)	Algharabata et al. (2017) found that 3D-quality determines perceptions of attitude toward presented product and attitude toward website, which would in turn influence users' satisfaction. The relationships between attitude towards presented product, attitude towards website and user's ssatisfaction would be moderated by virtual product experience (p. 213).
Papagiannidis, S., See To, E., Bourlakis, M.	2014	User Experience; Product Simulation; Product Authenticity; Enjoyment; Engagement; Purchase Intention	Qualitative within-subject experiment (N = 89)	Primary findings of Papagianni et al. (2014) were: The degree of control is not a critical determinant for higher engagement of users in simulated cars. So were the product authenticity. Bright colors do not generate higher engagement, while vivid graphics do. Whereas utilitarian values were not supported, hedonic values were supported. Engagement had a positive influence on the user's enjoyment of a simulated car. Hence engagement was associated with pleasure by users. Moreover, pleasure was positively related to user satisfaction which was in turn positively related to the intention to buy the car in the end.
E. Pantano, R. Servidio	2012	Technology; Management; Human–Computer Interaction; Retailing; Consumer behavior	Literature review; Quantitative survey in the form of a questionnaire, pilot study (N = 150; Undergraduate Students of University of Calabria, Italy)	Pantano et al. (2012) found that consumer satisfaction with "the introduction of immersive [technologies] in the traditional points of sale is influenced by three main dimensions: (1) perceived ease of use of the innovative tools, (2) provided enjoyment, and (3) new store perception" (p. 283).

(continued)

Table 3.1 (continued)

Author	Year	Field / Keywords	Study Design	Key Findings
Krasonikolakis, I. G., Vrechopoulos, A., & Pouloudi, A.	2011	Store Atmosphere; Virtual Reality Commerce; Retailing; Consumer Behaviour	In-depth interviews with field experts; online questionnaire survey (N = 104; experienced in virtual worlds)	In 2011, Krasonikolakis followed up on their work from 2009 and found that social dimension of v-commerce limits the customization possibilities (when more than two customers are present in the virtual store at the same time), but offers several innovative options to manipulate the store atmosphere. They grouped attributes of the store atmosphere into three factors: (1) store appeal (including window displays, theatrics, colors, music, and graphics), (2) innovative atmosphere (including crowds, product display techniques, and innovative store atmosphere services), (3) store design (single attribute).
Krasonikolakis, I. G., & Vrechopoulos, A.	2009	Information Systems; Marketing; User-Consumer Behavior; Virtual Reality Retailing; Store Atmosphere	Literature review and analysis of business practices on how the characteristics of the store atmosphere (layout, scent, sounds, etc.) influence shopping behavior at different stages of shopping in virtual reality environments	Krasonikolakis et al. (2009) found that virtual reality environments have characteristics of real and web environments. In addition, they found that the store atmosphere would significantly influence customer behavior in virtual reality environments. They also highlighted that the personalization of store atmosphere features (e.g. layout, colors, scent, music) would depend on the number of store visitors. They also emphasized that research into virtual reality environments is still in its infancy. In doing so, they highlighted that defining and exploring the role of factors that would determine store atmosphere in this emerging channel would be of great help in providing sufficient guidance on how retailers should design their virtual reality stores to meet customer needs and create certain emotions and feelings (p. 1444).
Lee, K. C., Chung, N.	2008	Shopping Mall; User Interface; Virtual Reality; Convenience; Enjoyment; Quality Assurance; Customer Satisfaction	Developed prototype of VR shopping mall, using 3D graphics and an avatar; Quantitative analysis (N = 102)	Lee et al. (2022) found that the virtual presence in a VR shopping center is significantly better than in an ordinary shopping center. In addition to quality assurance, enjoyment also has a significant impact on customer satisfaction. Furthermore, the VR shopping center has a stronger influence on customer satisfaction than the ordinary shopping center. The VR shopping center provides the customer with a sense of touch and presence that the ordinary shopping center lacks (p. 99).
Li, H., Daugherty, T., Biocca, F.	2001	N/A	Exploratory study; Protocol analysis (N = 30); interaction with four three-dimensional products and verbalization of virtual experience content	Li et al. (2001) derived that "virtual experience consists of vivid, involving, active, and affective psychological states occurring in an individual interacting with three-dimensional computer simulations. […] virtual experience is closer to direct experience than to indirect experience in terms of effective consumer learning" (pp. 27f.).
Chittaro, L. & Ranon, R.	2000	VR; Personalization Rule; Adaptive Feature; Background Music; Shelf Space	Between-groups experiment; Analyzed integration of real-world store features into VR store; Built customer profiles; Created a first prototype of a personalizable VR store called ADVIRT with so-called adaptive features	Chittaro et al. (2000) emphasized store design, creation of customer profiles, navigation, usability, interactivity, satisfaction of social needs and building sense of community as well as audio elements as important features of virtual stores (p. 96).

3.2.2 Research Project "Meta-Commerce" from Winter Semester 2022/23

In the winter semester 2022/23 of the e-commerce master's program at Hochschule Niederrhein University of Applied Sciences (HSNR), the author and three other fellow students developed a preliminary model of the determinants influencing user's technology acceptance of meta commerce as part of the research project "Meta-Commerce" (Hake et al., 2023). The question of which determinants might have an influence on Gen Z's acceptance of meta commerce was investigated. For this purpose, 12 participants (aged between 22 and 26) were recruited from the researchers' environment and invited into the IoT Lab of Prof. Dr. Ing. Alexander Korth from HSNR. There, a VR experiment was conducted with each of the participants, in which they were asked to try out two different virtual stores with the Meta Quest 2. The virtual stores were the Dyson VR demo store and the Burberry Virtual Flagship Store on Regent Street in London (Burberry, 2022; Dyson Limited, 2021).

After the experience, Hake et al. (2023) conducted qualitative in-depth interviews with each of the respondents individually in order to obtain information on their first impressions, expectations and problems relating to the two virtual store experiences and meta commerce in general. The aim of the study was to create a preliminary model of the determinants that might influence the acceptance of meta commerce in Gen Z. Overall, Hake et al. (2023, pp. 61–82) came to different conclusions regarding the determinants. One of the many determinants identified was CX. Within the main research model, CX represents a partial model for which the following three influencing factors were identified: the design of the virtual store, the technology itself, the HEM, that provides access to VR, and hedonic motivation (Hake et al., 2023, pp. 66–70). With regard to the design of virtual stores, the following aspects have proven to be particularly important: the addressing of senses, immersion, the participants' expectancies, product interactions, services, features and functions, the design and the atmosphere of virtual stores. The derived preliminary partial model of the CX is shown in Fig. 3.1. These results are also of high importance for the following Master's thesis and will further be used for the design of the research model, the conceptualization as well as the operationalization. In addition, further insights were gained about meta commerce and shopping in virtual stores. Some interviewees stated that they found the current visual design of virtual stores very simple.

They emphasized this by drawing a parallel to computer games. They also criticized the lack of interaction options. In general, the majority preferred the realistic replication of real brick-and-mortar stores as opposed to the creative, fictitious design of virtual stores. They also described reasons for or against shopping in virtual stores. The reasons they gave for shopping in virtual stores were brand awareness, product dependency, the purchase process phase and the variety of product ranges. Reasons such as social contact and price played a rather subordinate role. They also stated that they could imagine buying in virtual stores, particularly in the product categories of electronics, cars, furniture, shoes & accessories, games and decorative items. For products such as food, cosmetics, medicines & drugs, skincare products and travel bookings, they could imagine it less well. Opinions were very mixed when it came to fashion & clothing.

They also expressed wishes with regard to features and the design of virtual stores. They would like more interaction options, such as the feeling of actually being able to go into the store, walk around and look at, try on, touch and test products. They also wanted to be able to "check out" directly in the virtual store and not be redirected to the online store. They would find price details, product information such as product name or technical data on the products (scales) as well as reviews and product ratings important. They would also like to see videos in the form of tutorials. In addition, realism and appeal to the senses such as touch and smell would be important to them. The VR glasses, including the controllers, should also feel even less like VR glasses. Some participants would also be interested in personal purchasing advice at the touch of a button. The majority would prefer to go shopping with their own avatars in virtual cities or shopping malls than in stand-alone virtual stores. The findings will be incorporated into the conceptualization and development of the research model for this study. This research project can therefore be regarded as a qualitative preliminary study, the results of which are used as a basis for this work. In addition, another master's thesis by a graduate of the e-commerce master's program, Denise Bressau, also identified the CX as a determinant of the metaverse (Bressau & Zaharia, 2022, p. 58).

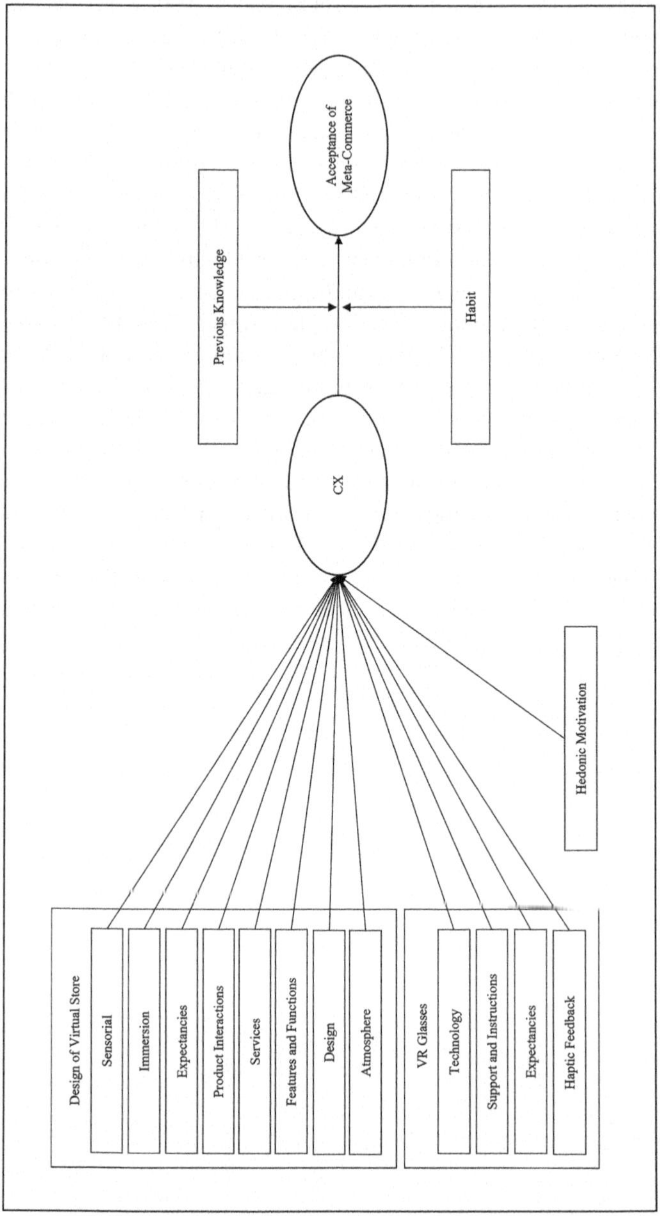

Fig. 3.1 Partial Model of CX in Meta-Commerce (*Note*. This figure shows the CX as a partial model of the acceptance of Meta-Commerce. Source. Author's own illustration adapted from Hake et al. (2023, p. 66))

3.2.3 Generation Z

As already mentioned in the past chapters, young people in particular, such as Gen Z, can be addressed via virtual shopping experiences. According to the "Trend Check Handel Vol. 3" study conducted by ECC Cologne in June 2022, young consumers (aged 18 to 29 in 2024) are particularly interested in new shopping experiences in the metaverse and see this as a relevant future development for online shopping (ECC Cologne & Salesforce.com, 2022, p. 13). In addition, 46% of them are already familiar with the Metaverse and 44% of them find the metaverse generally interesting.

While only 29% of older consumers are aware of the metaverse and 20% are interested in it (ECC Cologne & Salesforce.com, 2022, p. 10). Meffert, Burmann, Kirchgeorg, and Eisenbeiß (2024, p. 158) have also highlighted that for Gen Z in particular, positive CXs along all touchpoints of the customer journey are of particular importance.

At Roblox Investor Days 2023, Wootton (2023) mentioned that the primary reason why brands come to Roblox is to reach, appeal to and attract Gen Z as #1 top spending age group on Roblox (Roblox Corporation, 2023, p. 4; Wootton, 2023).

Gen Z has grown up online and is transitioning seamlessly from the physical to the digital world. Hence, Wootton (2023) emphasizes the relevance of Gen Z. In addition, Gen Z not only has great purchasing power, but also a great influence on everyone around them, not just their peers but also the older generations (Wootton, 2023). For virtual stores, this could mean that if Gen Z accepts and uses virtual stores in the future, other generations will follow.

Another survey conducted in December 2021 by Hub Entertainment Research in the USA for the Variety Intelligence Platform found that "a third of Gen Z said they would like to see brands develop virtual stores" (Petro, 2022). Regt and Barnes (2019, p. 20) also emphasize the relevance of younger generations in relation to v-commerce, highlighting various aspects such as their technological savviness, expressing their identity with brands, and their investment in experiential purchases.

Roblox conducted a survey about self-expression in 2023, 56% of Gen Z respondents said that it would be more important to them to style their avatar than themselves in the real world (Roblox Corporation, 2023, p. 5). Since avatars are currently the main way to enter the metaverse, it can be assumed that this will also influence the visit of virtual stores and the purchase of products in virtual stores. A study by the Fraunhofer Institute also found that of all generations (including baby boomers and older, Generation X and Generation Y), Gen Z is most likely to want AR/VR applications in brick-and-mortar stores (e.g., trying on clothes virtually with AR glasses or virtual shopping with VR glasses). This may indicate that they are also more inclined to want to use VR glasses not only in brick-and-mortar stores, but also in their own homes for shopping in virtual stores (Kemmer, Schweiger, & Taubert, 2023, p. 51). Another study by Razorfish and VICE Media Group found that one in three of Gen Z would like to be able to use virtual stores to browse or shop for products, as well as brands that sell skins and clothes for their avatars (Razorfish & Vice Media Group, 2022, p. 31). In their study I. Krasonikolakis et al. (2014, p. 35) also emphasize in their limitation section that it is necessary to investigate young consumers of people under the age of 25 years in particular with regard to virtual worlds. All of this underlines the suitability of Gen Z for shopping in virtual stores compared to other generations.

3.2.4 Research Gap and Research Questions

The study overview in Sect. 3.2.1 and the previous chapters show that, in principle, experiences in VR have already attracted attention in various fields and that the number of studies is also increasing. Nevertheless, the minority is concerned with CXs in virtual stores in VR. The demand for studies in this area is particularly high, as can be clearly seen from this year's call for papers for VAMR 2024 as part of the HCI International 2024 (2024).

Furthermore, the construct of CX has so far been rather conceptualized (e.g., Berry et al., 2002; Gentile et al., 2007; Lemon & Verhoef, 2016; Rose et al., 2011; Rose et al., 2012; Verhoef et al., 2009) and rarely operationalized and then empirically tested (except, e.g., Brakus et al., 2009, pp. 53–55; Bruhn & Mayer-Vorfelder, 2011, p. 4; Brun et al., 2017, pp. 323–325; Novak, Hoffman, & Yung, 2000; Schwertfeger, 2012, pp. 75–80; Zaharia & Schmitz, 2019, p. 2). When it has been conceptualized and operationalized in the context of virtual shopping experiences or virtual stores, the entire CX model was not used, but two dimensions of it, mainly the affective as well as the cognitive dimension, or as mentioned, the CX model was not considered at all (e.g., Jin et al., 2021, p. 9; I. Krasonikolakis et al., 2018, p. 1230). This means that the existing CX models need to be fundamentally adapted, revised and operationalized in the context of virtual shopping experiences. Some studies have already found that experiences in general can have a positive impact on customer share, customer satisfaction, customer engagement, purchase or behavioral intention. However, the majority of all these studies did not deal with German participants, but were carried out in Asia, Southern Europe or America.

As already shown in Sect. 3.2.3, some studies have found that Gen Z is the main target group of the metaverse and virtual stores. Therefore, the following work focuses exclusively on Gen Z. However, it remains to be shown how the CX in virtual stores (based on the examples from the use case list which can be provided upon request) influences the intention of the German Gen Z to use virtual stores for various purposes, e.g., to try out products, in virtual environments such as the metaverse. The investigation of this could reveal various implications for both, research and management. In addition to providing further important research insights, it could also pave the way for brands to use virtual stores by giving them initial insights into which C&F are important in virtual stores in order to create an unique and extraordinary shopping experience for customers. Moreover, it can show brands how they can improve their customers' online shopping experience with the help of virtual stores.

In addition, brands and companies could use virtual stores to clearly differentiate themselves from the competition in order to attract and win over Gen Z and other generations that follow Gen Z (see also Sect. 3.2.3).

Further benefits of virtual stores have already been discussed in Sect. 2.3.3. From all of this, the following research questions can be derived for this work:

Research Question 1.

What influence does the CX have on Generation Z's behavioral intention to use virtual stores and what are the determinants of the CX?

Research Question 2.

Is the effect between the customer experience, the general customer experience and the behavioral intention significantly different for:

a) *people with VR experience than for people without VR experience,*
b) *gamer than for non-gamer,*
c) *introverts than for extraverts?*

Research Question 3.

What should virtual stores look like in virtual environments such as the metaverse (including virtual store design, characteristics and features / stand-alone virtual stores, shopping centers, malls, or cities / physical products or NFTs)?

4 Model Development, Conceptualization, Hypotheses & Further Insights

Now that the relevant literature has been reviewed, the key terms of the work defined and the theoretical points of reference and research questions presented, an overview of the research model is given. The model is based on the S-O-R[1] approach from the neobehaviorism[2].

[1] The S-O-R approach is classified as an explanatory approach in psychology and can be used as a theory to explain the influence of the CX in virtual stores on BI.

[2] Neobehaviorism is a paradigm that is used to explain the behavior of individuals in behavioral research. In contrast to behaviorism, neobehaviorism is also based on non-observable variables. These non-observable variables are also understood as intervening variables and are interposed between stimulus and response. For example, consumers are exposed to various stimuli (S). When these stimuli encounter intervening variables in the organism (O), they lead to a behavioral response (R) (Foscht, Swoboda, and Schramm-Klein, 2017, p. 28).

Stimuli and behavioral response are observable, while the intervening variables are unobservable (Foscht et al., 2017, p. 23). Furthermore, the intervening variables can be divided into primarily activating, such as emotions, motivation and attitude (in the sense of a state of arousal that puts the consumer in a state of performance and readiness) and primarily cognitive, such as perception, learning and memory (in the sense of mental processes) processes (Foscht et al., 2017, p. 29; Kroeber-Riel, Weinberg, and Gröppel-Klein, 2009, p. 55).

Supplementary Information The online version contains supplementary material available at https://doi.org/10.1007/978-3-658-48634-1_4.

M. Hake, *Shopping in Virtual Stores*, BestMasters,
https://doi.org/10.1007/978-3-658-48634-1_4

For the present study, this means that stimuli in virtual stores and environmental stimuli (S) can have an effect on the consumer in the virtual store and trigger intervening variables (O), which in turn lead to a specific behavioral reaction (R).[3] The CX as the main construct of the research model represents the intervening variable that can be triggered by various stimuli. This includes both stimuli that can be controlled by the company in the form of C&F of the virtual stores, as well as stimuli that cannot be controlled by the company (see also Sect. 2.3). The focus of this work is on the C&F of virtual stores that can be controlled by the company. These are to be examined for their suitability to create the CX. The CX as an intervening variable in turn triggers behavioral reactions such as the behavioral intention to use virtual stores.

Based on the literature review, the CX models by Verhoef et al. (2009, p. 32), Gentile et al. (2007, p. 398), Novak et al. (2000), and Schmitt (1999, p. 60) were identified as the most established CX models. For this reason, these serve as the basis for the research model of this study. The CX models are suitable for determining the influence of the CX on the intention to use virtual stores insofar as they offer a solid basis for the development of the research model due to their multidimensionality and against the background of the still unexplored topic of the CX in virtual stores. The literature review in Sect. 3.2.1 also shows that researchers essentially rely on their understanding and conceptualization of the CX to strengthen their own understanding of the CX and to develop new approaches. In addition, the study overview also shows that the CX model not only has been adapted over time but also depending on the (scientific) context.

Nonetheless, there is no study to date that has dealt precisely with the topic of this work (see Sect. 3.2.4). In the context of this work, the established CX models lack essential aspects to capture the novel topic of virtual shopping experiences in the metaverse in conjunction with the use of new technologies such as VR glasses and the associated possibilities in their entirety. This is also reflected in recent literature (Wedel et al., 2020, p. 157; Xi & Hamari, 2021, p. 46).

Following the findings of Sect. 3.1.2, the established CX models incorporate various dimensions. The following work focuses on the most established dimensions: the sensory, emotional, cognitive, and social CX dimensions (Lemon

[3] Usually, the dimensions of CX are considered as organisms (O) rather than stimuli (S), e.g., Schwertfeger (2012). In this work, however, CX dimensions are based on features and characteristics of virtual stores that potentially lead to experiences, rather than the actual experiences that customers have had. In the latter case, the dimensions would be assigned to the organism (O) in the S-O-R model. In this work, this is the general customer experience. This is supported by A. Palmer (2010, pp. 198–199) who stated that emotions can be both, stimuli and outcomes.

& Verhoef, 2016, p. 70). However, in the context of CX in virtual stores, it requires the inclusion of a further dimension, the "immersive experience" (J. V. Chen et al., 2022, 5, 10, 12; Kim et al., 2023, p. 4; Li et al., 27; Wedel et al., 2020, p. 446; Xi & Hamari, 2021, p. 38; Yim et al., 2017, p. 91). Finally, the model consists of a total of seven constructs and can be seen in Fig. 4.1 below. As already mentioned, this work focuses on the CX. The CX is conceptualized as a multidimensional, higher-order construct and comprises the sensory (SED), emotional (EMD), cognitive (COD), social (SOD) and immersive (IMD) CX dimensions. The model postulates that various stimuli in terms of C&F of virtual stores generate CX. The work focuses on controllable stimuli. The model assumes that the dimensions of the CX have an influence on the overall CX which in turn leads to BI. This work therefore examines the effects of various C&F of virtual stores on the creation of CX.

Furthermore, according to the S-O-R approach, it is assumed that CX lead to behavioral reactions. This work focuses on the influence of the CX on the BI. It examines the extent to which the CX has an influence on general use, recommendation, the use of a virtual store for shopping, obtaining information about products or trying out products. The model also examines the effect of various consumer characteristics in terms of multigroup analyses (MGA) (previous experience with VR, personality and gaming).

In the following sections, the individual construct conceptualizations are presented, structured according to the three research questions derived in Sect. 3.2.4. The term conceptualization refers to the development of construct dimensions[4]. In this work, CX is conceptualized as a higher-order construct, more precisely as a second-order construct (Becker, Klein, & Wetzels, 2012, p. 363; Bruhn & Hadwich, 2012, p. 15; Gentile et al., 2007, p. 398).

[4] A basic distinction is made between single-factor and multi-factor conceptualizations. The former refers to the case where the construct is conceptualized using exactly one factor. Multi-factorial constructs, on the other hand, are captured by two or more factors. These multi-factorial constructs can be further differentiated into unidimensional and multidimensional constructs. If each factor is based on one and the same theoretical dimension, we speak of multifactorial unidimensional constructs, whereas in the case of multifactorial multidimensional constructs, the individual factors are assigned to different dimensions (Homburg and Giering, 1996, p. 6). In principle, constructs can be conceptualized formatively or reflectively (Bollen, 1989, p. 65).

4.1 Research Question 1—Conceptualization and Hypotheses

In this chapter, research question one, the conceptualization of the hypothetical constructs (latent variable) is undertaken. This involves describing a construct and its properties as concretely as possible and leads to the final construct definition on which this work is based.

4.1.1 Behavioral Intention to Use

Behavioral intention (BI; also referred to as conation) is defined as a "person's intention to perform various behaviors" (Fishbein & Ajzen, 1975, p. 12). According to Fishbein and Ajzen (1975), "the strength of an intention is indicated by the person's subjective probability that he [or she] will perform the behavior in question" (Fishbein & Ajzen, 1975, p. 12). It is distinguished from attitude, belief and (actual) behavior by Fishbein and Ajzen (1975). Warshaw and Davis (1985) followed on from this definition and defined BI "[...] as the degree to which a person has formulated conscious plans to perform or not perform some specified future behavior" (Warshaw & Davis, 1985, p. 214). Moreover, they distinguished it from the behavioral expectation, which they defined as "the individual's estimation of the likelihood that he or she actually will perform some specified future behavior" (Warshaw & Davis, 1985, p. 215).

Since the definition of BI by Fishbein and Ajzen (1975) is widely accepted and has been confirmed several times in the past (e.g., by Sheppard, Hartwick, & Warshaw, 1988, p. 340 or Warshaw & Davis, 1985, p. 214), it is also used in this work in order to determine Gen Z's behavioral intention to use virtual stores in the future.

Hence, behavioral intention refers to the person's intention to perform various behaviors in relation to virtual stores. These include the intention to use virtual stores, the intention to shop in virtual stores, the intention to recommend virtual stores to friends and acquaintances, the intention to try out products as well as the intention to search for product information in virtual stores. Moreover, the strength of the behavioral intention is indicated by the person's likelihood that he or she will perform the mentioned behaviors.

In literature, the BI is not only distinguished from the actual behavior, but is also considered as a predictor of actual behavior (Warshaw & Davis, 1985). For instance, Venkatesh, Morris, and Davis (2003) used BI as a predictor of actual behavior within their Unified Theory of Acceptance and Use of Technology (UTAUT) and extended UTAUT2 model (Venkatesh et al., 2003, p. 427; Venkatesh, Thong, & Xu, 2012, p. 160). Since both virtual stores and VR glasses are not yet so established in Germany and therefore few people have actually tried virtual stores or used VR glasses so far, the actual behavior will be not investigated in this research.

Several studies have confirmed that the CX (created by store design) has an influence on consumer behavior (e.g., Z. Chen & Dubinsky, 2003, p. 327; L.-D. Chen & Tan, 2004, p. 79; Haeusel, 2012, p. 635; Kim et al., 2023, p. 6; Li et al., 2001, p. 24; Nasermoadeli et al., 2013, p. 130; Papagiannidis, See-To, & Bourlakis, 2014, p. 886; Shen et al., 2021, p. 9; Sheth, Mittal, & Newman, 1999, p. 503; Xi & Hamari, 2021, p. 49; Zentes et al., 2017, p. 327). Thus, it is about finding out whether CX in virtual stores also has an influence on BI.

4.1.2 Customer Experience

Based on the definition (see Sect. 3.1.1) and the literature review (see Sect. 3.2), the term CX can be defined as follows for the purpose of this work:

> *The customer experience*[5] *refers to the sensory, emotional, cognitive, social and immersive experiences in a virtual store that can be evoked in users by various stimuli in the form of features and characteristics of the virtual stores when they visit a virtual store with VR glasses.*

[5] In German literature, there are two different translations of CX, namely "Kundenerfahrung" and "Kundenerlebnis". Both have a slightly different meaning. CX as "Kundenerfahrung" on the one hand, is the reflection of all experiences a customer made in the past. It is very long-term oriented. Furthermore, CX in this context often goes hand in hand with the acquisition of knowledge, skills, and abilities related to a product or service over an extended period of time. Moreover, by reflecting on the perceived experiences, the customer forms a judgment as to whether an experience made was perceived as positive or negative (Bruhn & Hadwich, 2012, p. 9). CX as "Kundenerlebnis" on the other hand, means the actual experiencing including all mental phenomena of a person, such as thinking, imagining, sensing, perceiving and feeling which is, different to the other meaning of CX, rather short-term oriented. These experiences are always accompanied by emotions. In this context, customer experience tends to emphasize the short-term, emotional experiences that the company provides for a customer and is predominantly discussed in an experience-oriented context (also referred to as experiential marketing. The following work refers to the second translation, customer experience as "Kundenerlebnis" (Bruhn and Hadwich, 2012, p. 9; Schwertfeger, 2012, p. 33).

The general characteristics of the CX have already been discussed in Chap. 3. In detail, these were subjectivity, appearance not only in brick-and-mortar stores but also in other sales channels, appearance throughout the customer's entire purchasing process and its multidimensionality. The multidimensionality of CX as a latent construct, following the holistic approach of Lemon and Verhoef (2016, p. 70), is also reflected in the definition of CX in this work. As already emphasized in Sect. 3.1.2, the consideration of CX as a holistic construct is supported by numerous studies. In this work, CX consists of a total of five dimensions: the sensory, emotional, cognitive, social and immersive dimensions. These dimensions represent the causes of CX and changes in the dimensions lead to changes in CX (Bruhn & Hadwich, 2012, p. 15). Each of them addresses different kinds of stimuli[6] in terms of the in Sect. 2.3 previously identified and thematized C&F of virtual stores (also see Appendix A).

In contrast to other definitions and conceptualizations of CX, this paper conceptualizes CX not only in terms of reactions, but also on the basis of the above-mentioned C&F that create experiences in virtual stores. It is about finding out which C&F lead to experiences. Furthermore, the construct CX is treated as a higher-order construct, as already mentioned in the introduction and which is also supported by previous studies (see e.g., Brakus et al., 2009; Bruhn & Mayer-Vorfelder, 2011) and from which the following hypothesis can be derived:

H1 The customer experience has a positive influence on the behavioral intention to use virtual stores.

The dimensions of the CX are explained in the following section.

4.1.3 Dimensions of Customer Experience

Chapter 3 has already identified the dimensions of CX on which this work is based: SED, EMD, COD, SOD and IMD. In addition, the C&F of virtual stores have already been identified and broadly discussed in Sect. 2.3 (see also Appendix A).

The next step involves matching the identified characteristics and features (C&F) of virtual stores with the dimensions of customer experience (CX). To this end, the CX dimensions are first defined below, followed by the detailed matching process. Table 4.1 presents the final matching of the C&F of virtual stores with the CX dimensions.

[6] Schmitt (2011, p. 75) also refers to them as experiential stimuli.

4.1.3.1 Sensory Dimension

Following Schmitt (1999, 2011), the "sense" module refers to the creation of sensory experiences that appeal to all the senses: sight, hearing, touch, smell and taste (Schmitt, 1999, p. 61). Gentile et al. (2007) agree with this definition and see the SED (to which they refer as sensorial component of CX) as "an offering, whose aim is to provide good sensorial experiences, [and that] can address sight, hearing, touch, taste and smell so as to arouse aesthetical pleasure, excitement, satisfaction, sense of beauty" (Gentile et al., 2007, p. 399).

Brakus et al. (2009, p. 54) also emphasize "aesthetics and sensory qualities" with regard to the sensory dimension of CX. As outlined in Sect. 2.1.2, Skarbez et al. (2021) distinguish between exteroceptive and interoceptive senses. Exteroceptive senses relate to those senses that come "from outside the body", i.e., the basic senses such as sight, hearing, touch, smell and taste, while interoceptive senses are senses that "monitor the body's internal state", like the proprioceptive and vestibular senses. Exteroceptive senses can nowadays be addressed and influenced relatively easily by computer-generated stimuli, which makes them very easy to control as well, unlike the interoceptive senses, which are non-manipulable (Skarbez et al., 2021, p. 3). This work therefore focuses on the interoceptive senses.

According to Schmitt (2009, pp. 703 ff.) sensory experiences are created with the help of so-called primary elements, styles, and motifs which are transferred to the customer in various ways. Within the scope of this work, the focus will be on primary elements. The primary elements refer to marketing-relevant, relatively basic elements of the five senses, such as color, shape, and typography for the sense of sight, specific sounds and music for the sense of hearing, and material and texture for the sense of touch. It has been scientifically proven that, in general, environmental factors such as store design, music, scents, lighting, store layout, and decoration have a positive influence on the shopping experience in brick-and-mortar stores or shopping malls (Mattila & Wirtz, 2001, p. 274; Wakefield & Baker, 1998, p. 531). The analysis of the C&F in Sect. 2.3 also showed that the senses are primarily addressed by the store design and the store atmosphere. The sense of *sight* is particularly appealed to by colors or color schemes. Gröppel-Klein (2012, p. 661) emphasize that in brick-and-mortar stores, colors in particular have a strong influence on the perceived attractiveness of a store.

Baek, Choo, and Lee (2018, p. 97), found out that stores which are visually warm (through the use of colors or materials) resulted in a higher perceived store intimacy among customers compared to cold designs. Another important element is lighting. In brick-and-mortar stores, it has been found that brighter lighting leads to longer and more frequent customer contact with the goods than dimmed lighting (Ahlert et al., 2020b, p. 305). This must be questioned in virtual stores, as there is also a dark mode on screens in addition to the light mode (Mantzios, 2023). However, in the research project mentioned in Sect. 3.2.2, it was found that the majority of participants preferred the Burberry Regent Street Virtual Flagship Store to the Dyson VR demo store because it had a brighter design and Dyson VR demo store was too dark for most of them (which was mainly due to the use of black as the base color) (Hake et al., 2023). Other elements that can appeal to the sight sense are sizes, shapes, forms (e.g., based on Feng Shui criteria), floor design as well as decorative elements (Ahlert et al., 2020b, pp. 303–305; Baek et al., 2018, p. 92; Gröppel-Klein, 2012, p. 655; Haeusel, 2012, pp. 640, 643; Schmitt, 2011, p. 76; Zentes et al., 2017, p. 332).

The sense of *hearing* can be addressed by acoustic elements such as music, audio advertising, or noises from other people (see e.g., Ahlert et al., 2020b, p. 304; Berekoven, 1995, p. 284; Gröppel-Klein, 2012, p. 647; Haeusel, 2012, p. 643; Mattila & Wirtz, 2001; Zentes et al., 2017, p. 332). Milliman (1982, p. 90) investigated in-store background music and found that "the tempo of instrumental background music can significantly influence [shopping behavior of consumers in terms of] both the pace of in-store traffic flow and the daily gross sales volume purchased by customers [...]". Moreover Milliman (1982) agreed with previously findings by Grayston (1974) about selecting the right music genre and its matching with intended objectives (Milliman, 1982, p. 91). However, it is not only the tempo and genre of the music that can have an influence on purchasing behavior and experience, but also the volume (Gröppel-Klein, 2012, p. 661). Loud music would distract from the purchase, while quiet music would make the customer feel unobserved in brick-and-mortar stores (Haeusel, 2012, p. 643). In 2018, Munir, Kear, Abdul, and J. (2018, p. 140), found that in virtual stores, "music has a significant effect on shopping behaviour, which is linked to shoppers' emotions". As part of the virtual store analysis, the volume of the music could be adjusted or the music could even be muted completely in the majority of virtual stores.

Olfactory elements such as scents, which appeal to the sense of *smell*, as well as tactile elements, which appeal to the sense of *touch*, or gustatory elements, which appeal to the sense of *taste*, are comparatively difficult to recreate and simulate in virtual stores (T. Pfeiffer, 2023, p. 37).

This is because they usually require more devices than just VR glasses. Nevertheless, there are several studies that have already investigated the appeal of senses other than sight and hearing (e.g., Ruusunen, Hallikainen, & Laukkanen, 2023). These are not investigated further in this work.

As such, in this work, the sensory dimension of the customer experience refers to the stimulation of the customer's senses of sight and hearing. It deals with C&F of virtual stores that appeal to the customer's visual and auditory senses.

According to the list, provided previously in Sect. 2.3, features such as virtual store design, store layout, store atmosphere, use of colors, decoration and furnishing, lighting and the quality of images can help to appeal to the *visual* sense. The sense of *hearing* can in turn be addressed by features such as sounds or background music. As already shown, elements that appeal to the sense of *sight* and *hearing* have a positive influence on the experience and consumer behavior. Hence, the following hypothesis can be derived:

H2 *The sensory dimension of the customer experience has a positive influence on the customer experience.*

4.1.3.2 Emotional Dimension

Following Schmitt (1999, 2011), the "feel" module relates to all affective experiences appealing to the inner feelings and emotions of the customer (Schmitt, 1999, p. 61). Gentile et al. (2007) define it as "a component of the Customer Experience which involves one's affective system through the generation of moods, feelings, emotions [...]" (Gentile et al., 2007, p. 399). According to Gentile et al. (2007), "an offering [like virtual stores] can generate emotional experience in order to create an affective relation with the company, its brand or products" (Gentile et al., 2007, p. 399). In literature, the affective system is also referred to as affective state (Jin et al., 2021, p. 3; Rose et al., 2011, p. 29). Both definitions refer to what Lemon and Verhoef (2016, p. 70) call the "emotional dimension" of the CX. Brun et al. (2017, p. 323) also uses the term emotional experience dimension and considers both, a positive as well as negative EMD.

The emotions they especially refer to are, e.g., interest, joy, and surprise as positive emotions as well as sadness, anger and disgust as negative (Brun et al., 2017, pp. 323, 340).

Jin et al. (2021, p. 16) did a sentiment analysis to find out how consumers feel about 360-degree-based VR videos, whether they feel more negative than positive emotions or vice versa. Both, negative (such as "blurry", "dizzy," "sore," "sick," and "headaches") as well as positive (such as "cool", "feel", "actual", and "enjoyed") emotions could be identified (see also Sect. 3.2.1; Jin et al., 2021, p. 16).

Fishbein and Ajzen (1975, p. 12) distinguish affect from cognition, conation and behavior. Affect refers to a person's feelings towards an object, a person, an issue or an event and their evaluation (Fishbein & Ajzen, 1975, p. 12). In this work, the affect mainly refers to the customer's feelings towards virtual stores and their evaluation.

Hence, the emotional dimension refers to emotions, feelings, and moods that can be evoked during a virtual store shopping experience. This dimension of the customer experience focuses on the hedonic and emotional aspect. The emotions that can arise during a virtual shopping experience can either be positive or negative.

The influence of the emotional dimension has also been investigated, e.g., previous studies have shown that positive emotions lead to positive consumer reactions and vice versa (e.g., Chang, Eckman, & Yan, 2011; Das & Varshneya, 2017; Eroglu, Machleit, & Davis, 2001). Jin et al. (2021, pp. 15–16) found that VR tends to evoke positive feelings compared to websites and that positive feelings have a positive influence on the perceived attractiveness of stores. This leads to the following hypothesis:

H3 *The emotional dimension of the customer experience has a positive influence on the customer experience.*

4.1.3.3 Cognitive Dimension

The third dimension of the CX is the COD. In Schmitt's (1999) CEM framework, this is related to the "think" module that focuses on intellect, and strives to create "cognitive, problem-solving experiences that engage customers" in creative ways (Schmitt, 1999, p. 61).

Gentile et al. (2007) define the COD as "a component of the Customer Experience connected with thinking or conscious mental processes" (Gentile et al., 2007, p. 399). In this case, C&F of the virtual store should encourage the customer to use his or her creativity. Furthermore, C&F of the virtual store should help the customer to solve his or her problems (in the virtual store) (Gentile et al., 2007, p. 399). The most important characteristics are usability, information availability and personalization (Interaction Design Foundation [IxDF], 2016b).

Usability is given, when the navigation is easy and intuitive, when customers are able to move freely in the virtual store, when they quickly find, what they are looking for, and when the structure of the virtual store is clear and concise (e.g., Barnes & Vidgen, 2002, pp. 115, 119; Childers, Carr, Peck, & Carson, 2001, p. 515; Rose et al., 2011, pp. 29, 39; Shen et al., 2021, pp. 10–11, 15; Yim et al., 2017, pp. 91, 100).

Quality would be another important characteristic in virtual stores, which is defined by Aladwani and Palvia (2002, p. 469) in the context of e-commerce stores as "users' evaluation of a web site's features meeting users' needs and reflecting overall excellence of the web site" (Sousa & Voss, 2006, p. 369). Information availability refers to information to be easy to find, and readily available. In addition, the cognitive experience can be created through other features that allow customers to easily ask questions about products and get quick answers with the desired information, e.g., by contacting salespeople, personalized assistance systems in the form of a virtual product comparison matrix (J. Pfeiffer, 2023, p. 15). Goel and Prokopec (2009, p. 118) derived the term "informativeness" from websites, which contain information and product descriptions, and transferred it to virtual worlds as the extent to which the channel provides information that the shopper finds useful. They found that virtual stores are less information-oriented and more experience-oriented. Unlike websites, which are more information-oriented. They emphasized that in virtual stores, brands would link to their websites for more information (Goel & Prokopec, 2009, pp. 119, 128). This could also be observed when analyzing the C&F of virtual stores. However, there were also many virtual stores that contained a lot of information, e.g., brand history, ingredients, product descriptions and others (see also Table 2.1, Appendix A). Another characteristic which can lead to cognitive experiences is personalization (Rose et al., 2012, pp. 310, 317). This can take the form of addressing the customer directly by name, personalized recommendations and product suggestions tailored to the customer.

In this work, the cognitive dimension of the customer experience refers to C&F of virtual stores that, on the one hand, relieve the customer cognitively and, on the other hand, stimulate the customer's thinking.

This can be done, e.g., through providing information, knowledge, intellectual stimulation to engage customer's thinking and problem solving abilities. In addition, clear product information, easy navigation, ease of use, search performance, search function, intuitive interfaces and control can help to create a cognitive experience for the customer. In the context of e-commerce, Z. Chen and Dubinsky (2003, p. 336) found that customers' perception of how easy an e-commerce store is to use and the provision of relevant information is highly associated with a positive online experience. This leads to the following hypothesis:

H4 *The cognitive dimension of the customer experience has a positive influence on the customer experience.*

4.1.3.4 Social Dimension

The SOD is based on Schmitt (1999) "Relate" module, which refers to the customer's desire to be part of a "social context" (e.g., brand community) (Schmitt, 1999, pp. 60–62). Gentile et al. (2007) define it as "a component of the Customer Experience that involves the person and, beyond, his [or her] social context, his [or her] relationship with other people or also with his [or her] ideal self. An offering can leverage on such component by means of a product which encourages the use [or] consumption together with other people or which is the core of a common passion that may eventually lead to the creation of a community or still a tribe of fans [...]" (Gentile et al., 2007, p. 399). This can include characteristics of virtual stores such as social presence, community building, social interactions, and (virtual) sales assistants (Brun et al., 2017, p. 340; I. Krasonikolakis et al., p. 10; Shen et al., 2021, pp. 11, 15; White Baker et al., 2019, p. 52).

Hence, in this work, the social dimension of the customer experience refers to social experiences in virtual stores, which can arise through social presence, social interaction and community building.

It is about how social presence, social interactions and the sense of community in virtual stores influence the CX.

A social experience can be created through features such as multi-usage, visual presence, social shopping, chat functions, social corners, social sharing functions and user-generated content that facilitate social connections and enhance the SOD of the CX.

A study by Razorfish and Vice Media Group (2022, p. 15) found that Gen Z would spend time with friends in the metaverse twice as much in real life (playing video games there in the first place). They also found that 65% have built new relationships through gaming and that 52% find it "easier to make new friends through gaming than in real life" (Razorfish & Vice Media Group, 2022, p. 16).

I. Krasonikolakis et al. (2014, p. 35) appeal to investigate social aspects such as the presence of others as influencing variables on the CX in virtual shopping environments. White Baker et al. (2019, p. 31) also found that a higher level of social presence leads to a higher level of perceived enjoyment. From this, the following hypothesis can be derived:

H5 *The social dimension of the customer experience has a positive influence on the customer experience.*

4.1.3.5 Immersive Dimension

In the context of CX in virtual stores, a fifth dimension, the IMD, should be taken into account. In contrast to the other four dimensions of CX, the IMD is not based on established CX models and has not been considered in any research in this form before. Nevertheless, various studies have found that virtual stores in particular create immersive experiences. According to Yim et al. (2017), who in turn refer to M. T. Palmer (1995) and Biocca and Delaney (1995), immersion is "the degree to which virtual systems make users feel absorbed in, involved with, and engrossed by virtual stimuli (Palmer 1995) or experience a sense of blocking out of stimuli from their physical world environment (Biocca and Delaney 1995)" (Yim et al., 2017, p. 92).

Immersion can be elicited through vividness, interactivity and telepresence (also referred to as presence, e.g., Lombard & Ditton, 1997). J. V. Chen et al. (2022) describe telepresence based on Minsky (1980) and Steuer (1992, p. 75) as "the feeling of being present in a mediated or virtual environment" (J. V. Chen et al., 2022, p. 5).

Schuemie, van der Straaten, Krijn, and van der Mast (2001) also refer to the feeling of "being there" (Schuemie et al., 2001, p. 187). However, Schuemie et al. (2001, pp. 198–199) emphasize that the investigation of presence alone is not sufficient and that further constructs such as interactions or interactivity, vividness as well as user characteristics (like involvement, focus, and gaming) should be taken into account when considering VR environments, in this case virtual stores. Accordingly, interactivity as well as vividness will be further considered. Steuer (1992, pp. 81, 89) identified both, vividness (subdivided into breadth and depth) and interactivity (subdivided into speed, range and mapping) as technological variables that would influence telepresence. While interactivity is defined as "the extent to which users can participate in modifying the form and content of a mediated environment in real time" (Steuer, 1992, p. 84), vividness represents "the representational richness of a mediated environment[7] as defined by its formal features, that is, the way in which an environment presents information to the senses [...], stimulus driven and entirely upon technical characteristics of a medium[8]" (Steuer, 1992, p. 81).

In this work, the immersive dimension of the customer experience represents C&F of a virtual store that create a sense of immersion and presence, allowing customers to feel deeply involved in the virtual store shopping experience.

---

[7] In this work, the mediated environment is the virtual environment, the virtual store.

[8] The medium refers to the device, in this work the VR glasses.

This can be elicited through C&F of virtual stores such as realistic store and product design, real colors and graphics, 360-degree views (e.g., to be able to inspect products from different angles), real-time interactions with products and the environment, customization and modification of content and environment (e.g., background, location, lighting, colors), and other technical features (such as scaling, imaging, resolution, or fidelity) and customer's control over what is displayed to him or her (see Sect. 2.3 and Appendix A).

Nevertheless, VR technology, such as VR headsets, also has a major impact on the creation of immersive experiences. Wedel et al. (2020) even refer exclusively to immersion as "a result of technical features of VR systems and devices" (Wedel et al., 2020, p. 446). However, this will not be considered further in this work, as it focuses on the C&F of virtual stores and not the technology behind it. According to Yim et al. (2017), "immersion has been understood to be a mediating enhancer in a variety of virtual experiences" (Yim et al., 2017, p. 92).

Wedel et al. (2020, p. 458), also call for a focus on creating virtual experiences that include interactive telepresence. This leads to the following hypothesis:

H6 *The immersive dimension of the customer experience has a positive influence on the customer experience.*

4.1.3.6 General Customer Experience

The general customer experience (GCX) was investigated by Zaharia and Schmitz (2019, p. 8) based on the "Customer Experience Pyramid" (also referred to as Customer Experience Index) by Forrester Research, Inc. (2014) which consists of three levels: (1) the fulfillment of customer needs, (2) the perception of the interaction as easy, and (3) the shopping experience as a pleasant activity.

> *In this work, the general customer experience is defined as the general perception of a shopping experience on the part of customers in virtual stores.*

It is considered as an independent variable that has an influence on the intention to use virtual stores. The GCX will be investigated in addition to the CX as a higher-order construct. Thus, it can be tested whether the CX has a general influence (as GCX) on behavioral intention to use virtual stores, apart from CX, which is composed of C&F of virtual stores that prove to have the potential to create experiences. From this, the following hypothesis can be derived (also see Table 4.3):

H7 *The general customer experience has a positive influence on the behavioral intention to use virtual stores.*

Table 4.1 Store Characteristics and Features x Customer Experience Dimensions

Characteristics	Features	Sensory Dimension	Emotional Dimension	Cognitive Dimension	Social Dimension	Immersive Dimension
Store Design / Store Atmosphere	Storytelling, Place / Background Scenes / Ambience, Theme, Style, Color Scheme, Fonts, Shapes and Forms, Quotes, Window Dressing, Attention Points, Presentation of Goods, Lighting, Sensory Feedback	x				
	Entrance, Orientation, Wayfinding, Direction	x		x		
	Favorites / Wishlist			x		x
Digital Signage, Multimedia and Technologies	Videos, Images, Illustrations, Displays, Banner	x		x		
	Animations, Graphics	x				x
	QR-Codes			x		
Audio	Music, Sounds, Volume Control	x		x		x
Store Layout	Qualitative Division of Store, Store-within-a-Store, Guidance system, Menu	x		x		
	Freedom of Movement			x		x
	Crowding and Dysfunctional Density (Prevention)			x		
	Escalator, Stairs	x				x
Quality	Resolution / Fidelity / Definition	x				
Usability	Ease of Use			x		
Information Availability	Usage-related			x		
	Product-related			x		
Interactivity	Social Interactions, AI Chatbot				x	
	Product Interactions, Real-time, Gift finder, Activities					x
Personalization / Customization				x		x
Gamification				x	x	
Loyalty Program				x		
Content / Education	Brand History, Brand's Heritage, Story, Product, Tutorials, How-to Videos, Styling Tips, Behind The Scenes / Making-off, Brand's Initiatives / Campaigns			x		
Access				x		
Checkout		x		x		
Product Offerings				x		
Other	Exclusivity, Omnichannel, Artists / Designer / Creators, Developer, Digital Service Provider, Avatar Creator, Events, Technology Partnerships					

Note. This table contains the mapping of the characteristics and features of virtual stores to the dimensions of CX. As can be seen from the table, some characteristics and features could not be assigned to any particular dimension, while others could not be assigned to any dimension.

4.2 Research Question 2—Influence of Moderator Variables

This chapter addresses the second research question that deals with the effect of consumer characteristics on the relationships between CX and BI, as well as GCX and BI. More precisely it will be investigated if the effects are significantly different for a) people with VR experience than for people without VR experience (Sect. 4.2.1), b) introverts than for extraverts (Sect. 4.2.2), and c) gamers than for non-gamers (Sect. 4.2.3).

4.2.1 Experience with Virtual Reality

Igbaria, Guimaraes, and Davis (1995) found that prior experience with computer has an influence on the usage of computer and the variety of usage (Igbaria et al., 1995, pp. 109–110). According to A. Palmer (2010, p. 198), who in turn refers to Sheth et al. (1999), also pointed out that prior experience with a product or service offering can have a great influence (A. Palmer, 2010, p. 198). Jin et al. (2021), investigated in their experiment whether users with VR experience and first-time users who had never used VR before were differently excited and pleased about the experience in the VR store. However, the regression results showed that there were no differences due to previous VR experience (Jin et al., 2021, p. 12). Nevertheless, as this work only considers Gen Z, the influence of previous experience with VR is tested. Hence, experience with VR is defined as previous experience with VR technology, such as VR glasses. This leads to the following hypotheses (also see Tab. 4.3):

H1-M1 *The influence of the customer experience on the behavioral intention to use virtual stores is moderated by the experience with VR, whereby the effect is stronger for VR-experienced people.*

H7-M1 *The influence of the general customer experience on the behavioral intention to use virtual stores is moderated by the experience with VR, whereby the effect is stronger for VR-experienced people.*

H8-M1 *People with VR experience have a greater behavioral intention to use virtual stores than people without VR experience.*

4.2.2 Personality

Schnack et al. (2021) investigated the impact of shoppers' personality (PERS) on their behavior in an immersive VR store environments in form of a 3D VR convenience store based on the "big five" personality dimensions (including agreeableness, conscientiousness, extraversion, neuroticism, and openness to experience) (Schnack et al., 2021, pp. 2–4). Their findings did not indicate any impact (Schnack et al., 2021, p. 6). Another study that explored Gen Z in relation to the metaverse found that those in the metaverse were "six times more likely to describe themselves as introverted [than] extraverted" (Razorfish & Vice Media Group, 2022, p. 8). Although, Schnack et al. (2021) could not find significant impact of personality in virtual stores, it will be investigated in this work. Therefore, based on the big fives, extraversion is defined as a personality type, mainly driven by characteristics such as talkative, energetic and assertive (Foscht et al., 2017, p. 135). Extraversion is also usually associated with sociability, i.e., extraverts enjoy being with people (Schnack et al., 2021, p. 3). On the other hand, introversion is defined through characteristics such as calm, reserved, shy (Foscht et al., 2017, p. 135). In a study by Nokia and Ipsos (2022, p. 18), Gen Z used an MBTI personality type to describe themselves alongside gender and other characteristics. MBTI stands for Myers–Briggs Type Indicator (MBTI) and is a questionnaire that is based on Carl Jung's theory of psychological type, including four dimensions, amongst others extraversion and introversion in which extraversion is associated with talkativeness, sociability and enjoying the attention of others, while introversion is associated with being reserved and observing others (The Myer-Briggs Company, 2024). PERS appears to have a moderating influence on the relationships between GCX and BI as well as CX and BI in the research model. For this reason, the following hypotheses are derived (also see Tab. 4.3):

H1-M2 *The influence of the customer experience on the behavioral intention to use virtual stores is moderated by personality, whereby the effect is stronger for introverted people.*

H7-M2 *The influence of the general customer experience on the behavioral intention to use virtual stores is moderated by personality, whereby the effect is stronger for introverted people.*

H8-M2 *Introverts have a greater behavioral intention to use virtual stores than extraverts.*

4.2.3 Gaming

In the Cambridge Academic Content Dictionary gaming (GAME) is defined as "the activity of playing games on computers and other electronic devices" ("Cambridge academic content dictionary," 2009).

Hence, in this work, gaming refers to people's activity of playing games on computers and other electronic devices.

GAME plays a big role in the metaverse. In the "Gaming Industry Survey 2022" conducted by EY, "97% of survey respondents believe[d] the gaming industry is the center of the metaverse" (Porter, Harrison, Ang, Golik, & Gupta, 2022, p. 6). This is also supported by Razorfish and Vice Media Group (2022, p. 4) who wanted to understand the metaverse from a gaming perspective. They analyzed gaming behavior to derive attitudes, beliefs and behaviors that can be assumed to motivate Gen Z to participate in the metaverse as well (Razorfish & Vice Media Group, 2022, p. 4). They found that "[one] in [three] Gen Z [...] play video games to build a more idealized version of the world" and for 56% "gaming [would be] an escape from real world issues". Similarly, Khan (2022) points out the importance of the gaming industry in relation to the metaverse. Campbell-Gross (2022), also emphasized that the metaverse primarily appeals to people who like to play games and that while shopping and using VR or AR technology, consumers would view "platforms [in the metaverse] as a way to enjoy games" (Campbell-Gross, 2022). It was found that "61% of shoppers are excited to use VR for shopping [...] and [that] they want to try out clothing, furniture, home appliances, and technology via AR or VR before buying" (Campbell-Gross, 2022).

Within the master's thesis of Djaiz and Zaharia (2022) about "Acceptance of Gamification Approaches in German E-Commerce"[9] at HSNR, the impact of gamification on the creation of online shopping experiences for consumers was also highlighted.[10] Furthermore, the gaming industry's main target group, alongside millennials and Gen Alpha, is Gen Z (Khan, 2022).

It can therefore be assumed that gamers tend to be more inclined to use virtual stores in the metaverse and strive to have experiences there. Hence, GAME is considered as a moderator that has influence on the relationships between the

[9] The original title is in German: "Akzeptanz von Gamification-Ansätzen im deutschen Online-Handel".

[10] No other similar studies or findings from the scientific literature could be found.

GCX and BI, as well as the CX and BI in the research model. This gives rise to the following hypotheses (also see Tab. 4.3):

H1-M3 *The influence of the customer experience on the behavioral intention to use virtual stores is moderated by gaming, whereby the effect is stronger for gamers.*

H7-M3 *The influence of the general customer experience on the behavioral intention to use virtual stores is moderated by gaming, whereby the effect is stronger for gamers.*

H8-M3 *Gamers have a greater behavioral intention to use virtual stores than non-gamers.*

Table 4.2 Overview of Definitions

Construct	Acronym	Definition (Short Form)
Behavioral Intention	BI	Behavioral intention refers to the person's intention to perform various behaviors in relation to virtual stores.
Customer Experience	CX	The customer experience refers to the sensory, emotional, cognitive, social and immersive experiences in a virtual store.
General Customer Experience	GCX	The general customer experience is defined as the general perception of a shopping experience on the part of customers in virtual stores.
Dimensions of Customer Experience		
Sensory Dimension	SED	The sensory dimension of the customer experience refers to the stimulation of the customer's senses of sight and hearing.
Emotional Dimension	EMD	The emotional dimension refers to emotions, feelings, and moods that can be evoked during a virtual store shopping experience.
Cognitive Dimension	COD	The cognitive dimension of the customer experience refers to features and characteristics of virtual stores that, on the one hand, relieve the customer cognitively and, on the other hand, stimulate the customer's thinking.
Social Dimension	SOD	the social dimension refers to social experiences in virtual stores, which can arise through social presence, social interaction and community building.
Immersive Dimension	IMD	The immersive dimension represents features and characteristics of a virtual store that create a sense of immersion and presence, allowing customers to feel deeply involved in the virtual store shopping experience.
Moderators		
Experience with VR	VREX	Experience with VR is defined as previous experience with virtual reality technology, such as VR glasses.
Personality	PERS	Personality is defined through the two personality types extraversion and introversion. While extraversion is defined as a personality type, mainly driven by characteristics such as talkative, energetic and assertive, introversion is defined through characteristics such as calm, reserved, shy.
Gaming	GAME	Gaming refers to people's activity of playing games on computers and other electronic devices.

4.3 Overview of Hypotheses and Research Model

Table 4.2 provides an overview of the derived definitions for each construct, while Table 4.3 summarizes the hypotheses to be tested in the following chapters. Figure 4.1 illustrates the overall research model.

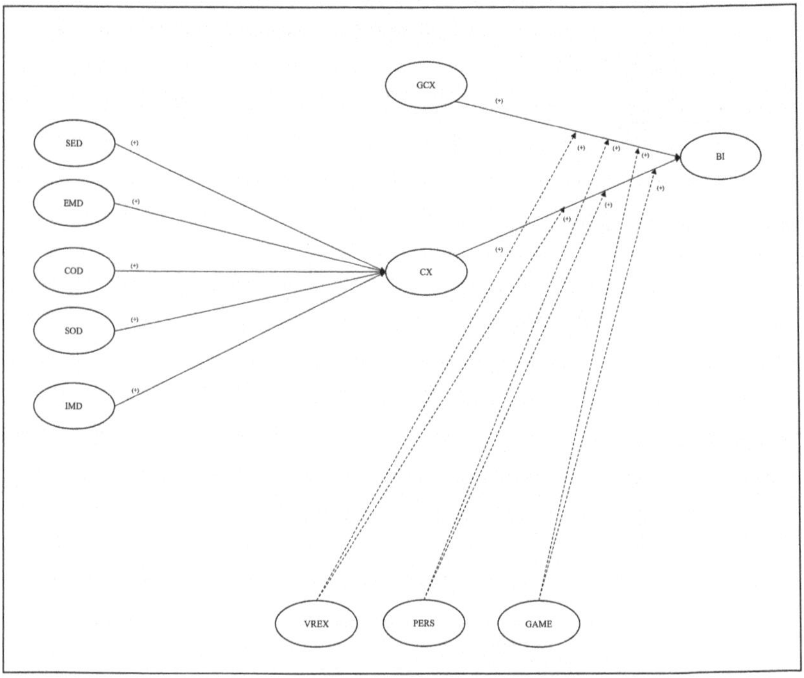

Fig. 4.1 Research Model and Hypotheses. (*Note*. This figure presents the research model developed in this study, including the hypothesized relationships. Source. Author's own illustration)

Table 4.3 Overview of Hypotheses

	Hypotheses
H1	The customer experience has a positive influence on the behavioral intention to use virtual stores.
H1-M1	The influence of the customer experience on the behavioral intention to use virtual stores is moderated by the experience with VR, whereby the effect is stronger for VR-experienced people.
H1-M2	The influence of the customer experience on the behavioral intention to use virtual stores is moderated by personality, whereby the effect is stronger for introverted people.
H1-M3	The influence of the customer experience on the behavioral intention to use virtual stores is moderated by gaming, whereby the effect is stronger for gamers.
H2	The sensory dimension of the customer experience has a positive influence on the customer experience.
H3	The emotional dimension of the customer experience has a positive influence on the customer experience.
H4	The cognitive dimension of the customer experience has a positive influence on the customer experience.
H5	The social dimension of the customer experience has a positive influence on the customer experience.
H6	The immersive dimension of the customer experience has a positive influence on the customer experience.
H7	The general customer experience has a positive influence on the behavioral intention to use virtual stores.
H7-M1	The influence of the general customer experience on the behavioral intention to use virtual stores is moderated by the experience with VR, whereby the effect is stronger for VR-experienced people.
H7-M2	The influence of the general customer experience on the behavioral intention to use virtual stores is moderated by personality, whereby the effect is stronger for introverted people.
H7-M3	The influence of the general customer experience on the behavioral intention to use virtual stores is moderated by gaming, whereby the effect is stronger for gamers
H8-M1	People with VR experience have a greater behavioral intention to use virtual stores than people without VR experience.
H8-M2	Introverts have a greater behavioral intention to use virtual stores than extraverts.
H8-M3	Gamers have a greater behavioral intention to use virtual stores than non-gamers.

5 Methodology

5.1 Research Design

This chapter deals with the definition of the research design. Homburg (2017) distinguishes between three research design types: descriptive research, exploratory research and causal research (also referred to as explicative research). Descriptive research is carried out if the facts relevant to the topic of the study are to be recorded and described as precisely as possible. However, no correlations between the variables are investigated (Homburg, 2020, p. 260; Kreis, Wildner, & Kuß, 2021, p. 33; Sarstedt & Mooi, 2019, p. 17). Exploratory research is carried out if the topic of the study is still relatively unexplored and must first be captured and structured. Correlations between the variables can then be analyzed. Exploratory research differs from causal research in that no hypotheses are made about the relationships between the variables before the data analysis (Homburg, 2020, p. 260; Kreis et al., 2021, pp. 31–33). Causal research is used when the causes of an observed phenomenon and the relationships between two or more variables are investigated (Sarstedt & Mooi, 2019, p. 18; Weiber & Sarstedt, 2021, p. 94). In contrast to exploratory research, hypotheses are formulated a priori and the relationships between the variables are then determined on the basis of the hypotheses. It is therefore mainly a matter of testing initial hypotheses and to uncover causality, i.e., the relationship between the cause and the effect, when the effect is a consequence of the cause (Homburg, 2017, p. 260; Kreis et al., 2021, pp. 34–36).

Supplementary Information The online version contains supplementary material available at https://doi.org/10.1007/978-3-658-48634-1_5.

M. Hake, *Shopping in Virtual Stores*, BestMasters,
https://doi.org/10.1007/978-3-658-48634-1_5

In the following work, causal research proves to be the most suitable research method. This is because the focus of this research is on investigating the causal relationships between the different variables on the basis of a priori formulated hypotheses. According to Sarstedt and Mooi (2019), the prerequisites for the application of causal research are (1) that there is a relationship between the cause and the effect, (2) that the cause occurs before the effect, (3) that other factors are controlled, and (4) that there is an upstream explanatory theory (Sarstedt & Mooi, 2019, p. 18). All of these requirements are met. Hence, causal research is applied.

5.2 Data Collection

Primary Research

Research is based on data. Data can be obtained by researchers using existing data (also referred to as secondary data) or by collecting new data themselves and tailoring it to their individual information needs (primary data) (Homburg, 2020, p. 285). So far, no comparable study has been conducted in German-speaking countries that investigates the influence of CX on the BI of Gen Z to use virtual stores in virtual environments such as the metaverse (see Sect. 2.1.1). Therefore, in order to empirically test the hypotheses of the research model, primary research will be conducted in which new data will be collected (Kreis et al., 2021, p. 36). Although secondary data is usually more affordable and readily available, unlike primary data it is not tailored to the research context and cannot be collected according to the researcher's information needs. Conversely, the planning and collecting of primary data often requires much more time and effort. It is also usually associated with higher costs (Sarstedt & Mooi, 2019, p. 30; Vomberg & Klarmann, 2022, p. 68). However, for the reasons mentioned before, the collection of primary data is necessary in this study.

Data Collection Method

The author has considered various options for collecting primary data. Following Homburg (2020), two different types of primary data collection methods can be distinguished: Survey methods or observation methods. Based on these methods, three different options for data collection were identified for this thesis. One of these proved to be potentially the most useful: The first would be a qualitative research method. The participants put on VR glasses, visit and experience a virtual store with the VR glasses and then the researcher conduct a structured in-depth interview with a short questionnaire in which socio-demographic criteria are queried. This has already been done as part of the research project mentioned in Sect. 3.2.2. Therefore, this might lead to redundant results.

The second method would be a mixture of qualitative and quantitative methods. Participants who already have VR experience and have their own VR glasses (at home) would have been surveyed. A link would have been shared with the participants. After opening the link, they can try out the virtual retail store experience and are then asked a list of questions to evaluate their experience.

This method is hybrid, qualitative, because participants need to try out the VR experience at first, and quantitative, as there is a subsequent online survey. Nonetheless, it may be difficult to find respondents, since VR glasses are not yet so well established in Germany.

The third option would be solely of quantitative nature. Participants are sent a link to an online survey. The online survey contains background information about virtual stores and a video in which the respondents are shown various examples of virtual stores. There are participants who already have VR experience, i.e., who can roughly imagine what it is like to wear VR glasses and can evaluate the experience in the form of a video based on previous experiences, and those who have not yet had any VR experiences.

The latter is the option used in this work, as it predominates after weighing up the advantages and disadvantages. An online survey might be much more cost-effective than qualitative in-depth interviews, especially, when it is done with a market research institute. Nevertheless, high case numbers can be achieved more quickly and it is possible to approach a higher number of respondents (online-shoppers, as well as both, people with and without VR experience). Gen Z people can also be found much more easier. It is also possible to use mixed media, e.g., audio and video. Moreover, VR glasses are not required as with the other methods.

Consequently, this method seems to be the most suitable for the current state of research and the given framework conditions. This is because only a few people in Germany have already gained VR experience and the minority are in possession of VR glasses (see e.g.,). Furthermore, as mentioned above, a qualitative preliminary study already exists (see Sect. 3.2.2), which only underlines the need to carry out a quantitative online survey. In addition, more targeted personalization and filter questions can be used in questionnaires (Homburg, 2020, p. 296). On the other hand, there are also some disadvantages such as potential biases (e.g., the user journey and VR experience is mostly guided by the researcher by means of text, image and video elements within the questionnaire, which makes the findings less trustworthy or credible), insufficient information about the population, and the risk of dubious answers due to anonymity. However, the latter is counteracted by collaborating with a market research institute (see Sect. 5.6).

So, the primary data is being gathered in form of an online survey conducted as a link provided on a website. Vomberg and Klarmann (2022) outlined that for researchers surveys are a flexible and powerful instrument for developing, testing and generalizing theories (Sarstedt & Mooi, 2019, pp. 22–45; Vomberg & Klarmann, 2022, p. 67).

Time Frame

As the aim is to find out whether Gen Z would currently use virtual stores and what influence the CX has on this, it is more useful to conduct a cross-sectional study than a longitudinal study. This is because the aim is not to observe changes over a longer period of time, as would be the case in a longitudinal study, but merely to examine the status quo. This means that the data is only collected once at one point in time over a certain period of time. Unlike a longitudinal study, which implies several observations over different periods of time (e.g., Kreis et al., 2021, pp. 42–44; Oehlrich, 2022, p. 196; Vomberg & Klarmann, 2022, p. 70).

5.3 Design of the Questionnaire

After determining the data collection method, the questionnaire used in the online survey has to be designed. Vomberg and Klarmann (2022, p. 93) recommend applying their questionnaire design process. The process of designing the questionnaire comprises a total of seven phases and, in addition to designing the questionnaire, also helps to avoid bias (Vomberg & Klarmann, 2022, p. 69). The online survey is conducted in German, however, all parts and contents of the questionnaire are presented in English in this work (e.g., items, further questions). A German equivalent can be found in Appendix D (full questionnaire) and Appendix C (operationalization). The underlying questionnaire design process is shown in Fig. 5.1.

5.3.1 Phase 1—Survey Content

The first phase of the questionnaire design process is about deciding on the content of the survey, which includes the key phenomena or constructs to be addressed in the survey (Homburg, 2020, p. 335; Vomberg & Klarmann, 2022, p. 94). According to Chap. 4, these are the *BI* as the dependent variable, the *CX* as a HCM with its dimensions *SED*, *EMD*, *COD*, *SOD*, and *IMD*, as well as the moderators *VREX*, *PERS* and *GAME*. Additionally, some socio-demographic criteria (age, gender, highest level of education, monthly net income) as well as psychographic criteria (online shopping frequency, early adopter, gaming, experience with virtual stores) are also investigated.

Next to the main variables of interests, there are further phenomena which are of high interest, including design style preferences of virtual stores, degree of realism of virtual stores, preferred virtual store features (see Sect. 2.3), preferred products and services, appearance of virtual stores, as well as preferred shopping channel (Sect. 2.1.3).

Within the first phase, the length of a questionnaire should also be considered. Vomberg and Klarmann (2022, p. 87) recommend a maximum of 25 questions in order to avoid biased responses such as response style or non-response biases. With regard to this, they also emphasize that the length of the questionnaire also depends on influential situational factors or the willingness to participate of the respondents (Vomberg & Klarmann, 2022, p. 95). As the survey is conducted by the market research institute INJ Partners who incentivize the respondents, their motivation as well as their willingness to participate might be higher than usually (Homburg, 2020, p. 324).

In addition, the author checked the length of the questionnaire with the market research institute INJ Partners who recommended a maximum survey length of 32 questions based on their experience. Hence, this rule of thumb is strictly followed.

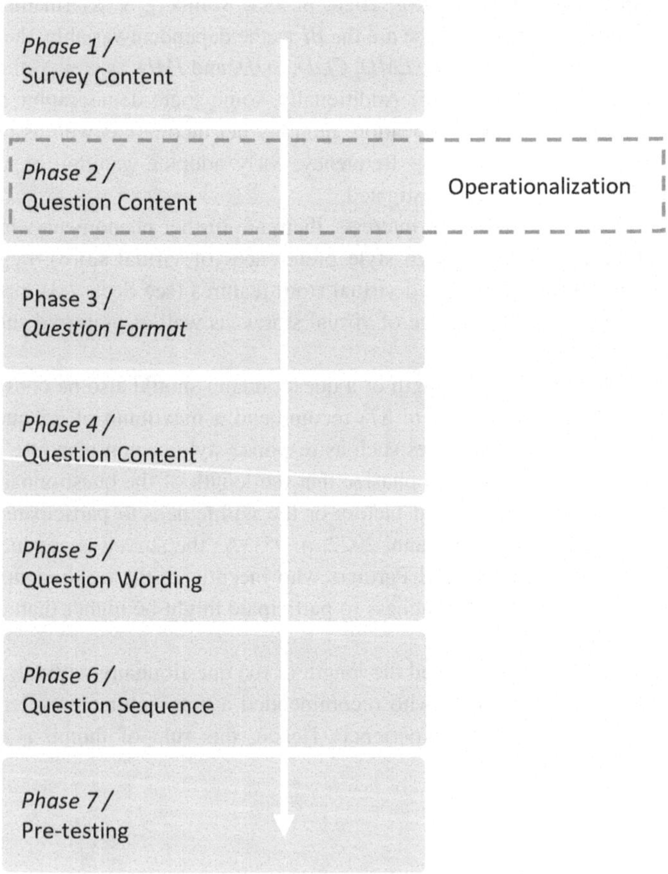

Fig. 5.1 Phases of the Questionnaire Design Process. (*Note*. This figure shows the seven phases of the questionnaire design process by Vomberg and Klarmann (2022, p. 93). Adapted from "Crafting Survey Research: A Systematic Process for Conducting Survey Research", by Vomberg, A., & Klarmann, M., 2022, in C. Homburg, M. Klarmann, & A. Vomberg (Eds.), Handbook of Market Research, p. 93. Cham: Springer International Publishing.)

5.3.2 Phase 2—Question Content

The second phase "Question Content" is dedicated to the constructs' operationalization[1], coming up with items for their measurement. Researcher have two options (1) relying on established scales or (2) create new ones.[2] It was searched for existing scales in the first place. Therefore, it was searched in manuals such as Handbook for Marketing Sales, on websites such as *inn-theoriezeit.org*, and especially in research papers published in leading journals (Bearden and Netemeyer, 2010, 1999; Homburg et al., 2011).

In this work, the researcher is faced with the lack of established scales (J. Hair, Black, Babin, & Anderson, 2010, p. 655). As already mentioned in Sect. 3.1, CX was often only conceptualized and not operationalized, especially not in the context of shopping experiences in virtual stores. Furthermore, existing scales usually refer to another context and content. Hence, the operationalization within this work is based on an hybrid operationalization approach, which incorporates both, items of established scales and newly developed items. Established items have been adapted to the context of this work.

For this, insights of the research project which is described in Sect. 3.2.2 and the use case list were also used. When designing and formulating the survey questions, the researcher had always paid attention to if respondents are able to understand and answer the particular question by e.g., using simple words. Hence, the use of foreign terms was tried to avoid, otherwise definitions, and examples, were given.

Apart from this, it needs to be decided, whether to use single or multiple items. According to Bergkvist and Rossiter (2007), as well as Diamantopoulos, Sarstedt, Fuchs, Wilczynski, and Kaiser (2012), it is acceptable to measure a construct using single items, when the construct can be captured by this single item accurately.

This applies, e.g., for demographic information such as the gender. If this is not the case, multi-item scales should be used which helps to control random measurement error and increases the overall reliability of the scale. In addition, through multi-item scales, the different facets of the constructs can be captured (J. F. Hair, Hult, Ringle, & Sarstedt, 2022, p. 10; Vomberg & Klarmann, 2022, p. 96).

[1] This chapter presents the final operationalization, which took place after the pretests had been carried out (see Sect. 5.3.7).

[2] Usually established scales are used as they are already widely accepted in scientific discourse and can later avoid issues in evaluating reliability and validity which can be evoked when developing new scales.

5.3.2.1 Operationalization of Behavioral Intention to Use

The BI is operationalized on the basis of Kim et al. (2023, p. 8) and Papagiannidis et al. (2014, p. 882). Kim et al. (2023), achieved a Cronbach's alpha of $\alpha = 0.96$ using the following three indicators (Kim et al., 2023, p. 8):

I would be willing to shop on this app.

The likelihood that I would shop on this app is very high.

I would be willing to recommend this app to my friend.

Papagiannidis et al. (2014, p. 882) used four indicators and achieved a Composite reliability of 0.84. The items of Kim et al. (2023, p. 8) and Papagiannidis et al. (2014, p. 882) were adapted to the context of this work. In order to find out more about the purposes for which respondents would use virtual stores, the scale was expanded to include trying out products as well as searching for and obtaining information about products. This was also based on the operationalization of Grewal, Baker, Levy, and Voss (2003, p. 267):

BI_01 I can imagine using virtual stores in the future.
BI_02 I would use virtual stores for shopping.
BI_03 I would use virtual stores to find out about products.
BI_04 I would use virtual stores to try out products.
BI_05 I would recommend virtual stores to my friends and acquaintances.
BI_06 If you had the opportunity, how likely is it that you would use virtual stores?

The BI is rated on a 5-point Likert scale with verbalized endpoints ranging from 1 = "strongly disagree" to 5 = "strongly agree", whereby BI_06 is rated from 1 = "very unlikely" to 5 = "very likely".

5.3.2.2 Operationalization of Sensory Dimension

The SED is operationalized by nine items from different measurement scales that are adapted to the context of this work. This is because the SED, similar to the COD, SOD and IMD, represents several C&F of virtual stores.

Both, visual as well as audio C&F are asked within the questionnaire. The characteristic store design is operationalized as follows:

SED_01 In a virtual store, the store design should be appealing.

The characteristic store atmosphere is operationalized based on Rose et al. (2012, p. 317) and adapted as follows:

SED_02 The look and feel of virtual stores would be important to me.

As the analysis of C&F has shown, image quality is also an important feature of virtual stores, so it is integrated as follows:

SED_04 In virtual stores, I would attach great importance to high-quality images.

The feature use of colors can be found in several works, e.g., Shen et al. (2021, p. 15), Papagiannidis et al. (2014, p. 882), Julia Baker, Parasuraman, Grewal, and Voss (2002, p. 131). In this work it is adapted and operationalized based on J. Baker, Grewal, and Parasuraman (1994, p. 337) as follows:

SED_03 The selection and arrangement of colors in Virtual Stores would be important to me.

The same applies to the features lighting, as well as the decoration and furnishings, which Baker et al. (1994) refer to as "merchandising".

SED_05 In virtual stores, lighting would be important to me.
SED_06 The decoration and furnishing of the Virtual Store would be important to me.

The audio features such as background music are also based on J. Baker et al. (1994, p. 337), but in addition to background music, audio and sound in general are also queried.

SED_07 Audio and sound effects, such as background music, could make the shopping experience in virtual stores even more pleasant.
SED_08 Audio and sound effects would be important to me in a virtual store.

In addition, addressing the sense of hearing is also queried, as the video shown in the questionnaire has no sound (see Sect. 5.3.1). It is operationalized based on Brun et al. (2017, p. 340) as follows:

SED_09 My sense of hearing should be addressed in a virtual store.

The SED is rated on a 5-point Likert scale with verbalized endpoints ranging from 1 = "strongly disagree" to 5 = "strongly agree".

5.3.2.3 Operationalization of Emotional Dimension

The operationalization of the EMD is based on I. Krasonikolakis et al. (2018, p. 1253) and adapted in the context of this work to investigate enthusiasm, fascination, drive, inspiration and interest, when visiting a virtual store. It was asked in form of a semantic differential as follows:

When visiting a virtual store, I would probably be...

EMD_01	1 = stressed	5 = relaxed
EMD_02	1 = frustrated	5 = enthusiastic
EMD_03	1 = bored	5 = fascinated
EMD_04	1 = passive	5 = active
EMD_05	1 = demotivated	5 = inspired
EMD_06	1 = disinterested	5 = interested

The EMD is asked in form of a semantic differential from 1 = negative emotion (i.e., stressed, frustrated, bored, passive, demotivated, disinterested) to 5 = positive emotion (i.e., relaxed, enthusiastic, fascinated, active, inspired, interested).

5.3.2.4 Operationalization of Cognitive Dimension

The COD is operationalized by eleven items from different measurement scales that are adapted to the context of this work. This is because the COD, similar to the SED and IMD, represents several C&F of virtual stores.

The ease of navigation and structure of layout are operationalized following Barnes and Vidgen (2002, p. 120) which leads to the following items:

COD_01 I would like to be able to move freely in Virtual Stores.
COD_02 Navigation in a virtual store should be simple and intuitive.
COD_03 In a virtual store, it would be important for me to find what I am looking for quickly.
COD_04 A virtual store should have a clear and concise structure.

Items COD_05 and COD_06 are taken from White Baker et al. (2019, p. 51) and Goel and Prokopec (2009, p. 127) and are adapted as follows:

COD_05 I expect information to be easy to find in virtual stores.
COD_06 I think it is important that information is easily available in virtual stores.

Item COD_08 is taken from Zaharia and Schmitz (2019, p. 9) and adapted as follows:

COD_08 I would prefer virtual stores that allow me to easily ask questions about products and get quick answers.

Items COD_07, COD_09, COD_10 and COD_11 are taken from the scale by Rose et al. (2012, p. 316) and adapted as follows:

COD_07 Virtual stores should offer real customer reviews and reports on product experiences.
COD_09 I would like to receive product suggestions and offers in the virtual store that are tailored to me personally.
COD_10 Virtual stores should recognize me and give me the feeling that they are talking to me personally as a user (e.g., "Hi Anna, how are you?" as a greeting).
COD_11 How important would personalized recommendations and offers in virtual stores be to you?

The COD is rated on a 5-point Likert scale with verbalized endpoints ranging from 1 = "strongly disagree" to 5 = "strongly agree", whereby COD_11 is rated from 1 = "not important at all" to 5 = "very important".

5.3.2.5 Operationalization of Social Dimension

The SOD is operationalized by five items from different measurement scales that are adapted to the context of this work. This is because the social dimension, similar to the SED, COD and IMD, represents several C&F of virtual stores. It starts with an introduction: "Imagine going shopping as an avatar in a virtual store and being able to meet other avatars there.". Then the following items follow:

Items SOD_01, SOD_03 and SOD_05 are based on Rose et al. (2012), Shen et al. (2021, p. 11) and I. Krasonikolakis et al. (2014, pp. 20–22) and formulated as follows:

SOD_01 I want to be able to talk to other people in virtual stores.
SOD_03 I want to meet new people in virtual stores.
SOD_05 In virtual stores, I would like to have the opportunity to share my experiences of products with other people.

Items SOD_02 and SOD_04 are based on Brun et al. (2017, p. 340), and Nasermoadeli et al. (2013, p. 132).

SOD_02 In virtual stores, I want to have the feeling of being part of a community.
SOD_04 I would like to be able to go shopping in virtual stores with friends and acquaintances.

The SOD is rated on a 5-point Likert scale with verbalized endpoints ranging from 1 = "strongly disagree" to 5 = "strongly agree".

5.3.2.6 Operationalization of Immersive Dimension

The IMD is operationalized by 12 items from different measurement scales that are adapted to the context of this work. This is because the IMD, similar to the other dimensions, represents several C&F of virtual stores.

The following items are taken from J. V. Chen et al. (2022, p. 10) and are adapted in the context of this work:

IMD_01 The design of the virtual store should be as realistic as possible.
IMD_02 The products in the virtual store should look real as if they could be touched.
IMD_03 In the virtual store, I want the products to look and feel like they do in real life.

IMD_04 The graphics and colors of the virtual store should give me an idea of what the products look like in real life.

IMD_05 In virtual stores, I want to be able to explore the environment and the products from all angles (360 degree view).

IMD_06 In virtual stores, I want to be able to interact with the products and the environment (e.g., pull out drawers, configure products, try on and try out products).

IMD_11 When I visit a virtual store, I want to be so immersed in the experience that I forget my immediate surroundings for a moment.

Items IMD_07 and IMD_08 are taken from Rose et al. (2012, p. 318) and adapted in the context of this work:

IMD_07 I would like to have control over what I do in virtual stores (e.g., via the controllers of the VR glasses) and what information is displayed to me.

IMD_08 I would like to be able to redesign a virtual store according to my own ideas and preferences (e.g., location, lighting, colors).

Item IMD_09 is taken from Papagiannidis et al. (2014, p. 882) and adapted in the context of this work as follows:

IMD_09 A virtual store should give me the feeling that I am shopping in a real store.

Items IMD_10 and IMD_12 are taken from White Baker et al. (2019, p. 51) and adapted in the context of this work as follows:

IMD_10 After visiting a virtual store, it should feel like I am returning to the real world after a journey.

IMD_12 The experience in a virtual store should be so realistic that it is almost as if I could actually touch the products and the environment.

The IMD is rated on a 5-point Likert scale with verbalized endpoints ranging from 1 = "strongly disagree" to 5 = "strongly agree".

5.3.2.7 Operationalization of General Customer Experience

The GCX is operationalized based on Zaharia and Schmitz (2019), who used the following multi-item scale to measure the GCX, achieving a Cronbach's Alpha of $\alpha = 0.924$ with the following six indicators (Zaharia & Schmitz, 2019, p. 12):

X exactly meets my needs.

X offers everything I need.

Shopping at X is altogether easy.

X does everything to make life easier for me as a customer.

As a customer, I always feel welcome at X.

X is constantly getting better at what they do for their customers.

The scale was adapted in the context of this work as the scale of Zaharia and Schmitz (2019, p. 12) is based on the evaluation of the experience at retailer X. For this, the indicator "*The site creates a positive experience for me*" of Barnes and Vidgen (2002, p. 120) was adapted and included. Furthermore, another item was integrated to evaluate the shopping experience and another two to find out, if virtual stores would enhance and provide an exceptional shopping experience.

An endpoint-verbalized 5-point Likert scale from 1 = "strongly disagree" to 5 = "strongly agree" is used to evaluate GCX_01 to GCX_05, while for GCX_06 the endpoints 1 = "very negative" to 5 = "very positive" are used.

GCX_01	Virtual stores would offer me a positive shopping experience.
GCX_02	A virtual store is exactly what I need.
GCX_03	Virtual stores could improve my shopping experience.
GCX_04	Virtual stores would offer me an exceptional experience.
GCX_05	Virtual stores would make my life as a customer easier.
GCX_06	How would you rate the experience in virtual stores?

5.3.2.8 Operationalization of Moderators

Regarding the moderators VREX, PERS and GAME, the participants are asked to evaluate themselves. The following questions are asked:

VREX Have you already had experience with VR technologies (e.g., VR glasses)?

○ Yes
○ No

PERS Would you describe yourself more as an extrovert or introvert?

○ Extraverted (sociable, communicative and outgoing)[3]
○ Introverted (less sociable, quiet and self-reflective)

GAME Would you describe yourself as a gamer?

○ Yes
○ No

5.3.2.9 Research Question 3—Further Insights into the Design of Virtual Stores

In order to address research question three and to gain further and deeper insights into the preferences of Gen Z in relation to virtual stores, it is necessary to ask further questions as part of the questionnaire, which could not be considered in the research model.

In their study "Metaverse—Unendliche Weiten für den Handel?", the *ECC Club* looked at the current German and US perspective on the metaverse and its opportunities for retailers (ECC Koeln, 2022). In this study, the majority stated that they could rather imagine buying physical products in the metaverse, which would then be delivered to their homes. This primarily includes product categories such as fashion & accessories (67%), home & furnishings (52%) and consumer electronics / electrical appliances (43%) ECC Koeln (2022, pp. 34, 37).

Only 36% of respondents would consider purchasing purely virtual products. They agreed with the following product categories in particular: Virtual music or videos (46%), tickets for virtual concerts (45%) and virtual clothing for their avatars (39%) ECC Koeln (2022, p. 26). In addition, they would predominantly like to see the following offers from retailers and brands in the metaverse: Coupons and discounts (39%), a walk-in online store (36%) and trying out products (34%). Respondents would find it particularly promising if the shopping

[3] The characteristics were selected based on Big Five and MBTI, as already mentioned in Sect. 4.2.2.

experience was designed like a VR shopping mall (59%) or a virtual showroom for fashion (55%). The majority of respondents could also imagine virtual test drives in (self-configured) cars (54%) (ECC Koeln, 2022, p. 39). Nevertheless, 78% of respondents still prefer real-life activities (ECC Koeln, 2022, p. 16).

As part of a further study, which was published as a white paper by the EHI Retail Institute, various decision-makers in German-speaking retail were interviewed on the topic of "Metaverse in retail" and possible applications from the German-speaking retail perspective were presented (Hofacker & Hübner, 2022, pp. 2, 7). The respondents assumed that the willingness to use the metaverse in retail would be greatest for the following industries in particular: fashion and accessories, furniture & furnishings and hobby & leisure. The majority are of the opinion that the potential benefits of metaverse for groceries' retail are low. In addition, around two thirds of those surveyed believed that their target group will only be very willing to use metaverse applications in ten years' time, and that the current willingness to use is still very low (Hofacker & Hübner, 2022, p. 25).

With regard to possible retail application scenarios in the metaverse, the authors found that 3D product demonstrations, virtual advice or shopping assistance as well as gamification as a means of improving brand perception would definitely represent the most sensible application scenarios (Hofacker & Hübner, 2022, p. 28). Ultimately, the respondents would really want to use the following application scenarios: 83% virtual advice or virtual shopping assistance, 76% 3D product demonstrations and 72% advertising in virtual spaces. The only application scenario that the majority of respondents could not currently imagine is virtual goods (Hofacker & Hübner, 2022, p. 27).

As part of a study published in "Trend Check Handel Vol. 3", 143 respondents were also asked about experiences and activities that they could well imagine in the metaverse.

Similar to the other two previously presented studies, it turned out that product presentations, shopping at retailers and manufacturers, virtual consultations and trying on and trying out products would be particularly suitable for the respondents in the area of "shopping in the metaverse". In addition, the respondents were quite inclined towards a unique world of experience and a walk-in online store. In this study, respondents were also asked about the products they could imagine purchasing in the metaverse. The majority of respondents (46%) stated that they could well imagine buying "fashion & accessories". Second place was shared by "living & furnishing" and "leisure & hobby" with 44% of respondents. "Consumer electronics" took fourth place with 41%. At the bottom of the metaverse is the purchase of "food". Similar to the EHI whitepaper, the majority of respondents cannot imagine buying groceries in the metaverse (ECC Cologne & Salesforce.com, 2022, p. 11).

It would therefore be interesting to find out what Gen Z in Germany thinks about this. The following additional questions are therefore asked in the online survey:

- What would you prefer?

  - Buying real products that are sent to my home.
  - Purchase of virtual products that exist purely in the digital world.
  - Purchase of real products that I get sent home and receipt of a digital twin (e.g., NFT) of the purchased product

- Which products and services would you want to use a virtual store for?

  - Medication / drugs
  - Configurator (e.g., cars, motorcycle, bicycle)
  - Electronic goods & household appliances
  - Pet supplies
  - Clothing, shoes & textiles
    - Cosmetic articles & body care
    - Groceries
    - Furniture, furnishings & household goods
    - Books and Magazines

- Which practical features and functions, which you may already know from online stores or real stores, would you like to see in a virtual store?

  - Check-out
  - Instructions, assistance, user manuals
  - Favorites / wish list
  - Search function
  - Search history
  - Product configuration
  - Virtual try-on / Virtual fitting of products
  - Mirrors
  - Filter and sorting options for products
  - Interactive floor plan of store (floor plan to departments like 1st floor, 2nd floor)

  - ○ Menu
  - ○ Product recommendations
  - ○ Product ratings and reviews
  - ○ Product interactions (e.g., trying on and trying out, touching)
  - ○ Virtual AI Sales Advisor
  - ○ Real Sales Advisor
  - ○ Digital screens and Product displays
  - ○ Gaming elements (e.g., Search and collect coins for discounts)
  - ○ Advertising
  - ○ Social / community corner (for exchange with other customers)

As virtual stores are a new shopping channel, it would be interesting to know which shopping channel they would prefer if they had the opportunity to shop in virtual stores. Hence, the following question is integrated:

- What would you prefer?

  - ○ Brick-and-mortar stores
  - ○ E-commerce stores
  - ○ Virtual store

In addition, Sect. 2.2 has shown that there are different types of virtual stores. In this respect, it would also be interesting to find out which types of virtual stores respondents would prefer:

- What would you prefer?

  - ○ Individual, mutually independent virtual stores
  - ○ Virtual shopping centers / malls
  - ○ Virtual shopping streets / cities

- Which design style do you prefer for virtual stores?

  - ○ Realistic (with detailed structures and lifelike elements)
  - ○ Minimalistic (Clear, simple and well-organized design)
  - ○ Futuristic (like in a science fiction movie)
  - ○ Abstract (with creative and artistic elements)

- Would you prefer a virtual shopping environment that offers an exceptional and creative shopping experience or should it be more of a replica of a real store?

  o Yes, I prefer an extraordinary and creative shopping experience.
  o No, I prefer a replica of a real brick-and mortar store.

It would also be interesting to find out whether they have already had experience with virtual stores in VR and which virtual stores they have visited and how satisfied they were with them:

- Had you already visited one or more virtual stores before this survey?
- If so, which one(s)?

The full questionnaire can be found in Appendix D.

5.3.3 Phase 3—Question Format

The third phase of the questionnaire design process deals with decisions about the question format. First, it must be decided whether to integrate open-ended questions or closed-ended questions. On the one hand, open-ended questions have several advantages such as allowing respondents to articulate their thoughts freely, giving "unusual and spontaneous" responses, as well as "insights into topics, the researcher has not considered" before (Vomberg & Klarmann, 2022, p. 99). However, answers to open-ended questions must be interpreted subjectively by the researcher, and participants may refuse to answer open-ended questions because they are more time-consuming and laborious to answer.

In addition, researchers are usually more familiar with the topic they are investigating than the participants, so it may be better to ask closed questions and more in-depth questions if necessary. Moreover, Vomberg and Klarmann (2022) experienced that the quality of open-ended questions in online surveys tend to be comparably low, hence, recommend to focus on closed questions in online surveys (Vomberg & Klarmann, 2022, p. 99). According to Schuman and Presser (1979), closed questions are comparable to open questions if they are adapted to the findings and feedback from pretests (Schuman & Presser, 1979, p. 698). Hence, closed-ended questions are primarily used. Following Gal and Rucker (2011), an open-ended question is asked at the end of the questionnaire to give participants the opportunity to provide feedback or share further information and insights about their answers. In addition, open-ended questions in the form of follow-up questions will be asked as part of the qualitative pretests. Another question that needs to be answered in this phase is which answer categories should be provided for the closed questions (Vomberg & Klarmann, 2022, p. 100).

Type of Scale

A large number of scale methods exist in the literature for constructing measurement scales, such as rank order scales, semantic differential scales, or Likert scales (Sarstedt & Mooi, 2019, p. 69; Weiber & Sarstedt, 2021, p. 127). In this study, the most popular scale type is primarily used to measure the latent constructs, the Likert scale (Sarstedt & Mooi, 2019, p. 69). This is because measurements using rating scales such as Likert scales, generally provide the minimum measure required by most statistical analysis methods, the metric scale level (at least interval scale level) (Weiber & Sarstedt, 2021, p. 129). Moreover, with this method, participants can easily evaluate statements themselves, usually in the form of (predefined) numerical values. A distinction is made between three different types of rating scales: (1) agreement scales, (2) intensity scales and (3) rating scales (Weiber & Sarstedt, 2021, p. 127). All three types are applied in this work. Another type which will be used in this work is semantic differential scale. In this type, opposing pairs of words (usually adjectives) are used, one of which is always at the other end of a scale. Participants rate how one word of each pair describes their feelings in relation to the object being rated (Sarstedt & Mooi, 2019, p. 69). This type is used for the EMD construct. The third type used in this work is rank order scales. Participants are asked to compare alternatives and rank them from highest to lowest. This type is used to get additional information on the SED.

Properties of Scale

When constructing rating scales, further considerations must be made and decisions taken. First of all, the number of response categories should be determined. In this work, there are both closed-ended questions with two answer categories (yes/no) (also referred to as dichotomous) as well as some with multiple categories (also referred to as multichotomous). As the latter allow for more variation and differentiation in the responses and prevent the trigger of different types of biases such as non-response, these are used primarily (Sarstedt & Mooi, 2019, p. 71; Vomberg & Klarmann, 2022, p. 100).

It was found that indicators with multiple response categories would tend to have higher reliability. In particular 5-point or 7-point Likert scales with a neutral middle response category proved to be very effective (Lietz, 2010, p. 260; Sarstedt & Mooi, 2019, p. 69; Vomberg & Klarmann, 2022, p. 100). Another decision that should be made is whether respondents should be forced to choose a positive or negative response (also known as a forced-choice scale) or whether they should also have the option to choose a neutral response (also known as a free-choice scale). As research has shown that the inclusion of neutral response categories minimizes response bias, a neutral category is included (Weijters, Cabooter, & Schillewaert, 2010, p. 244). In addition, care is taken to ensure that the response categories do not coincide, especially when designing age and monthly income questions (Sarstedt & Mooi, 2019, p. 72). The response categories are labeled by using endpoint labels only (i.e., "fully disagree" to "fully agree") (Weijters et al., 2010, p. 244). So, 5-point rating scales only labeled at the endpoints are used. Moreover, it is important to decide whether or not to include a "don't know" option. As this leads to more clarity overall and gives the respondents the choice to not answer, when he or she is not sure (Weiber & Sarstedt, 2021, p. 128). So this is also integrated at the end of each scale and additional. Lastly, equidistant scales are used, i.e., the number of positive and negative scale categories is equal (also referred to as quasi-metric scales) (Sarstedt & Mooi, 2019, p. 74).

5.3.4 Phase 4—Question Wording

When formulating questions, it is important to pay attention to ambiguous question wording, as this can distort the survey responses and cause bias (Vomberg & Klarmann, 2022, p. 100). For this reason, it is very important that respondents understand the questions correctly.

This can be ensured by formulating the questions simply, clearly and neutrally. Since negations and polar opposites can lead to confusion among respondents, they are not used. Moreover, according to the recommendations of Vomberg and Klarmann (2022), short sentences are used instead of long sentences, unnecessary variations in format and question structure are avoided, as well as computations (Vomberg & Klarmann, 2022, pp. 100–101).

5.3.5 Phase 5—Question Sequence

The fifth phase is about, where the questions should be placed and asked within the questionnaire. As respondents may tend to form opinions while answering the questionnaire, meaning that answers to questions at the beginning of the questionnaire could influence answers to later questions, researchers need to plan the sequence of questions carefully. It has been observed that different psychological processes start depending on the order, i.e., emotional (rather at the beginning) versus cognitive processes (rather at the end). All this can be steered by randomizing the order of the questions, i.e., presenting the same questions to the participants in a different order. However, this cannot guarantee that order effects do not occur at the individual level. Furthermore, randomization should be used with caution, as it can break the logical order of the questions (Vomberg & Klarmann, 2022, p. 102). Hence, the CX dimensions are asked before GCX and GCX before BI to ensure a causal relationship between them. This is because each construct determines the other (causal chain). The items are randomized between the dimensions of CX and within the latent constructs GCX and BI in order to avoid order effects as far as possible, but at the same time ensuring the logical order.

The questionnaire consists of a total of 28 pages following a clear structure. It begins with an introduction, three important screening questions on online shopping frequency, age and gender as well as the moderator question on experience with VR (including VR glasses). Participants are then given an introduction into the topic of the survey, key terms are defined and described using examples and illustrated with the help of images, a user journey[4] and a video. Among others, the Fig. 2.2 from Sect. 2.1.5 is also part of the survey.

The video contains several examples of virtual stores so that respondents know exactly what type of virtual stores the survey refers to.[5] This is followed by a filter question. Respondents are asked whether they have already visited such virtual stores and, if so, which ones. In the form of an open response option, respondents are asked to enter the brand name and rate how satisfied they were with these virtual stores on a 5-point Likert scale. This is followed by statements on the dimensions of the CX, additional questions (as described in Sect. 5.3.2.9) and statements on BI. Conversely, respondents who have never visited virtual stores are automatically taken to the statements on the CX dimensions.

Sensitive questions that are optional are asked at the end. However, always with the option "not to answer" to ensure that the online survey is not aborted due to sensitive questions (Vomberg & Klarmann, 2022, p. 103). At the end,

[4] The user journey introduces the respondents to the virtual store video and helps them to immerse into it. It can be found in Appendix D as part of the questionnaire.

[5] The video contains a filter that ensures that respondents who do not watch the video to the end a) have the opportunity to watch the video again to the end, b) if they have again not watched the video in full, are excluded from the survey. This is done to ensure that every respondent has the same basis for answering the follow-up questions.

respondents also have the opportunity to comment on the questionnaire in a text field and express further thoughts on the topic.

5.3.6 Phase 6—Survey Layout

Since the questionnaire was set up by the market research institute INJ Partners, the author does not have the full freedom in the design and layout of the survey. Nevertheless, the author has endeavored to make the questionnaire as clear, appealing and descriptive as possible in order to make it considerably easier for participants to complete. For example, headlines are written in bold, image and video content is used, or text content is written in line with storytelling. In addition, to make the flow of questions clear, a progress bar is integrated so that respondents know exactly how much they have already finished and how many questions are still to come. In this respect, the questionnaire follows a clean appearance that demonstrably arouses interest and underlines the author's trustworthiness (Iacobucci & Churchill, 2018, p. 221; Vomberg & Klarmann, 2022, p. 103).

5.3.7 Phase 7—Pretests

The last phase of the questionnaire design process is the obligatory pretest phase (Hulland, Baumgartner, & Smith, 2018, p. 104). Three different pretests were carried out to test the questionnaire. First, two qualitative pretests were conducted using the protocol method (Sect. 5.3.7.1). The questionnaire was then adapted with regard to the feedback. This was followed by a second qualitative pretest in the form of four cognitive interviews (also referred to as think-aloud technique) (Ericsson & Simon, 1980, p. 220; Presser et al., 2004, pp. 111–115) (Sect. 5.3.7.2). Finally, there was also a quantitative pretest with a total of 31 respondents (Sect. 5.3.7.3). All three pretests focused primarily on comprehension and lack of information, incompleteness of response categories, duration and length of the survey, and preliminary indicators of measurement validity and reliability, particularly in the quantitative pretest (Vomberg & Klarmann, 2022, p. 105). In summary, the questionnaire was empirically tested with the help of two qualitative pretests and one quantitative pretest which will now be explained in more detail.

5.3.7.1 Qualitative Pretest—Think-aloud Method

As part of the upstream qualitative pre-test, the questionnaire was initially tested with two participants. Both belonged to Gen Z in terms of age and also felt that they belonged to this generation. Same as in the quantitative pretest, participants were not selected based on representativity but on from whom the author expected valuable input (Vomberg & Klarmann, 2022, p. 105). The so-called protocol method was used in a first step (Vomberg & Klarmann, 2022, p. 104). Both pretests came to the conclusion that some of the wording of the items caused irritation among the respondents due to their similarity. Against this background, the corresponding items were revised. In addition, the questionnaire was modified in other sequences, including editing the video and shortening the introductory and information texts. The market research institute INJ Partners was then commissioned to program the modified version of the questionnaire. The researcher then checked the correct technical implementation of the revised questionnaire. The main focus was on randomization, filter guidance and the responsive design of the questionnaire on both desktop and mobile. As the researcher had to provide a German and an English version of the questionnaire, it was also checked for "copy and paste" problems or possible spelling mistakes.

5.3.7.2 Qualitative Pretest—Cognitive Interviews

Once the questionnaire had been successfully programmed, the researcher conducted further four qualitative cognitive interviews with other people who also belonged to Gen Z. Of the four participants, one had already gained experience with VR, while the other three had not yet had any experience with VR. The interviews were initiated by the market research institute INJ Partners. This minimized the risk of bias on the part of the researcher (Vomberg & Klarmann, 2022, p. 87).

The interviews were conducted individually via the cloud-based video conferencing service Microsoft Teams. The questionnaire was discussed in detail using the think-aloud method and through comprehension and category selection probing (Prüfer & Rexroth, 2005, pp. 5–8).

In the think-aloud method (also known as cognitive interviews) participants have to verbalize their thoughts when answering the questionnaire (Ericsson & Simon, 1980; Presser et al., 2004; Prüfer & Rexroth, 2005, p. 14). The researcher paid particular attention to the comprehensibility and correctness of the questionnaire, including its framework texts, instructions and questions as well as their scaling. The interviews lasted between 33 and 52 minutes which is below the maximum duration of 90 minutes recommended by Prüfer and Rexroth (2005, p. 16). All four interviews came to the conclusion that the questionnaire was already easy to understand overall and had a red path. To this end, mainly cosmetic corrections were made and texts were shortened and adapted for better understanding.

5.3.7.3 Quantitative Pretest

Furthermore, a quantitative pretest was carried out from 20.09.2023 to 27.09.2023 to check the data distribution for normality for all constructs and their corresponding items, as well as the scale reliability. The participants were recruited via the author's private environment and invited to take part in the online survey via online links previously provided to the author by the market research institute. When selecting the participants, the author did not necessarily focus on representativeness, but rather on the fact that the participants belong to Gen Z and can be expected to make valuable contributions (Vomberg & Klarmann, 2022, p. 105).

A total of 39 survey links were sent to Gen Z respondents. Eight of them were invalid due to filtering and exclusion, which is why a total of 31 valid and complete data sets were generated in the end. These were then analyzed using IBM SPSS Statistics. The data distribution was checked for normality and its skewness and kurtosis values were examined. In addition, a Shapiro-Wilk test was performed. Furthermore, the item correlations and outer loadings of each item as well as the reliability of each latent variable (using Cronbach's alpha) were examined (including SED, EMD, COD, SOD, IMD, GCX, and BI). Due to the lack of normal distribution and very low to negative Cronbach's alpha values, the operationalization of the constructs had to be completely revised and adapted. Appendix C, Tab. C-5 shows the first (pre-test) operationalization.

Following the research process by Vomberg and Klarmann (2022), after the design of the questionnaire, the next step would be the specification of the data collection including the sample structure, the sample size as well as the sample response rate. Sampling is described in Sect. 5.6.

First, the analysis method must be carried out. In this way, an insufficient sample size can be avoided. This is because a different minimum sample size is required depending on the model complexity and analysis method used (e.g., for PLS-SEM). Thereby, the basic guidelines of sampling theory are taken into account. In order to ensure sufficient statistical power of the results of the statistical method used (see Sect. 5.4), the adherence to minimum sample size guidelines is essential (J. F. Hair et al., 2022, p. 24; Vomberg & Klarmann, 2022, p. 105).

5.4 Analysis Method

There are several statistical analysis methods that can be considered, when data needs to be analyzed. First of all, it is emphasized that neither univariate nor bivariate analysis methods are suitable, as the research model consists of a total of seven latent constructs (with two endogenous and five exogenous constructs) as well as three moderator variables (J. F. Hair et al., 2022, p. 2). In order to be able to analyze the associated complex relationships between these constructs, multivariate data analysis methods should be used, which are explained in more detail below.

Multivariate data analysis methods can be roughly divided into so-called first-generation and second-generation techniques. Before specifying some of them, it must be mentioned that they are also differentiated into primarily exploratory or primarily confirmatory. Primarily confirmatory methods are typically used to test a priori formulated hypotheses based on existing theories and concepts, while researchers draw on primarily exploratory methods, when they have found little to no knowledge of how the construct variables within their research model relate to each other (J. F. Hair et al., 2017, p. 3; J. F. Hair et al., 2022, p. 2). In this work, there is no direct prior knowledge in the form of studies that have already examined the exact influence of CX on the BI of Gen Z to use virtual stores (see Chap. 3). Nevertheless, there are both, knowledge and concepts about the individual constructs themselves that serves as a basis, e.g., the CX model by Lemon and Verhoef (2016).

At first glance, it seems that explorative multivariate methods in particular are better suited for this work. But, J. F. Hair et al. (2022) indicate that it is often difficult to clearly distinguish between exploratory and confirmatory methods (J. F. Hair et al., 2022, p. 3). They use the example of regression analysis, which is primarily known as a confirmatory method as it is used to test hypothesis based on established knowledge and concepts. Nevertheless, the regression analysis can also be used exploratively to find out whether the tested model can be extended by additional independent variables (J. F. Hair et al., 2022, p. 3). This is also the case in this thesis, as the existing CX model by Lemon and Verhoef (2016) was modified by adding dimensions and excluding other dimensions. In order to evaluate the relationships outlined above in the research model between the two endogenous variables, BI and GCX, and the independent variables, the CX dimensions, multivariate analysis of variance and canonical correlation as first-generation methods therefore appear to be suitable analysis methods in the context of this thesis, as they include several dependent variables (J. Hair, Black, Babin, & Anderson, 2010, p. 17).

On the other side, these techniques come with some notable restrictions: Firstly, these methods assume a simple model structure, which does not apply to the research model of this thesis, as it implies a causal chain, i.e., dimensions of CX lead to GCX lead to behavioral intention to use virtual stores. Secondly, it is assumed that all variables can be regarded as observable. However, only in conjunction with an upstream independent validation such as a confirmatory factor analysis, which can lead to downstream limitations.

Finally, measurement errors, both systematic and random errors, as discussed in Sect. 5.3.2, are completely omitted (J. F. Hair et al., 2022, pp. 3–4; Sarstedt, Ringle, & Hair, 2022, pp. 592–594; Vomberg & Klarmann, 2022, pp. 74–89). Second-generation techniques, also known as structural equation modeling (SEM), do not have these limitations.

In contrast, complex relationships between multiple dependent and independent variables that are typically unobservable, multi-item variables, can be modeled and estimated simultaneously. Rather, complex relationships between several dependent and independent variables, which are usually unobservable variables that are typically measured by multiple indicators, can be modeled and estimated at once. Moreover, SEM considers measurement errors, which leads to more precisely measured theoretical concepts of interest (J. Hair et al., 2010, p. 19; J. F. Hair et al., 2022, pp. 4, 13). As a result, SEM is used as the statistical analysis method in the following work.

5.4.1 Partial Least Squares Structural Equation Modeling (PLS-SEM)

Currently, there are three primary SEM approaches, including covariance-based SEM (CB-SEM), partial least squares SEM (PLS-SEM; also known as variance-based SEM, and used to be called PLS path modeling), and a recently emerged approach, the generalized structure component analysis (GSCA) (J. F. Hair et al., 2022, p. 4; J. F. Hair, Sarstedt, Ringle, & Mena, 2012, p. 415; Latan, Hair, Noonan, & Sabol, 2023, p. 3). In literature, there are also a fourth and fifth method called regressions based on sum scores and the so-called PLS regression method (J. F. Hair et al., 2017, p. 12). The following work uses PLS-SEM. There are several reasons for using PLS-SEM over the other methods.

PLS regression

Starting with PLS regression, it is a multivariate analysis method that indicates similarities to PLS-SEM, but which cannot be equated with PLS-SEM.

PLS regression as a regression-based approach examines linear relationships between several independent variables and one or more dependent variables. In PLS regression aggregated variables or factors are formed by means of principal component analyses for the independent and dependent variables. In contrast, PLS-SEM uses the so-called ordinary least squares (OLS) regression that is based on predefined relationship networks between the constructs and between the constructs and their corresponding indicators.

Currently, this method is also the primary method for the development of theories and the explanation of variance (or the prediction of constructs) (J. F. Hair et al., 2017, pp. 12 ff.; Latan et al., 2023, p. 10). Since the relationships between the constructs of interest, i.e., BI, CX and its dimensions, and their relationships to the corresponding indicators are also predefined in the following work, this method will not be considered further.

Regressions based on sum scores

The regressions based on sum scores method represents a simplification of the PLS-SEM. However, this simplified method should be avoided because (1) sum scores assume that different indicators represent a latent construct, and (2) all indicators have the same relevance, meaning that each of the indicators has equal contribution to the formation of the corresponding composite (J. F. Hair et al., 2022, p. 16). According to J. F. Hair et al. (2017), this simplification, especially with regard to the equal relevance of all indicators in empirical applications, is unrealistic, which underlines the superiority of PLS-SEM in this respect (J. F. Hair et al., 2017, p. 47). In addition, regressions with sum scores have a lower test power than PLS-SEM (J. F. Hair et al., 2017, p. 19). Hence, this method is also not considered further.

CB-SEM, PLS-SEM or GSCA

So, which of the other SEM methods should be used to estimate the relationships in a SEM? To answer this question, after a brief definition, the main differences between the three remaining SEM methods, CB-SEM, PLS-SEM, and GSCA are highlighted (Latan et al., 2023, pp. 4–6; Weiber & Sarstedt, 2021, p. 79).

CB-SEM is the traditional SEM method and is defined as "a [variance-based method] for estimating structural equation models that assumes that the concepts of interest can be represented by common factors" (J. F. Hair et al., 2022, p. 309).

The PLS-SEM method was first developed by Wold (1966) as the partial least squares path modeling, PLS-PM method, and later advanced by Lohmöller (1989). In contrast to CB-SEM, PLS-SEM is "a composite-based method to estimate structural equation models [aiming] to maximize the explained variance of the endogenous latent variables" (J. F. Hair et al., 2022, p. 319). For a long time, CB-SEM was the predominant SEM method until PLS-SEM received more attention following the release of the SmartPLS software by Ringle and colleagues in 2005 (Ringle, Wende, & Becker, 2024b).

The third method, GSCA, is the most recently developed SEM method and is "a component-based structural equation modeling approach for analyzing complex inter-relationships between indicators and constructs [based on the alternate least squares (ALS) algorithm aiming to optimizing single criterions]" (Hwang & Takane, 2004; Latan et al., 2023, p. 6).

While CB-SEM relies solely on common variance and strictly focuses on model fit (i.e., goodness-of-fit indices), PLS-SEM relies on total variance and pursues the optimization of measurement and structural models with the goal of maximizing the prediction of variance in the dependent variables without forcing model fit (Latan et al., 2023, p. 5). PLS-SEM is therefore both confirmatory and predictive. Gregor (2006) describes this as PLS-SEM "implies both understanding of underlying causes and prediction, as well as description of theoretical constructs and the relationships among them", which underlines it superiority over the CB-SEM method (Gregor, 2006, p. 626).

Although the GSCA and PLS-SEM methods appear very similar at first glance, as both focus on "measurement and structural models that represent the relationships between the components and their indicators", they also have meaningful differences, e.g., in the research objective, the requirements for the sample size as well as in the cursivity of the model relationships. Unlike the PLS-SEM method, the GSCA method includes a third sub-model, the weighted relational model that considers its components as weighted sums of their related indicators. The model fit can then be tested by combining all three partial models into an overall model, the so-called equation (comparable to the GOFI of the CB-SEM) (Latan et al., 2023, p. 6). Another difference is that GSCA path models cannot only consider recursive but also circular relationships, whereas PLS-SEM can only account for recursive relationships (Latan et al., 2023, p. 9).

Latan et al. (2023) compared all three SEM methods and provided primary and secondary guidelines that help researchers select the most appropriate method for their research model (Latan et al., 2023). In the end, Latan et al. (2023) emphasized that they would recommend the use of the PLS-SEM method due to its rapidly expanding capabilities when researchers specify their research model and consider structural equation modeling (Latan et al., 2023, p. 10). J. F. Hair and Sarstedt (2019), recommend the application of both, either PLS-SEM or GSCA as an extended alternative method to PLS-SEM (J. F. Hair & Sarstedt, 2019, p. 621). Since PLS-SEM is the best known component-based SEM method,

GSCA is not considered further in this work (J. F. Hair & Sarstedt, 2019; Hwang, Sarstedt, Cho, Choo, & Ringle, 2023; Latan et al., 2023).

Therefore, it is discussed below whether the PLS-SEM should be applied as a composite-based SEM method in this work or the CB-SEM as a variance-based method.

Reasons for using PLS-SEM

In this thesis, PLS-SEM is used to analyze the data. Several reasons can be derived from the literature and the theoretical framework of this work as to why this method should be used and why it proves to be the method of choice. When deciding on using PLS-SEM, Sarstedt et al. (2022) recommend a total of six reasons that should be investigated (Sarstedt et al., 2022, p. 601). Four of these apply in the context of this work and are discussed below. In addition, J. F. Hair et al. (2022) have also drawn up some "rules of thumb for the choice between PLS-SEM and CB-SEM" (J. F. Hair, Jr. et al., 2021, p. 22; J. F. Hair et al., 2022, p. 32). These are also used to explain the reasons for using PLS-SEM instead of CB-SEM.

The first reason is that the aim of the research should be the prediction and explanation of a key target construct and/or the identification of its relevant antecedent constructs when considering the application of PLS-SEM (Sarstedt et al., 2022, p. 601). The aim of this work is to explore, predict and explain the relationships between the GCX and the BI as well as the relationship between the CX as a higher-order construct and the BI. In this case, the key target construct is the BI, while the GCX and the CX along with its dimensions represent the antecedent constructs of the BI. The second reason is that the path model is comparably complex, meaning that there are many constructs included (six or more) and indicators per construct as well (more than four indicators) (J. F. Hair et al., 2022, p. 32; Sarstedt et al., 2022, p. 601). At this point, J. F. Hair et al. (2022, p. 32) additionally mention the model relationships.

Also, they recommend not using PLS-SEM in case the model relationships are circular, since PLS-SEM can only consider recursive model relationships (J. F. Hair et al., 2022, p. 32). The research model of this work consists of seven constructs in total, as well as three moderator variables, and each construct has indicators ranging from five to 13. Relationships between these constructs are complex too, but recursive which calls for using PLS-SEM. The third reason relates to whether the path model contains not only reflective but also formatively measured constructs (J. F. Hair et al., 2022, p. 19; Sarstedt et al., 2022, p. 601). This is the case in this work, as the CX is a reflective-formative higher-order construct, in which all CX dimensions as lower order constructs are measured reflectively and the CX formatively (Becker et al., 2012, p. 363).

SEM-PLS should also be used when the sample size is either comparatively large or small or limited, which forms the fourth reason (J. F. Hair et al., 2022, pp. 24–27; Sarstedt et al., 2022, p. 601).

As this work focuses on Gen Z including participants who should already have had VR experience, the sample size is limited, because Gen Z makes up a small part of society and there are not that many people in Germany who have already gathered experience with VR. Moreover, as the CX construct is a higher-order construct which is formed by its dimensions (also referred to as lower-order constructs in PLS-SEM), the computation of latent variable scores and their use in further analyses is necessary, which only is possible with PLS-SEM. The last reason mentioned by Sarstedt et al. (2022) is not applicable to the context of this work, because this work is not based on secondary data (J. F. Hair et al., 2022, p. 32; Sarstedt et al., 2022, p. 601). In their rules of thumb, J. F. Hair et al. (2022) emphasize the predictive character of PLS-SEM (exploratory), which is also reflected in this work, while CB-SEM is aimed more at testing and confirming theories (confirmatory) (J. F. Hair et al., 2022, p. 32).

On the contrary, they recommend using CB-SEM rather than PLS-SEM, if the error terms need to be further specified. This is not the case in this work. Another recommendation is to use PLS-SEM rather than CB-SEM if there are problems with data distribution, e.g., if the data is not normally distributed. Conversely, it does not mean that the use of PLS-SEM is automatically excluded if the data is normally distributed. Plus, outliers and collinearity definitely cannot be ignored when using PLS-SEM (J. F. Hair et al., 2017, p. 19; J. F. Hair et al., 2022, p. 28). However, the last recommendation cannot yet be examined, as the analysis of the data distribution is part of Sect. 6.2, which follows. Additionally, J. F. Hair et al. (2022) recommend the use of CB-SEM over PLS-SEM, when a global goodness-of-fit criterion is required (J. F. Hair et al., 2022, p. 32). For this work, it is sufficient to use the fit measures that are provided by SmartPLS 4 including the standardized root mean square residual (SRMR), the bootstrap-based test (d_ULS and d_G), as well as the Normed Fit Index (NFI) and Chi-square (χ^2) test (Ringle et al., 2024b, p. 33).

Lastly, J. F. Hair and Sarstedt (2019) proved that it is better to "(incorrectly) [use] PLS-SEM to estimate common factor models […] than (incorrectly) [use] factor-based SEM to estimate composite models" and concluded that PLS-SEM appears to be the safer choice when estimating relationships between conceptual variables (J. F. Hair & Sarstedt, 2019, p. 621).

In light of all this, PLS-SEM is the method of choice, especially because of its predictive and confirmatory nature and the complexity of the path model, which includes not only reflective but also formative measurement models.

In addition, PLS-SEM is used instead of GSCA because PLS-SEM is the most prominent component-based SEM method, is better researched in the scientific community and additionally includes several advanced approaches, also known as "PLS-SEM tools", such as moderator analysis, multigroup analysis, higher-order constructs, or confirmatory tetrad analysis, which are essential for this work (J. F. Hair et al., 2022; J. F. Hair & Sarstedt, 2019; Hwang et al., 2023; Latan et al., 2023; Sarstedt et al., 2022).

5.4.2 Systematic Procedure for Applying PLS-SEM

When applying the statistical method PLS-SEM for data analysis, J. F. Hair et al. (2022, p. 32) suggest a systematic, multistage procedure, the PLS-SEM process. This process incorporates a total of eight stages starting with the first and second stage in which the structural model as well as the measurement models are specified. These stages are followed by stage three which deals with the collecting and examining of data. After this, in stage four, the application of the PLS-SEM algorithm is briefly introduced and the PLS path model is estimated as well as its results. Based on the results, both reflective (stage 5a) and formative (stage 5b) measurement models will be evaluated (stage 5). Assuming that the data for the measures is reliable and valid, the final step is to evaluate the structural model (stage 6). The seventh and eight stages involve the application of advanced analysis methods, such as multigroup analysis (MGA) or model comparisons, and the evaluation of the overall results and the resulting conclusions (J. F. Hair et al., 2022, pp. 33–34). This systematic approach is also used in this thesis and begins with the first stage in the next chapter.

5.5 Specifying the PLS-SEM Model

According to J. F. Hair et al. (2022), when applying SEM, it is important to first create a path model based on the theory and logic outlined above in Chap. 4. This forms the first two stages of the PLS-SEM process and is also referred to as the specification of the path model (J. F. Hair et al., 2022, p. 41).

The path model represents the previously formulated research hypotheses and relationships between the variables of interest, i.e., the latent constructs and their related indicators. A path model basically consists of two elements: a structural model and measurement models. The structural model (also known as "inner model" in PLS-SEM) represents the relationships between the latent variables, whereas measurement models (in PLS-SEM also known as "outer models") outline the relationships between latent variables and their measurements, i.e., indicators (J. F. Hair et al., 2022, pp. 41–46). Firstly, the structural model is specified (Sect. 5.5.1; stage one of the PLS-SEM process), then the measurement models (Sect. 5.5.2; stage two of the PLS-SEM process) and finally, after the sample has been determined (Sect. 5.6), it is continued with the examination of the collected data (Sect. 6.2; stage three of the PLS-SEM process).

5.5.1 Structural Model Specification

The first stage of the PLS-SEM process deals with the specification of the structural model. This is based on the research model illustrated in Sect. 4.3. J. F. Hair et al. (2022, p. 41) mention two aspects that should always be taken into account when specifying the structural model: the sequence of the constructs and the relationships between the constructs (J. F. Hair et al., 2022, p. 41). The sequence of the constructs, displayed from left to right, is derived from the theory, logic or practical experience of the researcher. In general, the independent (predictive) variables (also referred to as exogenous latent variables) are located on the left-hand side of the path model, as they are assumed to predict and precede the dependent variables (also referred to as endogenous latent variables) on the right-hand side (J. F. Hair et al., 2022, p. 42). There are a total of three latent variables in the structural model. These are (1) the *CX* and (2) the *GCX*, which are both exogenous independent variables, and (3) the *BI* which is the endogenous dependent latent variable. The relationship between these constructs is indicated by arrows pointing from *GCX* to *BI* and *CX* to *BI* (J. F. Hair et al., 2022, p. 42). As described in Chap. 4, the *CX* is a higher-order construct consisting of its higher-order component (HOC) *CX* and its lower-order components (LOC), which are the dimensions of *CX—SED, EMD, COD, SOD* and *IMD*. Although these are latent variables, they are not part of the structural model (Sarstedt, Hair, Cheah, Becker, & Ringle, 2019, p. 200).

However, they are considered as elements of the measurement model of the HOC CX, which will be discussed in more detail in the second stage of the PLS-SEM process (J. F. Hair et al., 2022, p. 279; Sarstedt et al., 2019, p. 198).

It should also be mentioned that the moderators *PERS*, *VREX* and *GAME* are not considered as variables in the structural model, as their influence is assumed to be on the entire model and not just on individual relationships. This will be investigated later using MGA in Sect. 6.4.3 (J. F. Hair et al., 2022, p. 47).

5.5.2 Measurement Model Specification

Once the structural model has been defined, the measurement models must be determined, which is Stage 2 of the PLS-SEM process. In comparison to structural models, which represent the relationships between latent variables, measurement models describe the relationship between constructs and their indicator variables. Accordingly, it deals with the measurement of constructs, which was part of the operationalization in Sect. 5.3.2.

In the context of PLS-SEM, it is particularly important to consider not only the formulation of the relevant measurement indicators for the constructs but also their measurement specifications, whether they are measured formatively or reflectively. This is important to avoid misspecification of the measurement models (Jarvis, MacKenzie, & Podsakoff, 2003). Therefore, J. F. Hair et al. (2022, p. 56) propose "guidelines for the choice of measurement model". Following these guidelines, five aspects must be taken into account when deciding between formative and reflective measurement models: (1) causal priority by Diamantopoulos and Winklhofer (2001), (2) trait or combination by Fornell and Bookstein (1982), (3) consequences or causes by Rossiter (2002), (4) similar change by Chin (1998), and (5) interchangeability by Jarvis et al. (2003) (J. F. Hair et al., 2017, p. 44; J. F. Hair et al., 2022, p. 56). These guidelines were also followed by the author.

Taking these aspects into account along with the definitions and the indicators determined, it can be concluded that GCX and BI are measured reflectively, i.e., the arrows go from the construct to the corresponding measurement indicators, considered as composite indicators (J. F. Hair et al., 2022, p. 53). This is because the causal priority between the constructs and the corresponding indicators runs from the constructs to the indicators (Diamantopoulos & Winklhofer, 2001, p. 274).

The construct is a trait of its indicators that explains the indicators and not a combination (Diamantopoulos & Winklhofer, 2001, p. 274; Fornell & Bookstein, 1982, p. 442). In addition, the indicators represent consequences of the constructs, and not causes (Rossiter, 2002, p. 314). Apart from this, a change in the underlying latent variable, such as the sensory dimension, does automatically lead to a similar change in all corresponding items (Chin, 1998, p. 307). Also, the items are interchangeable (J. F. Hair et al., 2022, p. 52; Jarvis et al., 2003, pp. 200, 203).

Since the CX is a hierarchical component model (HCM), it is not measured by its indicators, but by its five LOCs—SED (LOC_1), EMD (LOC_2), COD (LOC_3), SOD (LOC_4) and IMD (LOC_5)—each of which is measured by a set of reflective indicators. Furthermore, CX is defined collectively by its five LOCs, meaning that CX itself is measured formatively as a HOC. Therefore, the relationships go from the LOCs to the HOC, which is also referred to as collect model (J. F. Hair, Sarstedt, Ringle, & Gudergan, 2024, p. 37). Hence, according to Becker et al. (2012), *CX* is considered a multi-dimensional reflective-formative HCM (also referred to as Type II model) (Becker et al., 2012, p. 363; Jarvis et al., 2003).

All three moderator variables, VREX, PERS as well as gaming GAME are measured using single, dichotomous, binary-coded (1 = True, 0 = False) indicators. The PLS-SEM model is illustrated below in Fig. 5.2 and the HCM in Fig. 5.3.

5.6 Sampling

As path model and HCM model are finally defined, the sampling can be done. It starts with the definition of the target population and the sampling method, leading to the sample composition and the derivation of the sample size as well as sample quotas.

Target Population

The target population of this research study consists of German online shoppers who are at least 18 years old, belong to Gen Z (born between 1995 and 2012[6]) and regularly shop online (also referred to as sampling frame) (Beilharz, 2024; Turner, 2020, p. 8). "Regular" online shopping means purchasing online at least once a month (Rohleder, 2022, p. 2). Gen Z is selected because they are seen as the main target group of the metaverse and, as mentioned in Sect. 3.2.3, have just as much potential to exert a major influence on their own and other generations in terms of usage behavior (Wootton, 2023). Although Gen Z usually extends to the 2012 cohort, the age of 18 (born in 2005) was set as the minimum age

[6] The age group of Gen Z depends on the definition of the authors, some authors or studies also take years between 1997 or 2000 as the beginning and 2010 as the end, e.g., Maas (2019).

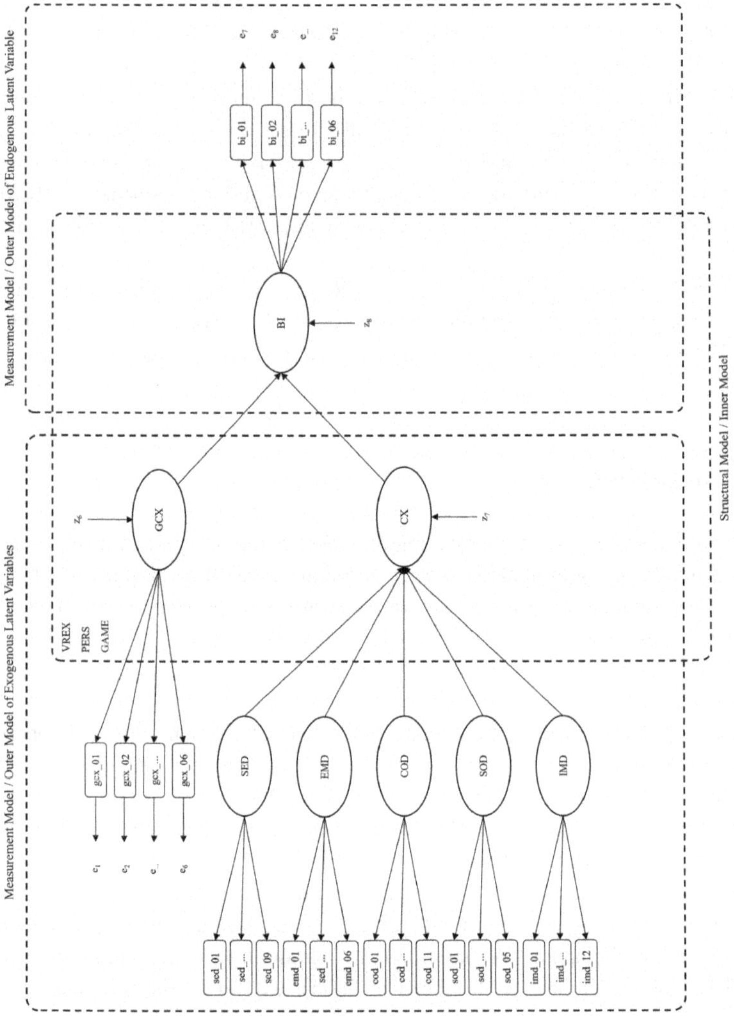

Fig. 5.2 PLS-SEM Path Model. (*Source.* Own illustration based on Hair et al., 2022, p. 87.)

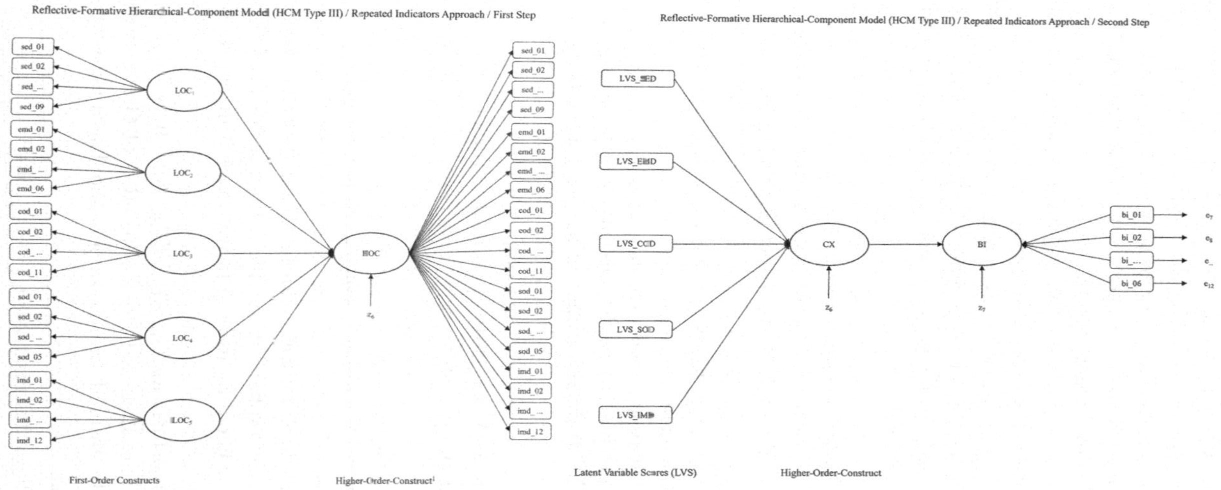

Fig. 5.3 Reflective-Formative Hierarchical-Component Model (HCM Type II). (*Note.* These figures show the repeated indicators approach which was used in this work. The left figure represents the first stage and the right the second stage. Source. Own illustrations based on Becker et al., 2012, p. 363, Hair et al., 2019, p. 199, and Hair et al., 2022, p. 279.)

(Maas, 2019, p. 11). This ensures that the generated study findings only relate to participants who are legally permitted to place online orders and make online purchases. This is because, according to section two of the German Civil Code (BGB), full legal capacity, which no longer requires the consent of the legal representative, only arises from the age of 18.

In addition, virtual stores, as well as VR glasses are not yet well established in Germany and only a few people have already had experience with VR (Bitkom e.V., 2023, p. 18). This suggests that German online shoppers have little or no experience with virtual stores and VR in general. The sample is therefore divided into people who have already had experience with VR and people who are still inexperienced in the field of VR.

Sampling Method and Sample Composition

Once the population has been defined, the sample must be determined. First, it must be decided whether all people in the target population (also referred to as a full survey) or only part of the target population (also referred to as a partial survey) are to be surveyed. For economic reasons, a partial survey is carried out instead of a full survey (Homburg, 2020, p. 276).

For this purpose, the auxiliary construction of a sample (sampling) is used, which is selected from the previously determined target population (Homburg, 2020, p. 277). Turner (2020) defines sampling as "[...] the selection of a subset of the population of interest in a research study" (Turner, 2020, p. 8). It can be carried out using both probability[7] and non-probability[8] sampling methods (Cochran, 1977; Sarstedt & Mooi, 2019, pp. 38–43; Turner, 2020, pp. 8–10). Since non-probability sampling methods (e.g., quota samples or judgmental sampling), are easier to carry out and generally more cost-effective than probability sampling methods (e.g., simple random sampling, or cluster sampling), non-probability sampling is used. Even if it is considered more unreliable and biased compared to its counterpart, because the selection of the sampling units is left to the interviewer alone and does not follow an impersonal, strictly defined procedure, as is the case with the probability sample (Moser & Stuart, 1953, p. 350). This weakness can be countered by using a proven market media study, such as the "b4p study", which enables precise planning of the samples (Gesellschaft für integrierte Kommunikationsforschung [gik], 2022). The aim of this work is to be able to draw conclusions about the target population of Gen Z. Accordingly, representativeness must be ensured, i.e., the sample population must represent the

[7] Also called random sampling (Moser and Stuart, 1953, p. 350).

[8] Also called non-random sampling (Moser and Stuart, 1953, p. 350).

generation as a whole. According to Moser and Stuart (1953), not only probability samples, but also non-probability samples can lead to representativeness, including the quota sampling method.

Due to this fact, its efficiency and its low cost, the quota sampling method is used in this work. In quota sampling, the sampling units are determined on the basis of predefined characteristics (Sarstedt & Mooi, 2019, p. 42). Representativeness exists if the sample population has the same distribution of characteristics as the target population of interest to be analyzed. For this, the sample statistics must match the target population's statistics (Sarstedt, Bengart, Shaltoni, & Lehmann, 2018, p. 651).

As Sarstedt et al. (2018) emphasize that quota sampling usually only confirms the representativeness of the tested characteristics instead of the target population (also known as specific representativeness), global representativeness, i.e., the equal distribution of all characteristics of interest for the research question and those that go beyond the researchers' specific research questions, as well as generalizability are often not given in quota sampling.

This can usually only be achieved with probability sampling methods (Sarstedt et al., 2018, pp. 652–654).

Furthermore, according to J. G. Lynch (1999), when using quota sampling, the composition of the sample should not interfere with the variables of the study, as this can jeopardize generalizability (J. G. Lynch, 1999, p. 369). Psychographic characteristics in particular, such as attitudes, perceptions and consumer behavior, should be selected carefully, as they almost always interfere with independent and dependent variables (e.g., Lucas, 2003; J. J. G. Lynch, 1982; J. G. Lynch, 1999). In order to minimize this risk, Sarstedt et al. (2018, p. 658) recommend to calculate sampling unit weights based on the current population characteristics, when using quota sampling. In this way, the underrepresentation of some population groups and the overrepresentation of others can be (at least partially) avoided (Sarstedt et al., 2018, p. 658).

Market Media Study

Following this recommendation of Sarstedt et al. (2018), the best for planning market media study b4p 2021 III, which has been published annually by gik since 2013, is used as the basis for determining sampling weights in order to subsequently determine underlying sample structure and composition (Gesellschaft für integrierte Kommunikationsforschung [gik], 2022).

With over 30,000 case numbers (in b4p 2021 III: 31,132 cases), the study collects representative data on the population of the German-speaking resident population aged 14 and over in Germany (in b4p 2021 III: 70.64 million people) (gik, 2021, p. 9). This study will be accessed with the help of Axel Springer's media planning program tool mds.

First, the population of 70,64 million people examined in the b4p study is filtered in mds according to the above-mentioned criteria: gender (female and male), age and purchase frequency on the Internet (at least once a month). The age grouping used was 18–20, 21–23, 24–26 and 27–28 years. With the help of the "target group" output function, a population of 4.11 million people (1,814 cases) could be determined on the basis of previous criteria. In addition, a structural analysis was issued via mds. The output of the structural analysis lays the foundation for the next step, the determination of the sample quotas. For this purpose, the characteristics of age and gender were cross-quoted.

Sample Size

Before the sample quotas can be determined, the required sample size at which the PLS-SEM test achieves an acceptable level of statistical power must first be calculated (also referred to as minimum sample size). In order to avoid an insufficient sample size, the minimum requirements for the sample size of the PLS-SEM are observed.

This is because a different minimum sample size is required depending on the model complexity and the analysis method used (e.g., for PLS-SEM). Thereby, the basic guidelines of sampling theory are taken into account. In order to ensure sufficient statistical significance of the results of the statistical method used (see Sect. 5.4), compliance with the minimum sample size is essential (J. F. Hair, Jr. et al., 2021, p. 15; J. F. Hair et al., 2022, p. 24; Vomberg & Klarmann, 2022, p. 105).

Various methods can be used to determine the minimum sample size. Three of these are explained in more detail below, based on the recommendations of J. F. Hair et al. (2022) in the context of PLS-SEM. The most common used method is the 10-time rule of Barclay, Thompson, and Higgins (1995, p. 292). Following this rule, the sample size should be as large as (1) ten times the highest number of formative indicators used to measure a single construct, or (2) ten times the highest number of structural pathways pointing to a particular construct in the structural model (J. F. Hair et al., 2022, p. 25). In the PLS-SEM context this means that the minimum sample size should be "ten times the maximum number of arrowheads pointing at a latent variable anywhere in the PLS path model" (J. F. Hair et al., 2022, p. 25). Applying this rule, the maximum number of arrows pointing to a formatively measured construct results from the measurement model for *IMD* with a total of 12 arrows. All other formatively measured constructs have fewer indicators and therefore a smaller number of arrows pointing to them. Moreover, the number of arrows pointing to the endogenous constructs *CX* and *BI* is also lower, with six arrows each. So, according to the 10 time rule, $12 \times 10 = 120$ cases would be required (Barclay et al., 1995).

However, the 10-time-rule only provides a rough estimate of the minimum sample size (J. F. Hair et al., 2017, p. 21). According to Marcoulides and Chin (2013), researchers should determine the minimum sample size for PLS-SEM taking into account the underlying population, model and data characteristics, which is not the case when using the 10 time rule (Marcoulides & Chin, 2013, p. 38). Accordingly, the required sample size should be determined by analyzing the test power (Marcoulides & Chin, 2013, p. 40).

Therefore, it is suggested to use Cohen's (1992) power tables or power analysis with programs such as G*Power by Faul, Erdfelder, Buchner, and Lang (2009).

These approaches consider the most complex regression in the (formative) measurement models and the structural model of a PLS path model as a reference point for the assessment of statistical power. As a rule, researchers aim for a statistical power of 80% and the most commonly used significance level of 5% (J. F. Hair et al., 2022, p. 25; Kock & Hadaya, 2018, p. 233; Sarstedt & Mooi, 2019, p. 154).

Following either the recommendations of Cohen (1992) for the multiple OLS regression analysis or carrying out an analysis of the statistical power using the G*Power program, this would result in a minimum sample size of 45 cases in order to identify R^2 values of around 0.25 with an assumed significance level of 5% and a statistical power level of 80% (J. F. Hair et al., 2017, p. 22). This is because the maximum number of independent variables in the measurement models and structural model is five (corresponding to the five CX dimension and the *GCX*).

However, Kock and Hadaya (2018) emphasize that the minimum sample size resulting from these approaches using the minimum R-squared method would still be too small and lead to inaccurate estimations. In this respect, they suggest the inverse square root method that is based on mathematical equations and "use the inverse square root of a sample's size for standard error estimation" (Kock & Hadaya, 2018, p. 228). Different to the other approaches, the estimation of the minimum sample size using the inverse square root method does not depend on the size of the most complex regression in the path model, but on only one path coefficient (Kock & Hadaya, 2018, p. 233). Moreover, Kock and Hadaya (2018, p. 245) differentiate between prospective (i.e., estimation of minimum sample size before data collection and analysis) and retrospective estimation (i.e., estimation after data collection and analysis). As the inverse square root method relies on model estimates, it is located in the latter. But, following Goodhue, Lewis, and Thompson (2012), they say that prospective is generally preferable to retrospective estimation (Kock & Hadaya, 2018, p. 245). To this end, it is proposed to derive the minimum expected effect sizes from previous research, e.g., by relying on research models with similar complexity or with a comparable conceptual background. In addition, a pilot study could also be used to derive the effect sizes (J. F. Hair et al., 2022, p. 26; Kock & Hadaya, 2018, p. 246).

As this research study has limited information on the expected effect sizes and no pilot study was conducted, J. F. Hair et al. (2022) consider it legitimate to use "ranges of effect sizes rather than specific values to determine the required minimum sample size" (J. F. Hair et al., 2022, p. 27). For this purpose, the minimum sample size requirements for different significance levels and ranges of the minimum path coefficient (p_{min}) listed in a table by J. F. Hair et al. (2022, p. 27). If it is assumed that p_{min}, which should be at least significant, is between 0.11 and 0.20, around 155 observations would be required to achieve the corresponding effect at 5% significance level. So, the recommended minimum sample size would be 155 cases according to J. F. Hair et al. (2022). Consequently, the minimum sample size should be 155 cases in this research study. Therefore, an effective sample size of 300 respondents is aimed for.

Sample Response Rate

According to Sarstedt and Mooi (2019), "it is helpful to calculate the response rate to find out how many surveys need to be send out" (Sarstedt & Mooi, 2019, p. 43). As a market research institute will be commissioned with the acquisition of an effective sample size of 300 respondents, the response rate does not need to be further considered by the author.

Sample Quotas

Now that the sample size that fulfills the minimum sample size requirement has been determined, the sample quotas can finally be calculated. Table 5.1 shows the calculated sample quotas for the data collection, cross-quoted in the characteristics of age and gender, e.g., in age group 18 to 20 years, 30 women and 30 men must be collected (also see Section "Market Media Study").

Table 5.1 Quota Sample

Age Group	Basis			Female			Male		
	MM.	Proportion	Quota	MM.	Proportion	Quota	MM.	Proportion	Quota
18 - 20 Years	0.84	20%	60	0.43	10%	30	0.41	10%	30
21 - 23 Years	1.03	25%	75	0.55	13%	39	0.49	12%	36
24 - 26 Years	1.25	31%	93	0.66	16%	48	0.6	15%	45
27 - 28 Years	0.98	24%	72	0.49	12%	36	0.5	12%	36
Total	4.11[a]	100%	300	2.12	51%	153	1.99	49%	147

Note. This table illustrates the calculation of the sample quotas for data collection, using cross-tabulation based on the characteristics of age and gender. The sample quotas were calculated on the basis of the market media study *b4p 2021 III* which has been published anually by gik since 2013.
[a] Figure is derived from the population (70.64 million people) from the market media study b4p 2021 III filtered according to the following criteria: "German-speaking population aged 14 and over, gender: male >>>—Potential: 5.8%, 1,814 cases, 4.11 million (MM)" (Gik, 2022).

Recruiting of Respondents

Participants will be recruited with the help of a market research institute. In commissioning the market research institute with the data collection and the acquisition of the sample, the author was financially supported by Capgemini Deutschland GmbH. Four potential market research institutes were identified. Individual meetings were held with each of them to discuss the general framework conditions and the market research process. In line with the internal guidelines of Capgemini Deutschland GmbH, the Indian market research institute INJ Partners was then commissioned with the acquisition of respondents and the programming of the questionnaire created by the author, including programming instructions. Based on the results from Sect. 5.6 "Sample size", the market research institute INJ Partners was commissioned to determine an effective sample size of 300 respondents.

Data Analysis

6

6.1 Tools

After specifying the PLS-SEM path model, this chapter proceeds with Stage 3 of the PLS-SEM process which deals with the collecting and examining of data (J. F. Hair et al., 2022, pp. 33–34). For this, various tools are used. The preparation of the data as well as the descriptive analysis of the sample and the test of data distribution for normality are done with Microsoft Excel and IBM SPSS Statistics 29.0.0.0 (Nie, Norman H., Bent, Dale H., Hull, C. Hadlai, 2022).

The preparation and cleaning of the data, as well as the statistical analysis (stages 3 to 7) are carried out using IBM SPSS Statistics 29.0.0.0 and the computer software SmartPLS v.4.1.0.0 (Nie, Norman H., Bent, Dale H., Hull, C. Hadlai, 2022; Ringle et al., 2024b).[1]

[1] As part of her master's thesis, the author also familiarized herself with statistical computing language R 4.3.2 (R Core Team, 2023) and the "seminr" package (v2.3.2; Ray, Danks, and Calero Valdez (2022) hosted on *CRAN* with the help of *RStudio* 2023.12.0 + 369 by *Posit*, following J. F. Hair, Jr. et al. (2021) and using the SEMinR vignette by Ray et al. (2022) and Ray and Danks (2020). R is a free, open source software and computational language that allows users to write and execute code to analyze data. *RStudio* is an integrated development environment (IDE) that makes it easy to carry out computational analyses with the R language (J. F. Hair, Jr. et al., 2021, p. 32). Within R, there are a number of pre-installed software packages that already include many of the standard functions and algorithms for statistical calculations (J. F. Hair, Jr. et al., 2021, pp. 39–40). One of those packages is the SEMinR package.

Supplementary Information The online version contains supplementary material available at https://doi.org/10.1007/978-3-658-48634-1_6.

M. Hake, *Shopping in Virtual Stores*, BestMasters,
https://doi.org/10.1007/978-3-658-48634-1_6

6.2 Data Collection and Examination

Starting with a brief summary of the data collected within the online survey, it is then prepared for the data analysis by checking for interviewer fraud[2], examining it for missing values, suspicious response patterns as well as outliers. This is followed by an analysis of the data distribution. At this point, it is worth mentioning that, in contrast to CB-SEM, normal data distribution is not essential in PLS-SEM (Lohmöller, 1989, p. 64). Nonetheless, it should be analyzed as well (J. F. Hair et al., 2022, p. 65).

6.2.1 Data Collection

The online survey was soft launched on October 13, 2023. Pilot data (10%) was received on October 20, 2023, interim data (50%) on November 07, 2023 and the final data (100%) was sent on November 25, 2023 by INJ Partners to the author. Apart from the data, INJ Partners also shared a project status report that include the key metrics of the data collection. Of 1,876 sent outs, a total of 302 cases were completed.

This leads to a sample response rate of approximately 16%. Vomberg and Klarmann (2022, p. 87) state that the average response rate today[3] is around 10% (based on Klarmann, 2008), which means that the response rate of around 16% is well above average. INJ Partners shared an incident rate of 62%, meaning that these persons were eligible to participate in the study. The average duration of the survey was 19 minutes, with the longest survey lasting ~ 33 minutes and the shortest ~ 13 minutes. Revilla and Höhne (2020) recently investigated the ideal length of an online survey in Germany according to respondents' opinions. They found out that the ideal online survey length is between ten and 15 minutes, and the maximum length between 20 and 28 minutes (Revilla & Höhne, 2020, p. 544). The average duration of this online survey was 19 minutes, which is

---

It is a software package that was specially developed for the R statistical environment and provides the user with a user-friendly syntax for the creation and estimation of structural equation models R Core Team (2021).

[2] INJ Partners was able to avoid interviewer fraud during the data collection process and safeguarded the data quality of data collection as well (also see Sect. 6.2.2).

[3] The response rate used to be higher (around 55.6% on average). Due to "oversampling" and people's reduced attention span (partly as a result of information overload), it is lower today, according to Vomberg and Klarmann (2022, p. 87) and Lorenz-Spreen, Mønsted, Hövel, and Lehmann (2019, p. 6).

between the ideal and maximum duration recommended by Revilla and Höhne (2020, p. 544).

6.2.2 Data Preparation and Cleaning

The collection of primary data, as is the case with online surveys, can lead to several problems that need to be overcome before applying PLS-SEM. According to J. F. Hair et al. (2022), these include missing data, suspicious response patterns, outliers and data distribution (J. F. Hair et al., 2022, p. 62). Sarstedt and Mooi (2019) also created an overview of potential issues that can occur, when data is cleaned (Sarstedt & Mooi, 2019, p. 107). According to INJ Partners, the data set provided has already been cleansed of respondents who did not completed the survey, suspicious response patterns and outliers by performing a quality check on the data using eight attributes. First, they integrated an attention check by adding a single choice question at the end of the screeners and at 70% of the survey, asking them to select a specific answer. Secondly, they did a front and back validation by asking the same question twice.

They therefore checked for speeders removing those who complete the survey in less than 50% of the median survey length (i.e., under 5.3 minutes). Moreover, they did a flatlining check. When respondents answered more than 50% (of the questions including a "Don't know" response option) with "Don't know" they have been removed.

Furthermore, they rejected respondents that selects all the options or only one option in "select all that apply type questions". Finally, INJ Partners took into account the "acquiescence response bias" and removed those answers where all response options are positive, e.g., "yes" for dichotomous questions or "strongly agree" for questions with a rating scale.

As a result, the data set of N = 302 provided by INJ Partners should already have been adjusted for the aforementioned aspects. Nevertheless, the author carried out an additional independent examination of the data quality based on the criteria proposed in the literature, which is described below.

Missing Data

Researchers usually have to face missing data issues on two different levels. J. F. Hair et al. (2022) mention so-called survey non-responses as one level, which happens, when surveys are not completed or entirely missing. The second level is referred to as item non-response. It occurs when participants do not answer certain questions at all, e.g., by not completing questions or refusing to answer them (including the selection of the “Don’t know” answer option). According to J. F. Hair et al. (2022), an observation should be removed from the data set if the amount of missing data per respondent is over 15%. At the same time, an indicator with more than 15% missing values should also be removed from the data set (J. F. Hair et al., 2022, p. 62; Sarstedt & Mooi, 2019, p. 101). So the first step is to check, if there are any observations or indicators with more than 15% of missing values. After this, the next step is to determine how to proceed with the remaining missing values in the data set. An option is to remove all observations that contain missing values. This option can lead to a strong loss of variation in the data and cause bias, especially if certain groups of observations have been systematically and unintentionally deleted (J. F. Hair, Jr. et al., 2021, p. 18).

Furthermore, there are a variety of other methods, including mean value replacement, listwise or pairwise deletion that can be used to overcome and deal with missing values (J. F. Hair, Jr. et al., 2021, p. 62). In contrast to the other methods, mean value replacement is easy to implement, because the missing values are just replaced by the mean of valid values of the indicator under consideration. On the other hand, this method reduces the variability of the data and lowers the probability of finding meaningful relationships (J. F. Hair, Jr. et al., 2021, p. 18; J. F. Hair et al., 2022, p. 62). Therefore, J. F. Hair et al. (2022) provide the rule of thumb that the mean value replacement should only be used, when an indicator has less than 5% missing values (J. F. Hair et al., 2022, p. 62).

For indicators that have more than 5% missing values, the other methods should be applied. Sarstedt and Mooi (2019, p. 101) created a process of missing data treatment that can be used to find out, which missing data treatment method fits best depending on whether the missing values occurred completely at random, or if there was some type of an underlying system, such as the missingness depended on one or more variables (J. F. Hair et al., 2022, p. 63). J. F. Hair et al. (2022) advise against both the use of listwise and pairwise deletion. Thus, in this work, the imputation method shared by J. F. Hair et al. (2022) is used, if there are indicators with more than 5% missing value, as it is known to be best suited for the application of PLS-SEM (J. F. Hair et al., 2022, p. 106).

To indicate missing values, researchers often use the value “−99” (J. F. Hair et al., 2022, p. 72). In this work the commonly used value of “−99” is used to indicate a missing value. With the help of the IBM SPSS tool “Missing Value Analysis” all missing values were identified. At this point it must be mentioned that the answer option “Don’t Know” was also considered a missing value. Whenever a missing value was identified, the −99 value was inserted right into that space as a missing value space holder. The data set contains 70 missing values. The indicators with the highest amount of missing values are sed_02 (2%), emd_05 (2.3%), cod_04 (2.0%), cod_10 (2.0%), sod_04 (2%) and imd_07 (2%). However, the missing values per indicator are all less than 5%.

Therefore, according to the rule of thumb of J. F. Hair et al. (2022), mean value replacement, person mean imputation or mean substitution can be carried out (Enders, 2010, p. 51; J. Hair et al., 2010, p. 53; J. F. Hair et al., 2022, p. 72). Person mean imputation means "imputing the missing values with the mean of a respondent's complete items". This does not work for formative measures as the missing items embody different facets (Enders, 2010, p. 51). Thus, the second method, mean substitution, is used, in which the missing values for an item are replaced by the mean value of this item calculated from all valid responses (J. Hair et al., 2010, p. 53).

The mean value replacement is performed in SmartPLS 4.0 with the missing value treatment option of "Mean Replacement", so that the missing values of the indicator variable are replaced by the mean value of the valid values of the indicators of this variable (Ringle et al., 2024b). Moreover, none of the indicators or observations have more than 15% missing values, meaning that no observation has yet to be deleted and the analysis of all 302 respondents can be continued.

Suspicious Response Patterns

Suspicious response patterns need to be identified before analyzing data. Sarstedt and Mooi (2019, p. 98) distinguish between two types of suspicious response patterns. The first is straight-lining (which is also referred to as flatlining), and the second is inconsistent responses. If a respondent selects the same responses for a high proportion of questions, it is called straight-lining. In online surveys, straight-lining is particularly common (Sarstedt & Mooi, 2019, p. 98). J. F. Hair et al. (2022) also mention diagonal lining and alternating extreme pole responses as suspicious response patterns (J. F. Hair et al., 2022, p. 64). In order to identify these suspicious response patterns, they recommend to either inspect the responses visually or analyze descriptive statistics such as mean, variance, and distribution of the responses (J. F. Hair et al., 2022, p. 64).

To find out, whether there were any suspicious response patterns in the data set, the mean value, the variance, and the distribution of responses per respondent were examined, but no suspicious patterns were found. In addition, the IRV, which stands for "intra-individual response variability", was used to detect straight-liners (Dunn, Heggestad, Shanock, & Theilgard, 2018, p. 118). The IRV values were calculated in IBM SPSS Statistics. Following the recommendation of Dunn et al.

(2018) to carefully examine the lowest IRV values, no suspicious comparatively low IRV values could be identified (Dunn et al., 2018, p. 118).

However, these statistics should not be considered solely. It is highly recommended to consider these statistics along with other statistics such as the duration it took the respondent to complete the survey or the plausibility of responses (J. F. Hair et al., 2022, p. 64). Respondents who finished the survey comparably quickly, also known as speeders, could be an indicator of low quality responses. As the average duration of this online survey was 19 minutes, all respondents with a duration of less than nine minutes could be flagged as speeders. However, no respondent was faster than nine minutes.

Inconsistency

Before analyzing the data, inconsistent answers must also be identified and dealt with. For this, Sarstedt and Mooi (2019, p. 99) recommend analyzing the screening questions, usually placed in the beginning of the questionnaire, to ensure that only participants who meet the specified criteria have actually participated.

Although filters were programmed for such questions in the questionnaire of this online survey, the individual observations are nevertheless examined in this respect. Also, if a respondent gives different answers to very similar questions, this can be a cause for concern (Sarstedt & Mooi, 2019, p. 99).

Firstly, the screening questions were examined. In fact, only those participants who meet the specific criteria determined in Sect. 5.6 are among the 302 participants. All others were therefore correctly screened out. Conversely this means that only qualified participants completed the survey. A control question was integrated in the middle of the questionnaire to check whether the participant was attentive. The participant had to select answer option D from five answer options from A to E. All 302 participants selected the correct answer option D. This gives an initial indication that the participants completed the online survey carefully.

Outliers

J. F. Hair et al. (2022) see outliers as extreme replies either to a specific question or even to all questions (J. F. Hair et al., 2022, p. 64). Sarstedt and Mooi (2019) differentiate three different types of outliers. The first type can occur when collecting data or due to input errors. The second type refers to exceptionally low or high values and the third type to exceptionally rare combinations of values (Sarstedt & Mooi, 2019, p. 100). According to Schamberger, Schuberth, Henseler, and Dijkstra (2020), outliers are very common in empirical research and are known to cause biased and questionable results if ignored. They must therefore be given special attention (Schamberger et al., 2020, p. 308). Schamberger et al. (2020,

p. 309) define outliers in the context of PLS-SEM as "observations that differ significantly from the rest of the data". They differentiate two types of outliers: unsystematic (also referred to as random outliers) and systematic outliers. While unsystematic outliers occur randomly and do not follow a systematic structure, this is the case with systematic outliers (Schamberger et al., 2020, p. 309). Just like missing values and suspicious response patterns, outliers should be identified and interpreted before applying PLS-SEM (Sarstedt & Mooi, 2019, p. 100). J. F. Hair et al. (2022) suggest to use standard statistical software packages, e.g., IBM SPSS Statistics, to identify outliers (J. F. Hair et al., 2022, p. 65).

To detect outliers, Sarstedt and Mooi (2019) as well as J. F. Hair et al. (2022) refer to univariate, bivariate and multivariate methods (i.e., the use of graphs and statistics) (J. F. Hair et al., 2022, p. 64; Sarstedt & Mooi, 2019, p. 101).

In this work, box plots, also known as box-and-whisker plots and which belong to the univariate methods, are used to detect outliers. Sarstedt and Mooi (2019) define box plots as "graph[s] representing a variable's distribution and consists of elements expressing the dispersion of the data" (Sarstedt & Mooi, 2019, p. 109). With the help of IBM SPSS Statistics, box plots per indicator could be created quickly (J. F. Hair et al., 2022, p. 65). According to Sarstedt and Mooi (2019), "observations that range between 1.0 and 3.0 interquartile ranges away from the box" can be referred to as outliers (Sarstedt & Mooi, 2019, p. 110). While "observations that range more than 3.0 IQR away from the box" represent extreme values, also can be recognized by the fact that they are outside the whiskers (Sarstedt & Mooi, 2019, p. 110). Hence, many observations could be identified as outliers. These values were indicated in form of an circle, so IBM SPSS Statistics used the inter-quartile range rule which uses a multiplier of 1.5 to detect outliers. But Hoaglin and Iglewicz (1987) stated this rule as inaccurate. There is an alternative approach which can be used in IBM SPSS Statistics based on the interquartile range rule (IQR) of three to examine and identify potential outliers marked in IBM SPSS Statistics as stars instead of circles (Nie, Norman H., Bent, Dale H., Hull, C. Hadlai, 2022). So looking at the frequency, more explicitly the histogram, and using IQR three, these values do not seem as outliers anymore, rather as potential influential observations. As a consequence, all observations of 302 respondents can be retained.

Data Distribution

A special characteristic of PLS-SEM is that it does not make any assumptions about data distribution, which is the case in CB-SEM (J. F. Hair et al., 2022, p. 11). Therefore, PLS-SEM was labelled as soft modeling, while CB-SEM as hard modeling by Lohmöller (1989) (see Lohmöller, 1989, p. 64). Even though

PLS-SEM is very robust against both normal and extremely non-normal data, the data distribution should still be tested for normality (see J. F. Hair, Jr. et al., 2021, pp. 18–19).

This is because, according to J. F. Hair et al. (2022), extremely non-normal data can still cause problems in PLS-SEM analysis, e.g., when assessing the significance of the parameters or during bootstrapping (J. F. Hair et al., 2022, p. 65). J. Hair et al. (2010, p. 73) propose to carry out statistical tests such as the Kolmogorov-Smirnov and Shapiro-Wilk test to assess whether data is normally distributed. Additionally, skewness and kurtosis can be examined (J. F. Hair et al., 2022, p. 65). These two distribution measures make it possible to evaluate the extent to which the data deviate from normality (J. Hair et al., 2010, p. 71).

The data distribution was also checked with IBM SPSS Statistics. Therefore, both Kolmogorov-Smirnov and Shapiro-Wilk tests, as well as skewness and kurtosis were investigated for each item (Cleff, 2019, p. 324). The Shapiro-Wilk test is generally used when the sample size is comparatively small (< 50 cases). However, it can also be used for larger sample sizes. In contrast, the Kolmogorov-Smirnov test is used for $n \geq 50$ cases (Janssen & Laatz, 2017, p. 249).[4] In both of the above tests, the null hypothesis states that the data originates from a normally distributed population. If $p > 0.05$, the null hypothesis is accepted and the data is classified as normally distributed (Cleff, 2019, p. 325). The skewness is a measure of the symmetry or, more precisely, the lack of symmetry of the normal distribution, while the kurtosis is a measure of the peakedness of a distribution (J. F. Hair et al., 2022, p. 66). When the values for skewness and kurtosis equal zero, data is normally distributed. But as this situation is very rare, there is a guideline which can be followed. The further the values are from zero, the less likely the data is normally distributed. According to J. F. Hair et al. (2022, p. 66), skewness values between -1 and $+1$ are considered as excellent. However, skewness values between -2 and $+2$ are also generally considered acceptable. Likewise, skewness values above the -2 and $+2$ range are an indicator of nonnormally distributed data (J. F. Hair et al., 2022, p. 66). As with skewness, the general guideline for kurtosis is that the values should be within the -2 and $+2$ range. Distribution is considered as too peaked if the kurtosis is greater than $+2$. Similarly, a kurtosis of less than -2 indicates a distribution that is too flat (J. F. Hair et al., 2022, p. 66).

[4] In its null hypothesis, the Shapiro-Wilk test assumes that the tested variable is normally distributed. Consequently, the aim is not to reject the null hypothesis, but to accept it. As the Shapiro-Wilk test has a higher test power than the Kolmogorov-Smirnov test, the Shapiro-Wilk test should be preferably used, e.g., Janssen and Laatz (2017, p. 249).

Both tests Kolmogorov-Smirnov as well as Shapiro-Wilk show a high significance level of $p < 0.01$. Accordingly, the null hypothesis of a normal distribution is rejected. However, a visual inspection of the histogram shows that the residuals are approximately normally distributed.

Furthermore, Backhaus, Erichson, Gensler, Weiber, and Weiber (2021, p. 121) point out that a normal distribution can be assumed for samples with an $n > 40$. In addition, both the kurtosis and skewness values of all indicators are consistently below -1 and $+ 1$, which are excellent values for demonstrating normal distribution.

6.2.3 Descriptive Analysis, Representativeness and Comparability of the Sample

In addition to preparing and examining the data, it is important to check the representativeness of the data. This involves examining whether the data matches the sample quotas calculated in Sect. 5.6. Furthermore, the demographics of the sample, including socio-demographic criteria as well as psychographic criteria, are discussed. To check the consistency of the sample quotas, a cross-tabulation[5] for age and gender was created in IBM SPSS Statistics (Sarstedt & Mooi, 2019, p. 146). A chi-square test was also carried out[6] to confirm the representativeness of the sample and to ensure that there is no significant relationship between gender and age group (H0). The chi-square test shows that the difference between the observed and expected values is not statistically significant, as the Pearson chi-square significance value is 0.990, meaning that H0 is true. The cross-tabulation also shows that the distributions of the socio-demographic characteristics of gender and age group correspond to the expected distribution (as provided in Sect. 5.6; see Appendix E). Thus, the sample is representative for German Gen Z.

In the following, the descriptive analysis of the sample is examined and subdivided based on the segmentation criteria proposed by e.g., Freter, 2008, pp. 93, 106ff.; Homburg, 2020, p. 520; Meffert et al., 2024, p. 222, which are usually also used for market and customer segmentation. Fig. 6.1 shows the sample details.

---

[5] The cross-tabulation alongside the Chi-square test results can be found in Appendix E.

[6] Since no respondents had to be eliminated and the sample should therefore correspond to the sample quotas, it was not actually necessary to check the sample composition using a chi-square test (Backhaus et al., 2021, p. 390; Moser and Stuart, 1953). Nevertheless, a chi-square test was used to check whether there was a significant correlation between gender and the Gen Z age group (Cleff, 2019, p. 317).

Socio-Demographics
50.7% of respondents are female and 49.3% are male. The majority (30.8%) is aged between 24 and 26. In addition to socio-demographics such as age and gender, the survey also asked about socio-economics, including educational background and monthly net income (in EUR). Table 6.1 provides a detailed overview of the sample details.

Table 6.1 Sample Details

Variables	Descriptive Statistics
Socio-Demographics	
Gender	50.7% were female and 49.3% were male.
Age (years)	20.2% belonged to the 18-20 years age group, 25.2% to the 21-23 years age group, 30.8% to the 24-26 years age group and 23.8% were between 27-28 years.
Education	3.3% still a pupil; 20.9% advanced technical college certificate (Fachhochschulreife); 19.2% abitur; 21.2% vocational training; 11.9% technical college degree; 11.3% bachelor's degree[a]; 12.3% master's degree[a].
Monthly Net Income (in EUR)	0.7% no own income; 1.7% 250 to less than 500; 7.9% 500 to less than 1,000; 26.5% 1,000 to less than 1,500; 28.8% 1,500 to less than 2,000; 11.6% 2,000 to 2,500; 12.3% 2,500 to less than 3,000; 4.6% 3,000 to less than 3,5000; 6.0% 3,500 to less than 4,000.
Psychographics	
Online Shopping Frequency	6.0% daily; 11.6% several times a week; 20.2% once a week; 24.2% several times a month; 38.1% once a month
Personality	57.0% extraverted and 42.2% introverted; 0.7% did not know.
Early Adopter	76.5% yes and 23.5% no.
Gamer	81.8% yes and 17.9% no; 0.3% did not know.
VR Experience	66.6% yes and 33.4% no.
Visited VR Stores	13.6% yes and 86.4% no.

Note. This table shows the demographics and details of the sample, including socio-demographic as well as psychographic criteria.

[a] or equivalent.

In the sample, 3.3% of respondents are still pupils[7]. 20.9% have a "Fachhochschulreife"[8] and 19.2% are have an "Abitur"[9] degree.

There are also 21.2% with a "Berufliche Ausbildung"[10] and 11.9% with a "Fachschulabschluss"[11]. No one has a "Hauptschulabschlus"[12] or has finished school without a qualification. The proportion of students is 23.6%, of which 11.3% have a Bachelor's degree and 12.3% a Master's degree as their highest educational qualification. Therefore, the sample is very diverse in terms of educational background. The majority of respondents have a monthly net income of 1,500 to under 2,000, which is also in line with the stated educational background.

Psychographic Criteria

The psychographic criteria of the sample include personality and the characteristic of being an early adopter. In the sample, 57% considered themselves to be extraverted and 42.2% introverted, of which 0.7% were unable or unwilling to make a self-assessment. 76.5% would call themselves "early adopter". Early adopter was defined in the questionnaire as being usually among the first to use a new product, especially a new technology. This means that the majority of participants have an early adopter mindset, which suggests that they would also be among the first to use VR glasses.

Behavior-oriented Criteria

The last are the behavioral criteria, including gaming and online shopping. All respondents are online shoppers, the majority of whom shop online once a month (38.1%) and the second largest group (24.2%) several times a month. The minority shop online daily (6%). Further results were that 66.6% already have VR experience, of which 13.6% have already visited VR stores. In contrast, 33.4% have no experience with VR. This proportion of participants is reasonable, and is also consistent with their characteristic of being early adopters. 81.8% see themselves as gamers, while only 17.9% not and 0.3% do not know. This only confirms that Gen Z is a gaming generation, as the clear majority call themselves

---

[7] German term is "Schüler:in".

[8] There is no direct equivalent in English, which is why the German term is used. However, it can be translated to "advanced technical college certificate" or "entrance qualification for universities of applied sciences".

[9] There is no direct equivalent in English, which is why the German term is used.

[10] Direct English equivalent is "vocational" or "professional education".

[11] Direct English equivalent is "technical college degree".

[12] There is no direct equivalent in English, which is why the German term is used. However, it can be translated to "secondary school certificate".

gamers (also see Sect. 3.2.3). Furthermore, it also shows that the sample is well suited for examining and testing the research model (Sect. 4.2.3).

6.3 Path Model Estimation

The collection and examination of data is followed by Stage 4 "Model Estimation and the PLS-SEM Algorithm" of the PLS-SEM process. The estimation of the PLS path model is based on the PLS-SEM algorithm, which is part of the SmartPLS software (Ringle et al., 2024b). In this, the PLS-SEM algorithm generally requires three basic parameter settings in order to run (J. F. Hair et al., 2022, p. 96). Before these could be determined, a further decision had to be made regarding the approach to be used to estimate the HCM.

Following the recommendation by Becker et al. (2012) and Wilson (2010), in the first stage, the repeated indicator approach was used to estimate the LOCs and in the second stage, the latent variable scores (LVS) from the first stage were used to estimate the HOC (Ringle et al., 2012; Wilson, 2010). This methods was preferred over using the repeated indicator's approach only, as the two-stage approach is known to provide better parameter recovery of the paths (Becker et al., 2012, p. 368).

The three basic parameter settings were made in line with the "rules of thumb for initializing the PLS-SEM algorithm" by J. F. Hair et al. (2022, p. 96). First, the indicator weighting schemes (Mode A or Mode B) need to be specified. To estimate the HCM, Mode B was used for the HOC in both stages and the measurement Mode A for all LOCs in the first stage. For the other reflectively specified measurement models, GCX and BI, the indicator weighting scheme Mode A was also used (Becker et al., 2012, p. 372; Chin, 1998, pp. 305–307; J. F. Hair et al., 2022, p. 89; J. F. Hair et al., 2024, p. 44; Sarstedt et al., 2019, p. 200). As the weighting method, the path weighting scheme was selected (Becker et al., 2012, pp. 372, 377; Chin, 1998, p. 309; Sarstedt et al., 2019, p. 200). For all outer weights, the value + 1 was used as the initial value as all indicators have the same orientation. The stop criterion of $1 \cdot 10^{-7}$ and the maximum number of iterations were automatically chosen by SmartPLS (J. F. Hair et al., 2022, p. 96). In addition, the missing values, which were specified as −99, were treated with the mean value replacement option (see Sect. 6.2.2). A weighting variable was not necessary as the representativeness of the sample was already ensured and confirmed through the data collection and preparation (Cheah, Roldán, Ciavolino, Ting, & Ramayah, 2021). Afterwards the PLS-SEM algorithm was started. The PLS-SEM algorithm runs in two stages to estimate the model parameters (i.e., outer weights, outer loadings and path coefficients). In the first stage, the construct scores are estimated, followed by the second stage, which involves the estimation of the structural model relationships (J. F. Hair et al., 2022, p. 88).

To assess the reflectively measured LOCs, indicator loadings, average variance extracted (AVE), composite reliability and discriminant validity (DV) must be tested and reported (Becker et al., 2012, p. 377; J. F. Hair et al., 2022, p. 110). Hereby, the loadings should be obtained from the correlation between first-order constructs and its manifest variables (also referred to as indicators). Since the HOC is measured formatively, indicator weights, significance of weights, as well as the multicollinearity of indicators need to be assessed and reported. The only difference is that the weights are not obtained from the relations between the HOC and its manifest variables, but from the relations between the HOC and its LOCs. For GCX and BI, as for the LOCs, indicator loadings, the AVE, composite reliability and DV must be tested and reported.

To estimate the model, the PLS algorithm was used. Before analyzing the results in the next chapters, it must be checked whether the algorithm has converged, i.e., whether the stop criterion has been reached and the number of iterations is below the previously defined maximum number of iterations (300 iterations) (J. F. Hair et al., 2022, p. 127). In this case, the algorithm ran 210 iterations until it has converged. Hence, the latter can be confirmed. The path model estimated in *SmartPLS*, including the algorithm settings, can be found in Appendix F (Ringle et al., 2024b).

6.4 Assessing PLS-SEM Results

This chapter deals with Stage 5 and Stage 6 of the PLS-SEM process, in which the measurement models and the structural model are evaluated. Since the confirmation of the reliability and validity of the measurement models (also known as measurement theory) is a necessary condition for the evaluation of the structural model, this forms the first part of this chapter (see Sect. 6.4.1). Meaning that only if the measurement models are statistically reliable and valid, the structural model can be then tested (J. F. Hair, Jr. et al., 2021, p. 7). Once the measurement theory has been successfully evaluated, the structural theory is tested (Sect. 6.4.2). Finally, an advanced analysis method, the MGA and a brief model comparison is applied (see Sects. 6.4.3 and 6.4.4).

Confirmatory Tetrad Analysis
Firstly, the "Confirmatory Tetrad Analysis" (CTA-PLS) was done. The CTA-PLS is an advanced analysis method to test, whether the measurement models were specified correctly (Gudergan, Ringle, Wende, & Will, 2008; J. F. Hair et al., 2022, p. 281). Hence, with the help of CTA-PLS, a measurement model misspecification can be avoided. (J. F. Hair et al., 2022, p. 281).

The results of the CTA-PLS show that all constructs (i.e., the five CX dimensions as well as GCX and BI) were measured correctly, as at least 80% of the p-values of their indicators are not significant, suggesting that they need to be measured reflectively[13], which was the case (Ringle et al., 2024b, p. 285). Hence, it can be continued with the evaluation of the measurement models.

6.4.1 Evaluation of the Measurement Models

The next step was to evaluate the measurement models (also referred to as outer models) (J. F. Hair et al., 2022, p. 13). According to J. F. Hair et al. (2022, p. 116), the reflective measurement models are tested first, followed by the formative measurement models. Therefore, the validity and reliability of the reflective measurement models (which are the LOCs as well as GCX, and BI) were tested in the first place (J. F. Hair et al., 2022, p. 110). Afterwards, the validity of the formative measurement model which is the HOC was estimated[14] (Henseler, Ringle, & Sinkovics, 2009, p. 298).

There are several approaches, how HCMs can be specified and estimated, e.g., with the (extended) repeated indicators approach, or the two-stage approach, which can be further subdivided into the embedded and disjoint two-stage approach (Sarstedt et al., 2019, p. 198). Since in this work the CX as a reflective-formative HOC does not functions as both independent and depend, but only independent construct to the BI, the two-stage approach with the repeated indicators approach in the first stage can be applied (Sarstedt et al., 2019, p. 199). Using this approach, all indicators of the LOCs are assigned to the HOC (as can be seen in Fig. 5.3).

[13] Hence, in this case, the null hypothesis of the CTA-PLS method cannot be rejected, since it assumes a reflective measurement model specification (Hair et al., 2022, p. 285).

[14] The reliability is not tested for formative measurement models (Diamantopoulos, 2006, p. 11; Rossiter, 2002).

Evaluation of the Lower-Order Components

The LOCs and the other reflectively measured constructs, *GCX* and *BI* were evaluated in terms of their indicators. The same criteria for evaluating measurement models were applied to the evaluation of LOCs, GCX and BI as for reflective measurement models in standard PLS-SEM analyses (J. F. Hair et al., 2022, p. 110; Sarstedt et al., 2019, p. 200). First, the indicator reliability was investigated, followed by the internal consistency, the convergent validity and finally the DV (J. F. Hair et al., 2022, p. 110).

Step 1: Indicator Reliability

In order to check the reliability of the indicators, the estimates for the outer loadings were required. These were delivered by running the PLS-SEM algorithm as outlined in Sect. 6.3. The minority of the outer loadings of the reflective constructs SED, EMD, COD, SOD, IMD, GCX and BI are above the recommended threshold of 0.708 by J. F. Hair et al. (2022). As most of the scales were newly developed, indicators with weaker outer loadings below 0.708 should not be automatically eliminated (Hulland, 1999, p. 198). Conversely, it should be investigated the effect of removing the indicator on other reliability and validity measures, such as the Cronbach's alpha, composite reliability measures, AVE or HTMT. Hence, an indicator should only be eliminated if its omission "leads to an increase in internal consistency reliability or convergent validity" (J. F. Hair et al., 2022, p. 117). Its effect on content validity is also important. If an indicator has a weaker outer loading but a high contribution to content validity, it is reasonable to retain it. Especially in social sciences lower outer loadings are accepted (J. F. Hair et al., 2022, p. 117). Nevertheless, indicators that have very low outer loadings of less than 0.40 should always be excluded from the corresponding construct (Bagozzi, Yi, & Phillips, 1991; Joe F. Hair, Ringle, & Sarstedt, 2011, p. 146; Hulland, 1999, p. 198).

Accordingly, all indicators with external loadings below 0.3 were definitely eliminated and below 0.4 were gradually eliminated if their removal increased internal consistency reliability or convergent validity. Finally, the following items had to be eliminated: sed_04, sed_08, sed_09, emd_02, emd_05, cod_05, cod_06, cod_07, cod_08, cod_11, sod_04, sod_05, imd_06, imd_07, imd_08, imd_11, gcx_02, gcx_06. All others were retained as shown in Table 6.4.

Step 2: Internal Consistency Reliability

The next step was to test internal consistency reliability. There are three main measures that can be considered: Cronbach's alpha (α), the reliability coefficient (ρ_a), as well as the composite reliability values (ρ_c). According to J. F.

Hair et al. (2022, p. 119), the Composite reliability (pc) is too liberal and the Cronbach's Alpha too conservative. Hence, they recommend considering the Reliability coefficient p_A (J. F. Hair et al., 2022, p. 120). Nevertheless, all measures were analyzed and reported. In exploratory research, values of 0.60 and 0.70 are acceptable, while values below 0.60 indicate a lack of internal consistency reliability. Higher values indicate higher levels of reliability (J. F. Hair et al., 2022, p. 119).

The values of Cronbach's alpha (0.659 for SED, 0.783 for EMD, 0.809 for COD, 0.650 for SOD, 0.856 for IMD, 0.780 for GCX, as well as 0.644 for BI) are all within the threshold of 0.60—0.90 (Bagozzi et al., 1991).

The same applies for the reliability coefficient p_A (0.623 for SED, 0.875 for EMD, 0.873 for COD, 0.677 for SOD, 0.865 for IMD, 0.846 for GCX, and 0.710 for BI) as well as for the composite reliability (pc) (0.771 for SED, 0.830 for EMD, 0.846 for COD, 0.811 for SOD, 0.889 for IMD, 0.815 for GCX, and 0.807 for BI).

Since, all values for Cronbach's alpha, the reliability coefficient p_A and the composite reliability (pc) are acceptable, it can be assumed that for all constructs internal consistency reliability is given. Thus, it is continued with the analysis.

Step 3: Convergent Validity

The third step was to evaluate the convergent validity using the AVE as a measure to establish convergent validity (J. F. Hair et al., 2022, p. 120). According to J. F. Hair et al. (2022), "an AVE value of 0.50 or higher indicates that, on average, the construct explains more than half of the variance of its indicators, [while] an AVE of less than 0.50 indicates that, on average, more variance remains in the error of the items than in the variance explained by the constructs" (J. F. Hair et al., 2022, p. 120). As can be seen in Table 6.4 the AVE values of EMD, SOD, IMD, GCX and BI are all above the threshold of 0.50. This means that these constructs explain more than 50% of the variance of its indicators. The AVE values of SED and COD are less than 0.50, but according to Lam (2012, p. 1331) an AVE value below 0.4 is acceptable, when internal consistency reliability and DV are given, which is the case as can be seen in Table 6.2, Table 6.3 and Table 6.5.

Step 4: Discriminant Validity

The next step was to analyze the DV. The DV shows, whether the constructs distinct from each other in terms of empirical standards (J. F. Hair et al., 2022, p. 129). Therefore, the Fornell-Larcker-criterion (FL) as well as the Heterotrait-monotrait ratio (HTMT) were analyzed (J. F. Hair et al., 2022, pp. 121–123). The DV assessment using the HTMT criterion is shown in Table 6.2. The HTMT values should not exceed 0.85 (which is the more conservative value; below 0.90 is also acceptable), as HTMT values above the threshold values of 0.85 and 0.90 imply a lack of DV (J. F. Hair et al., 2022, p. 123; Henseler, Ringle, & Sarstedt, 2015, p. 129).

As can be seen in Table 6.2, the HTMT values are well below 0.85 in most cases and below 0.85 in all cases. Therefore, DV is given (J. F. Hair et al., 2022, p. 123). DV can also be confirmed in terms of the stricter FL criterion (see Table 6.3). In other words, all constructs differ from the other constructs in the model.

Table 6.2 Discriminant Validity Assessment using the HTMT Criterion

	BI	COD	CX	EMD	GCX	IMD	SED	SOD
BI								
COD	0.134							
CX	0.312	0.770						
EMD	0.065	0.115	0.549					
GCX	0.104	0.108	0.216	0.091				
IMD	0.239	0.116	0.790	0.096	0.113			
SED	0.155	0.147	0.701	0.168	0.141	0.141		
SOD	0.253	0.104	0.501	0.102	0.163	0.126	0.174	

Note. All values are below the threshold values of 0.85 and 0.90 based on J. F. Hair et al. (2022, p. 123) and Henseler et al. (2015, p. 129).

Table 6.3 Discriminant Validity Assessment using the Fornell-Larcker Criterion

	BI	COD	EMD	GCX	IMD	SED	SOD
BI	0.766						
COD	-0.042	0.644					
EMD	-0.023	-0.017	0.749				
GCX	0.099	-0.029	0.036	0.734			
IMD	-0.182	0.064	0.055	-0.037	0.710		
SED	-0.089	-0.012	-0.078	-0.090	0.085	0.603	
SOD	-0.167	0.061	0.033	0.090	0.064	0.087	0.769

Note. All values are below the threshold of 0.90 based on Becker et al. (2019, p. 203).

According to J. F. Hair et al. (2022, p. 123), it must be also tested whether "HTMT statistic is significantly different from a certain threshold value" (J. F. Hair et al., 2022, p. 123). For this, the bootstrapping procedure was carried out in form of a two-tailed test with an assumed significance level of 10% and with 10,000 subsamples (J. F. Hair et al., 2022, pp. 124, 134). The results of the bootstrap confidence intervals (CFI) indicate that all HTMT values are significantly lower than the corresponding threshold values of 0.85 and 0.90. Hence, they also clearly demonstrate the DV of the constructs as all values are significantly lower than the more conservative threshold value of 0.85 (J. F. Hair et al., 2022, p. 134).

In summary, the results of the bootstrap CFI of the HTMT criterion provide clear evidence for the DV of all constructs in addition to the FL criterion and the HTMT ratio. This allows to proceed with the creation of latent variable scores (LVS; that are the indicators of the HOC) for the evaluation of the HOC, which represents the second stage of the two-stage approach to evaluate the HCM (Sarstedt et al., 2019, p. 201). For this purpose, the LVS of the CX dimensions were saved and added as new variables to a new data set, which forms the basis for further analysis in SmartPLS 4 (Sarstedt et al., 2019, p. 199).

Evaluation of the Higher-Order Component

After calculating the LVS (including LVS_SED for SED, LVS_EMD for EMD, LVS_COD for COD, LVS_SOD for SOD and LVS_IMD for IMD), a new model based on the LVS for measuring and evaluating the HOC was built in *SmartPLS*

4 (left model in Fig. 5.3). Then, the PLS-SEM algorithm was run again (with the same settings as before) to obtain the results required for further analysis.

According to Becker et al. (2012, p. 377), in order to evaluate the formatively measured HOC, the indicator weights, significance of weights and multicollinearity of indicators must be taken into account. These are reflected in the relationships between the HOC and its LOCs (Becker et al., 2012, p. 378).

Step 1: Collinearity between LOCs as Indicators of the HOC

The first step was therefore to check whether the measurement model of the HOC is negatively influenced by high collinearity. For this purpose, the variance inflation factor (VIF) was used as a measure of collinearity. A high level of collinearity is present when the VIF values are five or even higher, while the more common threshold value is three. Therefore, VIF values should be close to or below three (J. F. Hair et al., 2022, p. 147). In this work, all VIF values are between 1.011 (for LVS_COD) and 1.021 (for LVS_SED), which indicates no potential collinearity issues.

Step 2: Significance and Relevance of the Outer Weights

In a second step, the significance and relevance of the relationships between the LOCs and the HOC were tested, which are the outer weights as the HOC is formatively measured. This was done by running a one-tailed bootstrap analysis with 10,000 subsamples. The results of the analysis show that LVS_SOD and LVS_IMD have a pronounced (LVS_SOD: 0.670; LVS_IMD: 0.733) and significant ($p < 0.001$) positive effect on CX with absolute as well as relative importance.

For LVS_SED, LVS_EMD and LVS_COD, the outer weights are not significant. According to J. F. Hair et al. (2022, p. 151), when the outer weights are not significant, the formative indicator's outer loading (≥ 0.5) and its significance need to be analyzed in a next step. This was done for LVS_SED, LVS_EMD, and LVS_COD. As the outer loading of LVS_SED is < 0.5, but statistically significant ($p < 0.05$), it is retained. Also, because of its content validity. Conversely, not only the outer weights of both, LVS_EMD and LVS_COD are nonsignificant, but also their outer loadings are relatively low. Thus, they neither have relative nor absolute relevance for CX. Usually, LVS_EMD and LVS_COD must be deleted, but, as they contribute highly to the content validity, they are retained in the HOC's measurement model (see Hair et al., 2022, pp. 151f.). These results clearly support the validity of the reflective-formative HOC. All estimates of the HOC are summarized in Table 6.5.

As the outer weights as well as outer loadings of LVS_SOD and LVS_IMD are significant on 0.01% significance level, they have both, relative as well as absolute relevance. Hence, the hypotheses H5 and H6 are supported and can be confirmed. Although the outer weight of LVS_SED is not significant, its outer loading is significant, indicating an absolute relevance of LVS_SED for CX. Thus, H2 can also be confirmed.

There is no significant influence for LVS_EMD and LVS_COD. Consequently, H3 and H4 are not supported and rejected. The values for F-squared and R-squared from the CX dimensions and CX cannot be interpreted due to the repeated indicators approach (Becker et al., 2012, p. 366; Sarstedt et al., 2019, p. 199).

Table 6.5 summarizes all findings of the evaluation of the HOC. It is continued with the evaluation of the structural model.

6.4.2 Evaluation of the Structural Model

Finally, the structural model is examined, i.e., the relationships between GCX → BI and CX → BI, by applying the standard structural model assessment criteria for PLS-SEM (Sarstedt et al., 2019, p. 200). In general, the evaluation of the structural model follows a five step procedure (J. F. Hair et al., 2022, p. 188).

Step 1: Assessment of Structural Model for Collinearity
Usually, it starts with the assessment of the structural model for collinearity issues. No collinearity issues could be identified between the constructs as all VIF values are far below the threshold of three.

Step 2: Significance and Relevance of the Structural Model Relationships
In the second step, the significance and relevance of the relationships in the structural model are examined. For this, researchers usually report either the t-values, p-values or the bootstrap CFI (J. F. Hair et al., 2022, p. 193).

Following the recommendation of J. F. Hair et al. (2022), bootstrap CFIs are reported, as these also allow conclusions to be drawn about the stability of the coefficient estimates (J. F. Hair et al., 2022, p. 193). For this, the total effects of CX and GCX on BI were analyzed. Table 6.6 shows the total effects. It could be found that CX has a significant negative effect on BI ($p < 0.001$), whereas the effect of GCX on BI is not significant ($p = 0.156$). However, as these results contradict the postulates, both H1 and H7 are rejected.

Along the examination of the significance of relationships, it is also important to analyze the relevance of the significant relationships (J. F. Hair et al., 2022, p. 193). Thus, a change in CX by one standard deviation unit changes the BI by

Table 6.4 Reliability and Validity Statistics

Latent Variable	Indicators	Convergent Validity			Internal Consistency Reliability			Discriminant Validity
		Loadings	Indicator Reliability	AVE	Cronbach's Alpha	Reliability rho_a	Composite reliability rho_c	HTMT
		> 0.70[a]	> 0.50	> 0.50	0.60 – 0.90[b]	0.60 – 0.90	0.60 – 0.90	Significantly lower than 0.85 (0.90)[c]
SED	sed_01	0.709	0.503	0.364[d]	0.659	0.623	0.771	YES
	sed_02	0.525	0.276					
	sed_03	0.697	0.486					
	sed_05	0.606	0.367					
	sed_06	0.466	0.217					
	sed_07	0.576	0.332					
EMD	emd_01	0.921	0.848	0.561	0.783	0.875	0.830	YES
	emd_03	0.858	0.736					
	emd_04	0.587	0.345					
	emd_06	0.563	0.317					
COD	cod_01	0.792	0.627	0.414[d]	0.809	0.873	0.846	YES
	cod_02	0.647	0.419					
	cod_03	0.732	0.536					
	cod_04	0.567	0.321					
	cod_05	0.745	0.555					
	cod_07	0.553	0.306					
	cod_08	0.585	0.342					
	cod_10	0.455	0.207					
SOD	sod_01	0.864	0.746	0.592	0.650	0.677	0.811	YES
	sod_02	0.773	0.598					
	sod_03	0.657	0.432					
IMD	imd_01	0.810	0.656	0.504	0.856	0.865	0.889	YES
	imd_02	0.784	0.615					
	imd_03	0.821	0.674					
	imd_04	0.696	0.484					
	imd_05	0.677	0.458					
	imd_09	0.675	0.456					
	imd_10	0.597	0.356					
	imd_12	0.580	0.336					
GCX	gcx_01	0.888	0.789	0.538	0.780	0.846	0.815	YES
	gcx_03	0.888	0.789					
	gcx_04	0.537	0.288					
	gcx_05	0.536	0.287					
BI	bi_02	0.894	0.799	0.587	0.644	0.710	0.807	YES
	bi_03	0.713	0.508					
	bi_04	0.672	0.452					

Note. This table illustrates the summary of results for the reflective measured lower-order constructs based on Hair et al. (2022, p. 135).

[a] Bagozzi et al. (1991).

[b] Bagozzi (1980).

[c] J. F. Hair et al. (2022, p. 135).

[d] Lam, 2012 (p. 1331).

Table 6.5 Higher-order Construct Estimates

Higher-Order Construct	Latent Variable Scores	Outer Weights (Outer Loadings)	t Value Outer Weights	t Value Outer Loadings	p Value Outer Weights	p Value Outer Loadings	95% Percentile Confidence Interval Outer Weights	95% Percentile Confidence Interval Outer Loadings	Significance ($p < 0.05$)[a]
	LVS_SED	0.249 (0.355)	0.437	1.930	0.092	0.027	[-0.084, 0.523]	[0.010, 0.611]	*YES*[b]
	LVS_EMD	0.040 (0.089)	0.192	0.436	0.424	0.331	[-0.314, 0.369]	[-0.261, 0.411]	*NO*
CX	LVS_COD	0.104 (0.132)	4.269	0.569	0.331	0.285	[-0.308, 0.476]	[-0.274, 0.491]	*NO*
	LVS_SOD	0.607 (0.670)	1.328	4.013	0.000	0.000	[0.230, 0.805]	[0.301, 0.844]	YES
	LVS_IMD	0.665 (0.733)	3.454	5.217	0.000	0.000	[0.337, 0.844]	[0.417, 0.874]	YES

Note. This table illustrates the outer weights significance testing of the formative measurement models as latent variable scores derived from the lower-order constructs SED, EMD, COD, SOD and IMD of the higher-order construct CX (J. F. Hair et al., 2022, p. 181).
[a] For significance testing, it is referred to the bootstrap confidence intervals.
[b] According to J. F. Hair et al. (2022, p. 118), when the outer weights are not significant, the outer loading ($\geq$ 0.5) and significance of the formative indicator's outer loading need to be evaluated. This is the case for LVS_SED. As its outer loading is lower than 0.5, but statistically significant, it is retained. Also because of its high contribution to content validity. Conversely, the outer weights of both LVS_EMD and LVS_COD are nonsignificant, and their outer loadings are relatively low, thus they do not have any relative or absolute relevance. But, as they contribute highly to the content validity, they are retained (Hair et al., 2022, pp. 151f.).

the size of −0.250, when all other constructs and their path coefficients remain constant.

Table 6.6 Significance Testing Results

Reflective-Formative

Relationships	Path Coefficient / Total Effect	t Value	p Value	95% Percentile Confidence Interval	Significance ($p < 0.05$)
CX → BI	-0.250	5.388	0.000	[-0.351, -0.202]	YES
GCX → BI	0.102	1.012	0.156	[-0.142, 0.207]	NO

Note. Path coefficients and total effects are the same as these are the only relationships in the model. Moreover, there is no multicollinearity affecting the model and the standardized path coefficient is actually the correlation of the two constructs (J. F. Hair et al., 2022, p. 193).

Step 3: Assess the Model's Explanatory Power

In order to evaluate the explanatory power of a model, the coefficient of determination (also referred to as R-squared; R^2) should be analyzed. The assessed R^2

value of BI of 0.072 is very weak and does not align with the threshold value of 0.10 and rule of thumb by J. F. Hair et al. (2022, p. 195). However, the reason for this could be that there are only two exogenous variables that predict BI in the model, as well as the fact that one of them is an HCM (forum.smartpls.com, 2022; J. F. Hair et al., 2022, p. 195).

In addition, the effect sizes of the two exogenous constructs are also comparatively weak with values of 0.011 for GCX and 0.067 for CX, which indicates that there is no measurable effect (J. F. Hair et al., 2022, pp. 196, 219).[15] This suggests that the model does not have strong explanatory power and is unable to capture the available data by quantifying the strength of the relationship indicated by the PLS path model (J. F. Hair et al., 2022, p. 194).

Step 4: Assess the Model's Predictive Power

According to Shmueli (2010), in order to assess the overall performance of the model, it is necessary to evaluate not only the explanatory power but also the predictive power of the model (Shmueli, 2010, 295, 305).

The fourth step therefore refers to the predictive power of the model, which indicates whether generalizable findings can be obtained with the model (J. F. Hair et al., 2022, p. 196). For this, J. F. Hair et al. (2022, p. 196) recommend the $PLS_{predict}$ approach of Shmueli, Ray, Velasquez Estrada, and Chatla (2016), recommending the analysis of the Mean Absolute Error (MAE) and the Standardized Root Mean Square Residual (RMSE) in comparison to a linear regression model (LM) benchmark. The $PLS_{predict}$ analysis in was also performed in SmartPLS and the guidelines of J. F. Hair et al. (2022, p. 203) were followed. The results of the analysis are shown in Table 6.7.

Table 6.7 Results of $PLS_{predict}$

BI	$Q^2_{predict}$	PLS-SEM_RMSE	PLS-SEM_MAE	LM_RMSE	LM_MAE
bi_02	0.029	0.955	0.761	0.962	0.767
bi_03	0.008	0.857	0.687	0.87	0.697
bi_04	0.005	0.999	0.831	1.013	0.839

Note. This table illustrates the results of $PLS_{predict}$.

[15] According to Cohen (1988, p. 477), effect sizes of f-square ≥ 0.02 are considered as small, f-square ≥ 0.15 as medium and f-square ≥ 0.35 as large.

As can be seen in Table 6.7, the values of the $Q2_{predict}$ of the three indicators bi_02, bi_03 and bi_04 are larger than zero, suggesting that the PLS path model outperforms the most naïve benchmark.

The comparison of the RMSE values of the PLS-SEM analysis with those of the naïve LM benchmark model reveals that the PLS-SEM analysis delivers lower RMSE values (also known as prediction values) than the LM for all three indicators of BI. This indicates that the model has a high predictive power, with PLS-SEM analysis outperforming the naïve LM benchmark model for all BI indicators (J. F. Hair et al., 2022, p. 203).

Model Fit

Furthermore, the overall model fit was tested. For this purpose, the model fit indices output by the PLS algorithm were considered, as shown in Table 6.8.

However, according to Ringle et al. (2024b), the values of d_ULS and d_G are not meaningful in themselves as "only the Bollen-Stine bootstrapping results of the bootstrap-based test for the exact overall model fit, as provided by my SmartPLS, allow an interpretation of [the] results" (see Table 6.9).

Table 6.8 Results of the PLS-SEM Algorithm

	Saturated model	Estimated model
SRMR	0.068	0.068
d_ULS*	0.364	0.364
d_G*	0.123	0.123
Chi-square	218.755	218.755
NFI	0.605	0.605

Note. This table shows the results of the PLS-SEM algorithm for evaluating the overall model fit.

The carrying out of the bootstrap-based test showed that the model has good fit, as the upper bound of the CFI is larger than the original value of both, the d_ULS and d_G fit criteria (see Table 6.9). Moreover, the difference between the correlation matrix implied by the model and the empirical correlation matrix is not significant ($p > 0.05$) (Ringle, Wende, & Becker, 2024a).

Table 6.9 Bootstrapping Results

Criteria	Original sample (O)	Sample mean (M)	95%	99%
SRMR				
Saturated model	0.068	0.067	0.134	0.161
Estimated model	0.068	0.067	0.134	0.161
d_ULS				
Saturated model	0.364	0.395	1.392	2.014
Estimated model	0.364	0.395	1.392	2.014
d_G				
Saturated model	0.123	0.131	0.346	0.457
Estimated model	0.123	0.131	0.346	0.457

Note. This table shows the bootstrapping results based on Ringle et al. (2024a).

6.4.3 Multigroup Analysis

In Sect. 4.2 it was hypothesized that the relationships from GCX to BI and CX to BI are affected by the customer characteristics: Experience with VR (VREX), personality (PERS) as well as gaming (GAME). Hence, VREX, PERS as well as GAME are considered as grouping variables, each of which divides the sample into two subsamples (J. F. Hair et al., 2022, p. 244). For VREX this means, a subsample with participants who had experience with VR (coded as 1) and another with participants who had not (coded as 0). The same applies for PERS which divides the sample into a subsample with participants who are introverts (coded as 1) and participants who are extraverts (coded as 0). Lastly, GAME splits the sample into a subsample with participants who see themselves as gamers (coded as 1) and those who not (coded as 0). Accordingly, the CX model will be estimated for each subsample. The main objective is to find out, whether the differences between each subsamples are statistically significant and meaningful (J. F. Hair et al., 2022, p. 287).

A MGA, which also forms Stage 7 of the PLS-SEM procedure by J. F. Hair et al. (2022, p. 33) and is subsumed as an advanced analysis method in PLS-SEM, helps to find out exactly this. Within a MGA, the "null hypothesis H_0 that the path coefficients are not significantly different (e.g., $p_{13}^{(1)} = p_{14}^{(2)}$)" is tested, i.e., "the absolute difference between the path coefficients is zero $\left(H_0 : \left|p_{13}^{(1)} = p_{14}^{(2)}\right| = 0\right)$.

The corresponding alternative hypothesis H_1 is that the path coefficients are different (i.e., $H_1 : |p_{13}^{(1)} \neq p_{14}^{(2)}$ or, put differently, $H_1 : |p_{13}^{(1)} = p_{14}^{(2)}|\rangle 0$)" (J. F. Hair et al., 2022, p. 287).

There are both, the parametric approach as well as several non-parametric approaches, such as the permutation test by Chin and Dibbern (2010), the Welch-Satterthwaite test by Satterthwaite (1946) and Welch (1947) or the PLS-MGA by Henseler et al. (2009, p. 309) for conducting a MGA. In this work, the recommendation by J. F. Hair et al. (2022, p. 289) is followed using the PLS-MGA for *VREX* and *GAME* (J. F. Hair et al., 2022, p. 289). For *GAME*, the Welch-Satterthwaite test is performed because the difference between the sizes of the two subsample groups is greater than the difference that the PLS-MGA can handle to obtain valid results[16] (i.e., the difference is greater than one-third of the observations in one group and two-thirds in the other) (J. F. Hair et al., 2022, p. 290). The sizes of the sub-sample groups can be found in Table 6.10.

[16] In other words, the subsample groups of *GAME* are highly unequal compared to the subsamples of *VREX* and *PERS*.

Table 6.10 Sizes (in Cases) of Sub-Sample Groups

Group Name	Cases
VREX	302
VR-Experienced	201
VR-Inexperienced	101
PERS	300
Extraverts	172
Introverts	128
GAME	301
Gamer	247
Non-Gamer	54

Note. This table shows the number of cases in each sample group and its subsample groups.

VREX

There are a total of 302 participants in the VREX group. It can be divided into 201 VR-experienced and 101 VR-inexperienced. Both subgroups were compared with each other applying the PLS-MGA. No significant differences were found neither in the relationship between CX and BI ($p = 0.135$) nor in the relationship between GCX and BI ($p = 0.444$). Since the subgroups are relatively unequal, a non-parametric Welch-Satterthwaite test was also carried out for comparison, assuming that the variances are unequal (also known as heteroskedastic) (J. F. Hair et al., 2022, p. 289). Again, no significant differences were found neither in the relationship between CX and BI ($p = 0.252$) nor in the relationship between GCX and BI ($p = 0.494$) as the path coefficients of both subgroups are not significantly different. Hence, it can be concluded that the GCX as well as the CX affecting the BI are more or less equal for participants with VR experience as well as for people without VR experience. Thus the hypotheses H1-M1 and H7-M1 are rejected.

In addition, the R-squared was compared between participants with VR experience and participants without VR experience. Contrary to the assumption that VR-experienced people ($R^2 = 0.072$) have a greater intention to use virtual stores, it turned out that VR-inexperienced people have a greater intention to use them ($R^2 = 0.127$). In this respect, H8-M1 is also rejected.

PERS

The PERS group incorporates a total of 300 participants, of which 172 see themselves as extraverts and 128 as introverts. As with VREX, both subgroups of PERS were compared with each other applying the MGA-PLS. In contrast to VREX, a significant difference could be found for the relationship between CX and BI ($p = 0.039$) with a difference between introverts and extraverts of −0.173, while the relationship between GCX and BI ($p = 0.055$) was nonsignificant. This means that for extraverts the impact of CX on BI is higher than for introverts. Therefore, the hypotheses H1-M2 as well as H7-M2 are not being supported either.

The R-squared was also examined here. However, the analysis showed that introverts ($R^2 = 0.166$) have a higher BI than extraverts ($R^2 = 0.068$). This finding underlines the postulated assumption. H8-M2 can therefore be confirmed.

GAME

The GAME group consists of a total of 301 participants, of whom 247 see themselves as gamers and only 54 do not. As with VREX and PERS, no significant differences were found between the two relationships CX to BI ($p = 0.148$) and GCX to BI ($p = 0.309$) using the Welch-Satterthwaite test. As a result, hypotheses H1-M3 and H7-M3 are also not supported.

As with the other two moderators, the effect of the R-squared was also examined for GAME. It was found that gamers ($R^2 = 0.064$) do not have a higher BI than non-gamers ($R^2 = 0.223$). Conversely, non-gamers have a higher BI. Therefore, H8-M3 is rejected.

Table 6.11 shows the results of the MGA. Table 6.12 on the next page provides an overview of the results of the hypotheses tests.

6.4.4 Model Comparison

Due to the negative influence of CX on BI and the low explanatory power of the model examined, an alternative model was examined in which CX was not considered as HOC, but instead the direct influence of the dimensions of CX (measured reflectively) on BI was examined.

This not only revealed a significant influence of also the *COD* of CX ($p < 0.05$) on BI, but also resulted in a higher R-squared ($R^2 = 0.112$) overall. However, the influence of EMD on BI ($p = 0.694$) as well as GCX on BI stayed insignificant ($p = 0.290$). Moreover, except for COD, all other dimensions have a negative influence on BI with small effect sizes[17] (F-square ≥ 0.02; including COD).

The alternative model can be found in Appendix F containing Figure F-4, showing the alternative model generated by the PLS-SEM algorithm to obtain the outer loadings and effect sizes, along with Figure F-5 showing the alternative model generated through a bootstrapping procedure to get the significance levels.

6.5 Analysis of Further Insights

This section deals with the third research question of the Master's thesis and aims to examine the eleven additional questions (ADQ) that are intended to provide insight into further preferences in relation to virtual stores on the part of Gen Z. The analysis and evaluation of these additional questions were mainly carried out in IBM SPSS Statistics and Microsoft Excel.

ADQ 01

Right at the beginning, after the introductory text and the video about virtual stores, the participants were initially asked whether they had ever visited one or more virtual stores before the survey. Out of 302 participants, 41 respondents stated that they had already had experience with virtual stores. This corresponds to a proportion of 13.6%.

ADQ 02

In addition, the 41 respondents were asked to indicate in an input field which virtual stores they had actually visited. Therefore, all respondents indicated the specific brand name of the virtual stores. Table 6.12 summarizes the virtual stores previously visited by the respondents, sorted by the most frequently mentioned virtual stores visited: Ikea (nine cases), Zalando (nine cases) and Nike (eight cases).

[17] According to Cohen (1988, p. 477), effect sizes of f-square ≥ 0.02 are considered as small, f-square ≥ 0.15 as medium and f-square ≥ 0.35 as large.

Table 6.11 Results of Hypotheses Testing

Results of Hypotheses Testing

	Hypotheses	Results
H1	The customer experience has a positive influence on the behavioral intention to use virtual stores.	Not supported
H1-M1	The influence of the customer experience on the behavioral intention to use virtual stores is moderated by the experience with VR, whereby the effect is stronger for VR-experienced people.	Not supported
H1-M2	The influence of the customer experience on the behavioral intention to use virtual stores is moderated by personality, whereby the effect is stronger for introverted people.	Not supported
H1-M3	The influence of the customer experience on the behavioral intention to use virtual stores is moderated by gaming, whereby the effect is stronger for gamers.	Not supported
H2	The sensory dimension of the customer experience has a positive influence on the customer experience.	Supported
H3	The emotional dimension of the customer experience has a positive influence on the customer experience.	Not supported
H4	The cognitive dimension of the customer experience has a positive influence on the customer experience.	Not supported
H5	The social dimension of the customer experience has a positive influence on the customer experience.	Supported
H6	The immersive dimension of the customer experience has a positive influence on the customer experience.	Supported
H7	The general customer experience has a positive influence on the behavioral intention to use virtual stores.	Not supported
H7-M1	The influence of the general customer experience on the behavioral intention to use virtual stores is moderated by the experience with VR, whereby the effect is stronger for VR-experienced people.	Not supported
H7-M2	The influence of the general customer experience on the behavioral intention to use virtual stores is moderated by personality, whereby the effect is stronger for introverted people.	Not supported
H7-M3	The influence of the general customer experience on the behavioral intention to use virtual stores is moderated by gaming, whereby the effect is stronger for gamers.	Not supported
H8-M1	People with VR experience have a greater behavioral intention to use virtual stores than people without VR experience.	Not supported
H8-M2	Introverts have a greater behavioral intention to use virtual stores than extraverts.	Supported
H8-M3	Gamers have a greater behavioral intention to use virtual stores than non-gamers.	Not supported

ADQ 03
Furthermore, they were asked, how satisfied they had been with the experience in these virtual stores. On a scale of one to five, three of 41 respondents were very satisfied with the experience, 15 were satisfied, the majority (21 respondents) were neither satisfied nor dissatisfied, and two were dissatisfied. The average level of satisfaction in each virtual store is also indicated in Table 6.12.[18] In addition, the Composite Customer Satisfaction Score (CSAT) was calculated to find out which virtual store the participants were most satisfied with. The results are shown in Table 6.13. According to Bishop (2024), a CSAT score between 75% and 85% is considered good and a score above 90% as exemplary, but they also emphasize that these values are subjective and that can vary depending on the industry or business. For online retailers, they recommend a score of 80% as a good CSAT score, and a score of 75% for general merchandise retailers.

Since virtual stores can fall under both categories, a score between 75% and 80% is recommended in this work.[19] As can be seen from Table 6.13, the recommended CSAT score was only achieved by Nike, Dyson (VR Store demo) and Gucci.

The next step was to analyze whether the use case list already contains virtual stores for Nike, Dyson and Gucci. Only one virtual store from Nike is included, the virtual platform store "Nikeland" on Roblox (NIKE, Inc., 2021). To this end, further research was conducted to find out, whether there are other Nike virtual stores. This was done in the form of a search engine analysis in Google with the keywords "virtual store nike", "nike vr store", and "nike virtual reality store".

Apart from a brand community site called https://www.swoosh.nike/ through which customers get the chance to personalize and create their own EA SPORTS experiences as well as an AR experience called "Need it now", no other virtual stores could be found for Nike (JD Sports, 2020; NIKE, Inc., 2020, 2023). The Dyson VR Store demo is also included in the use case list and was also part of the research project by Hake et al. (2023) (also see Sect. 3.2.2). The participants in the research project had mixed opinions about the Dyson VR Store demo. On the one hand, they liked that it was very interactive, but on the other hand, they did not like that the store design was comparatively dark. As part of the use case analysis, three virtual stores from Gucci were also found. All three virtual stores are virtual platform stores on The Sandbox as well as on Roblox (Gucci, 2021,

[18] Satisfaction was measured in the form of a five-point Likert scale with verbalized end points ranging from 1 = "very dissatisfied" (in German: "sehr unzufrieden") to 5 = "very satisfied" (in German: "sehr zufrieden").

[19] Nevertheless, as the amount of respondents who already had experience with virtual stores is comparably small, these cannot be perceived as representative.

2022, 2024). Moreover, a Google search analysis with the keywords “virtual store gucci”, “gucci vr store”, and “gucci virtual reality store” was used to search for other virtual stores. Hereby, “Gucci Visions” was found (Gucci, 2023). However, this is not a virtual store, but an immersive virtual brand exhibition experience (Burgos, 2023).

Virtual stores from IKEA and BMW were also found within the use cases analysis (Demodern, 2017a; Ready Player Me, 2023a). For Prada could not be found any virtual store, neither within the use cases analysis nor the follow-up analysis. In contrast, for Adidas, another virtual store could be found in addition to the ones already included in the use case list: The virtual flagship store “The Adidas Oxford Street Store Basement” which is a virtualized version of the real Adidas’ flagship store on Oxford Street in London. It was created by Matterport in 2016 and can be visited via VR as well as desktop and mobile (Adidas AG, 2016; Dingwall, 2016). The virtual flagship store from adidas was included in the use case list (Adidas AG, 2023).

Lastly, for Zalando, within a Google search analysis searching, a virtual fitting room experience could be found, in which customers are able to try on clothes on a self-created 3D avatar that can have the same height, weight and gender as themselves (Zalando SE, 2023). As this is more like a web and mobile and not a VR application, it was not included in the use case list.

ADQ 4

As part of the questionnaire, participants were also asked to rank the five senses according to their importance in virtual stores. For the analysis, a Friedman’s ANOVA test was carried out in IBM SPSS Statistics.

Table 6.12 Visited Virtual Stores and Satisfaction

Virtual Store	Cases[a]	Average Satisfaction
IKEA	9	3.22
Zalando	9	3.22
Nike	8	3.88
Gucci	6	3.75
Dyson	4	3.75
Adidas	3	3.33
BMW	2	3.00
Prada	2	3.50

Note. This table shows the virtual stores already visited by the participants, sorted by the frequency. The average satisfaction with this stores was also calculated. *Source.* Author's own illustration based on online survey results.
[a] Cases ($n = 43$). Two participants had visited two different virtual stores, which is why there are two more virtual stores than there are participants with virtual store experience ($n = 41$).

Table 6.13 Composite Customer Satisfaction Scores (CSAT)

Virtual Store	CSAT Score
Nike	77.50%
Dyson	75.00%
Gucci	75.00%
Prada	70.00%
Adidas	66.67%
IKEA	64.44%
Zalando	64.44%
BMW	60.00%

Note. This table contains the CSAT scores of the virtual stores in descending order. The CSAT score was calculated as follows. (Number of satisfied customers (4 and 5)/ Number of cases with virtual store) $\times$ 100 = % of satisfied customers. *Source.* Author's own illustration based on online survey results.

The analysis showed that there is a statistically significant difference in which sensory perceptions are most important to participants when visiting a virtual store, $\chi2 = 110.654$, $p < 0.001$ (see also Table 6.12). The test also calculated the average rank (also referred to as mean rank) of all senses. This was used to rank the senses in descending order. The sense with the lowest mean rank (MR) was placed in first place, the sense with the second lowest mean rank in second place and so on. Sight is in first place (MR = 2.49), followed by hearing in second place (MR = 2.70), touch in third place (MR = 2.79) and taste in fourth place (MR = 3.48). Smell (MR = 3.54) brings up the rear in fifth place.

IBM SPSS Statistics was also used to determine the percentage of respondents who placed each sense in a particular rank. Here, 31.1% of the participants ranked sight in first place, 23.5% ranked hearing in second place, 20.9% ranked touch in third place, 24.2% ranked taste in fourth place and finally 30.8% ranked smell in fifth place.

ADQ 5

Furthermore, respondents were asked what design style they would prefer for virtual stores. The clear majority, almost two thirds (63.58%), prefer a realistic design (with detailed structures and lifelike elements) in virtual stores.

21.85% prefer a minimalist design style (clear, simple and uncluttered design), while 12.58% would prefer a futuristic design style (like in a science fiction movie). The clear minority, only 1.99% prefer an abstract design style (with creative and artistic elements).

ADQ 6

In addition to this question, they were asked whether they would prefer a virtual shopping environment that offers an exceptional and creative shopping experience or rather a replica of a real store, as previous analysis had shown that virtual stores of both exist. In line with the responses of the previous question, the majority, around 58% of respondents prefer a replica of a real store (57.95%). In contrast, 41.39% prefer an exceptional and creative shopping experience in virtual stores. Two respondents had no preference at all.

ADQ 7

Respondents were also asked whether they would prefer individual, mutually independent (also referred to as stand-alone) virtual stores, virtual shopping malls or virtual shopping cities. The majority (59.60%) prefer stand-alone virtual stores, while 24.17% prefer shopping centers and 16.23% prefer shopping cities.

ADQ 8

Since the analysis of C&F had shown that virtual stores can include features that are already known from both, brick-and-mortar and e-commerce stores, respondents were also asked to select those features, they would like to see in virtual stores as well. Fig. 6.1 provides an overview of the preferred features of virtual stores, sorted in descending order. The top five features are 1. Product configuration (n = 226), 2. Gaming elements (n = 215), 3. Search function (n = 205), 4. Search history (n = 204) and 5. Product reviews (n = 202). In contrary, the less preferred features are 1. Advertising (n = 14), 2. Social / Community Corner (n = 50), 3. Real shopping assistant (n = 70), 4. Interactive floor plan of store (n = 82) and 5. Virtual try-on / virtual fitting of products (n = 94).

ADQ 9 and ADQ 10

Apart from questions about the design of virtual stores, respondents were also asked for which products and/or services they would use virtual stores, as well as in which form they would like to receive the products. The top five products and services are 1. Clothing, shoes and textiles (n = 265), 2. Electronic goods and household appliances (n = 223), 3. Furniture, furnishings and household goods (n = 208), 4. Groceries (n = 191) and 5. Cosmetics and body care (n = 145).

Medicines and drugs were on the last place (n = 31). Furthermore, only around 7% of respondents prefer to buy virtual products that exist purely in the digital world. In this respect, the vast majority would like to buy real products that are sent to their homes (around 68%) while 26% would prefer to buy real products that are sent to their homes along with a virtual equivalent rather than buying only real products (also see Fig. 6.2).

ADQ 11

As virtual stores represent a completely new shopping channel alongside brick-and-mortar and e-commerce stores, respondents were also asked where they would prefer to shop if they had the opportunity to use virtual stores in the future. While around 26% of respondents would continue to shop in e-commerce stores, only around 18% would shop in brick-and-mortar stores. Meanwhile, one in two (around 56%) would use virtual stores for shopping in the future. This is more than double the number of people who would continue to use e-commerce stores and even three times as many people compared to brick-and-mortar stores.

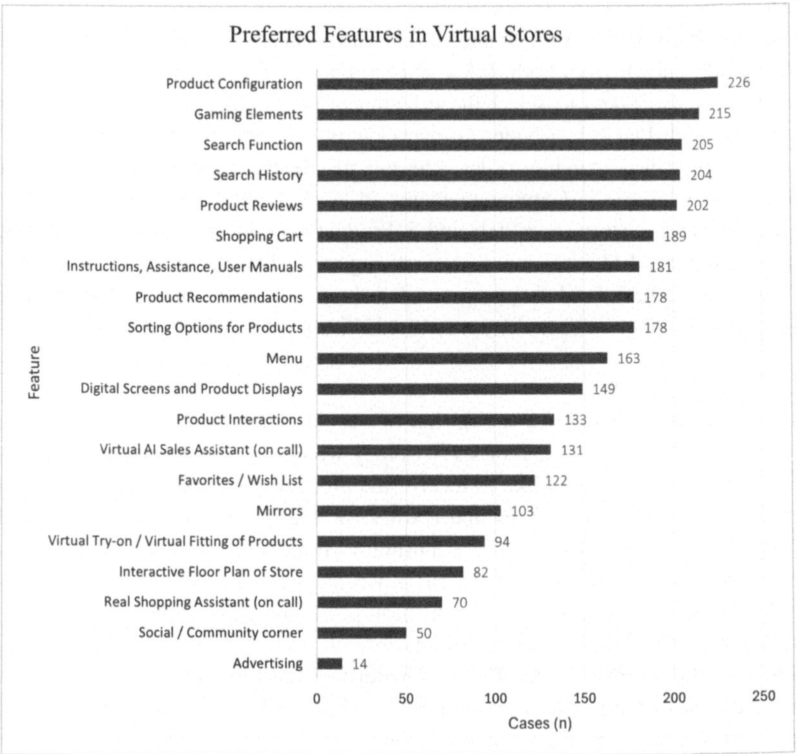

Fig. 6.1 Preferred Features of Virtual Stores. (*Note.* This table shows the results of ADQ 8: "What practical features and functions, which you may already know from online stores or physical stores, would you like to see in a virtual store? Please select all answer options that apply" (N = 302). Source. Author's own illustration based on online survey results)

Feedback of Participants

As already mentioned in Sect. 5.3.5, at the end the participants had the opportunity to comment on the questionnaire in a text field and express further thoughts on the topic. These were also evaluated. In addition to positive feedbacks on the questionnaire itself, some interesting insights into virtual stores were also gained.

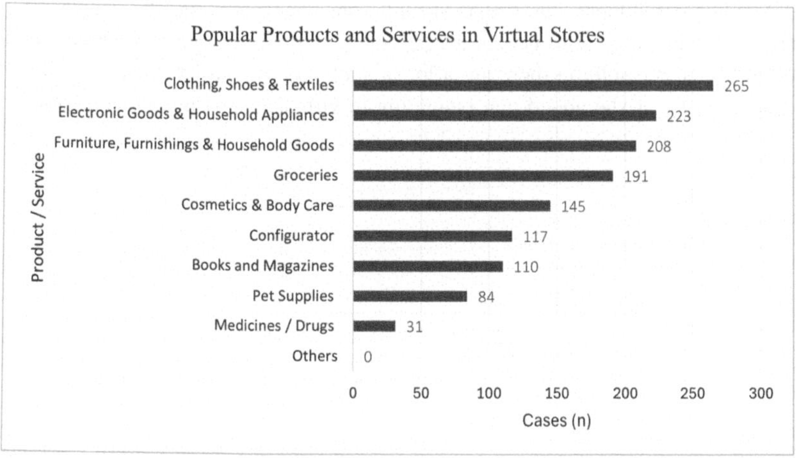

Fig. 6.2 Popular Products and Services in Virtual Stores. (*Note*. This table shows the results of ADQ 9: "For which products and / or services would you use virtual stores? Please select all answer options that apply" (N = 302). Source. Author's own illustration based on online survey results.)

Three comments express critics with regard to virtual stores. One participant commented that in his or her opinion physical stores would be more reliable.[20]

Another wrote that he or she thinks that currently only a few people know about virtual stores and that even if they would be aware of virtual stores, they would prefer physical stores nonetheless.[21] A third stated that he or she thinks that virtual stores do not have big potential and that they would fail as other virtual assets / services such as Doge(coin)[22,23]

[20] The German original statement was: "Meiner Meinung nach sind die physischen Geschäfte für die Menschen zuverlässiger".

[21] The German original statement was: "Ja, ich denke, dass die Menschen im gegenwärtigen Szenario nicht so viel über virtuelle Geschäfte wissen. Und selbst wenn sie es wüssten, würden sie immer noch lieber in physische Läden gehen".

[22] Doge(coin) is an "open-source peer-to-peer cryptocurrency" based on blockchain technology (Dogecoin, 2024).

[23] The German original statement was: "Ich glaube nicht, dass die virtuellen Läden ein großes Potenzial haben. Sie könnten wie andere virtuelle Güter wie Doge untergehen".

Another participant shared that virtual store concepts would be a niche and that it could last long until people get this method.[24] Lastly, one participant wrote that in his or her opinion there are a lot of such surveys, which focus on similar aspects and he or she added that (shopping in virtual stores) is a great vision.[25]

[24] The German original statement was: "Obwohl das Konzept eine Nische ist, wird es lange dauern, bis die Menschen diese Methode verstehen".

[25] The German original statement was: "Meiner Erfahrung nach gibt es eine ganze Reihe von Umfragen, bei denen diese Aspekte im Vordergrund stehen. Großartige Vision!".

7 Conclusion

7.1 Summary of Main Results

This chapter concludes with (1) a summary of the core results to answer the research questions posed in Sect. 3.2.4 (Sect. 7.1), (2) the derivation of strategic implications (Sect. 7.2) and (3) a discussion of the limitations of the work and the identification of starting points for further research projects (Sect. 7.3).

The primary research objective was to find out whether the CX has an influence on Gen Z's intention to use virtual stores in the future and if there are differences between people who are more inclined to use virtual stores. Beyond that, the work aimed to find out which features of the experience that are known from both brick-and-mortar and e-commerce stores also apply to virtual stores from the consumer's point of view and which other features can be used in virtual stores to provide initial starting points that encourage companies to create and make use of virtual stores. In addition, a timeless research model should be created and further insights generated that can be used by researchers as well as companies and brands for the design of virtual stores. Companies should be paved the way into the metaverse for the creation of virtual stores. They should be able to successfully exploit the potential of virtual stores and offer consumers a unique shopping experience in order to stand out from the competition and position themselves successfully on the market in the long term. The research questions initially posed were answered using the research model, the standardized online survey of Gen Z online shoppers and the descriptive evaluation, structural equation modeling and multi-group analysis.

Supplementary Information The online version contains supplementary material available at https://doi.org/10.1007/978-3-658-48634-1_7.

M. Hake, *Shopping in Virtual Stores*, BestMasters,
https://doi.org/10.1007/978-3-658-48634-1_7

Research Question 1.

> *What influence does the customer experience have on Generation Z's intention to use virtual stores and what are the determinants of the customer experience?*

First, 95 existing virtual stores were analyzed. From this, eleven different types of virtual stores were derived. In addition, characteristics of virtual stores were identified. Furthermore, the characteristics and features of brick-and-mortar and e-commerce stores were examined and finally compared with the characteristics of virtual stores. The CX and its dimensions were then defined and conceptualized based on the matching process of characteristics with the CX dimensions. In the end, the research model was derived.

The results show that the research model of CX in virtual stores can only explain 7.2% of the variance in Gen Z's behavioral intention to use virtual stores. However, it should be noted that the reason for this may lie in the consideration of only two predictor variables, the GCX and CX as HOC. This is because a comparison of an alternative research model, in which the direct influences of the dimensions of CX on the intention to use were examined, achieved a higher explanatory power with an R^2 of 0.112 (Sect. 6.4.3). Apart from the lack of explanatory power, the original research model has a solid predictive power. Nevertheless, CX has a negative influence on the intention to use, which is in contrast to the previously postulated findings and research results from other studies (see Sect. 4.1.1).

In addition, the determinants of CX were identified. In the original research model, significant influences of the sensory, social and immersive dimensions on the CX were identified. While the social as well as the immersive dimension showed both absolute and relative importance, the sensory dimension only showed relative importance. IMD had the strongest influence. No significant influences were found for either the emotional or the cognitive dimension. In contrast to the original model, the alternative model was able to demonstrate a significant influence of the cognitive dimension in addition to the sensory, social and immersive dimensions. Only the influence of the emotional dimension on BI remained insignificant. From this it can be deduced that the levers of these four dimensions should be considered in particular for the creation of experiences in virtual stores (see also Sect. 7.2).

The non-significant influence of the emotional dimension could be due to the fact that, unlike the other dimensions, the emotional dimension did not ask about characteristics and features of virtual stores, but was intended to evaluate feelings that could be evoked in virtual stores. The clear majority (86.4%) had no experience with virtual stores.

It may have been difficult for these participants to assess what emotions can be evoked when visiting a virtual store with VR glasses if they have not had any previous experience with virtual stores. The cognitive dimension primarily asked about characteristics and features relating to the receipt of information and usability in the virtual store. This dimension is therefore strongly oriented towards the characteristics and features of e-commerce stores. However, the results of the research model and the other findings show that virtual stores are more similar to brick-and-mortar stores. This is because significant influences were found for the sensory, social and immersive dimensions, all of which are more aligned with the characteristics of brick-and-mortar stores.

Like brick-and-mortar stores, virtual stores are more about hedonistic aspects and less about utilitarian aspects. Particularly in brick-and-mortar stores, which are experience-oriented, retailers are keen to avoid information overload and take the cognitive burden off the customer. Customers want to be surprised and their shopping motive is primarily experience-oriented, which is why the availability of information in any form is of secondary importance. Unlike in e-commerce, where customers are more information, benefit and price-oriented and attach great importance to information in the form of customer reviews and product descriptions (Gröppel-Klein, 2012, p. 651). The cognitive dimension tends to include those features that are familiar from e-commerce. This shows that the characteristics and features of brick-and-mortar stores should be used when designing virtual stores in the first place, as virtual stores are less similar to e-commerce and more similar to brick-and-mortar stores.

Research Question 2.

Is the effect of customer experience and general customer experience on behavioral intention significantly different depending on different consumer characteristics?

A multigroup analysis was carried out to answer the second research question. With regard to the relationship of *CX* and *GCX* to *BI*, no differences were found between VR-experienced and VR inexperienced or between gamers and non-gamers. Only for *PERS* could a significant difference in the relationship of *CX* on *BI* be determined with a difference between introverts and extraverts of −0.173. This means that for extraverts the impact of CX on BI is higher than for introverts. However, the analysis showed that introverts ($R^2 = 0.166$) have a higher behavioral intention to use virtual stores than extraverts ($R^2 = 0.068$). This is also in line with previous findings (see Sect. 4.2.2).

In addition, it turned out that contrary to the assumption that VR-experienced people ($R^2 = 0.072$) have a greater intention to use virtual stores, it turned out that VR-inexperienced people have a greater intention to use them ($R^2 = 0.127$). This finding is consistent with the findings of Jin et al. (2021, p. 12) (also see Sect. 4.2.1).

Moreover, the analysis showed that non-gamers have a higher behavioral intention to use virtual stores than gamers, which is contrary to the assumptions made in Sect. 4.2.3. Against this background, it can be concluded and assumed that there are other consumer characteristics than gaming and previous VR-experience that could have a greater influence, e.g., shopping motives. These are discussed in Sect. 7.3.

Research Question 3.

What should virtual stores look like in virtual environments such as the Metaverse (including virtual store design, characteristics and features / stand-alone virtual stores, shopping centers, malls, or cities / physical products or NFTs)?

Within the analysis of use cases in Chap. 2, eleven different virtual story types could be identified: (1) Virtual Retail Stores, (2), Virtual Flagship Stores, (3) Virtual Store-in-Stores, (4) Virtual Designer Outlets, (5) Virtual Shopping Malls, (6) Virtual Pop-up Stores, (7) Virtual Holiday Stores, (8) Virtual Showrooms, (9) Virtual Platform Stores, (10) Virtual Store Shopping Apps, and (11) Virtual Product Configurators. Moreover several C&F of brick-and-mortar, e-commerce and lastly virtual stores could be found. It became clear that virtual stores can have C&F of both, brick-and-mortar and e-commerce stores. Based on these findings, it was aimed to find further insights into preferences of Gen Z with regard to virtual stores. This was done in form of additional questions that were also asked within the online survey. Various insights could be gained.

First of all, out of 302 participants, 41 respondents stated that they had already had experience with virtual stores. This corresponds to a proportion of 13.6%. The most frequently mentioned virtual stores visited have been Ikea ($n = 9$), Zalando ($n = 9$) and Nike ($n = 8$). On a scale of one to five, three out of 41 respondents were very satisfied with the experience in virtual stores, while 15 were satisfied, the majority ($n = 21$) were neither satisfied nor dissatisfied and two were dissatisfied. The virtual stores of Nike, Dyson and Gucci were particularly popular and achieved a CSAT score of between 75% and 80%.

In terms of store design, it was found that the clear majority, almost two thirds (63.58%), prefer a realistic design (with detailed structures and lifelike elements) in virtual stores. 21.85% prefer a minimalist design style (clear, simple and uncluttered design), while 12.58% prefer a futuristic design style (like in a science fiction movie). The clear minority, only 1.99%, prefer an abstract design style (with creative and artistic elements).

In addition, the majority, around 58% of respondents, prefer a replica of a real store (57.95%). In contrast, 41.39% prefer an unusual and creative shopping experience in virtual stores. In this regard, Gen Z would prefer to be addressed via the sense of sight in virtual stores, followed by the sense of hearing and the sense of touch. As expected, touch and smell were in the last two places. It is remarkable that the selected rankings can be traced back to those senses that can be addressed with VR glasses.

To date, VR glasses and other HEMs have primarily been able to address the senses of sight and hearing, and to a limited extent the sense of touch (e.g., T. Pfeiffer, 2023, 37). While touch and smell can hardly or not at all be addressed, and if so, require additional hardware to the VR glasses. Accordingly, participants may have ranked the senses less according to their preferences and more according to their logical thinking in terms of what is possible.

The majority (59.60%) also prefer stand-alone virtual stores, while 24.17% prefer shopping centers and 16.23% shopping cities[1]. The majority can imagine using virtual stores for products and services such as clothing, shoes and textiles (n = 265), electronic goods and household appliances (n = 223), furniture, furnishings and household goods (n = 208), and even groceries (n = 191). Apart from groceries and the clear majority in favor of clothing, these results also coincide with those from the qualitative preliminary study as part of the research project (see also Sect. 3.2.2). In addition, only around 7% of respondents prefer to buy virtual products that only exist in the digital world. The vast majority would like to buy real products that are sent to their homes (around 68%), while 26% prefer to buy real products that are sent to their homes together with a virtual equivalent rather than just buying real products (see also Figure 6.2). Respondents were also asked where they would prefer to shop if they had the opportunity to use virtual stores in the future. While around 26% of respondents would continue to shop in e-commerce stores, only around 18% would shop in brick-and-mortar stores. By contrast, one in two, i.e., more than half (around 56%), would shop in virtual stores in the future.

[1] This finding differs from the research project, in which the majority of participants preferred shopping malls or cities (see Sect. 3.2.2; Hake et al., p. 105).

The five most important features preferred in virtual stores are: 1. product configuration (n = 226), 2. gaming elements (n = 215), 3. search function (n = 205), 4. search history (n = 204) and 5. product reviews (n = 202). In contrary, the less preferred features are 1.advertising (n = 14), 2. social / community corner (n = 50), 3. real shopping assistant (n = 70), 4. interactive floor plan of store (n = 82) and 5. virtual try-on / virtual fitting of products (n = 94). It was surprising that AI-based virtual shopping assistants (n = 131) are preferred over real shopping assistants (n = 70). It is also clear that the social aspect is important in virtual stores, but not in the form of a social corner.

These findings also underline the results of the literature research and the analysis of the use cases that virtual stores can combine the best of both worlds, i.e. C&F of brick-and-mortar stores (product configuration, store design) and e-commerce stores (search function, search history, product ratings) as well as game elements that originate from the gaming industry.

7.2 Implications for the Design of Virtual Stores

The online survey showed that Gen Z has a strong interest in using virtual stores in the future, regardless of whether a strong correlation between the CX and the intention to use them could be found. More than half stated that they would prefer virtual stores to brick-and-mortar stores and e-commerce stores as soon as they have the opportunity to use virtual stores. According to Gen Z, virtual stores are particularly suitable for companies that offer and sell products such as clothing, shoes and textiles, electronic goods and household appliances or furniture, furnishings and household goods and even groceries. In this respect, those companies and brands in particular should definitely aim to use virtual stores in the future if they want to win over Gen Z. What companies and brands should pay particular attention to is explained in more detail below.

First of all, as with any other channel, the design and use of virtual stores depends strongly on the goals being pursued with virtual stores and what is intended with virtual stores (also see Sect. 2.3; Ahlert et al., 2020b, p. 296). There are several types of virtual stores that companies and brands can create, e.g., virtual retail stores, virtual platform stores and others (see Sects. 2.2 and 7.1). In particular, stand-alone virtual stores are preferred, i.e. virtual stores that can be visited independently of other virtual stores.

These can be individual virtual stores that can be visited via the company's own website, individual apps or even individual virtual stores on platforms such as Roblox. It is important that the virtual stores are independent of each other and are not located in virtual shopping malls or shopping cities.

With regard to the design of virtual stores, the majority of Gen Z prefers a realistic design (with detailed structures and lifelike elements) over abstract, futuristic, and minimalist design of virtual stores. Moreover, the majority (58%) prefer a replica of a real store, whereas 41.39% prefer an unusual and creative shopping experience in virtual stores. For companies and brands this means that the best option is to experiment with different degrees of realness. For instance, retailers with brick-and-mortar stores could create a virtual replica of a real store, but can make use of futuristic and fictious elements (e.g., a slide made of chocolate, or perfume fountains) at the same time which would be hardly possible in real life. Gen Z is particularly interested in having products sent to their homes in physical form and less interested in receiving only digital products, e.g., in form of skins exclusively for clothing for their avatars (also see Sect. 2.1.5), or both. Companies could use virtual stores as an alternative to their e-commerce store, but connect them with the help of APIs to all systems and processes in the same way as the e-commerce store, e.g., virtual stores must be linked to the product information management (PIM) system (see Sect. 2.4). In this way, the products and their availability can be updated regularly. Virtual stores, just like brick-and-mortar and e-commerce stores, require regular adjustments due to constant changes in the product range, so that out-of-stock situations in particular are avoided (Ahlert et al., 2020b, p. 295; Ahlert & Kenning, 2007, p. 269).

From the results of the research model, it can be deduced that sensory, social and immersive experiences in particular lead to a shopping experience. To create a sensory experience, companies and brands should appeal to the senses of sight, hearing and touch in particular. With regard to the sense of sight, store design, appearance and atmosphere, as well as the arrangement and selection of colors, lighting, decoration and furnishings play a particularly important role. With the help of Table 2.1 and Table 4.1 on the characteristics and features of virtual stores, appropriate measures can be derived. In addition to the sense of sight, the sense of hearing has also been shown to play an important role. The video shown in the survey deliberately had no sound in order to find out whether participants would miss something. In fact, some people gave feedback at the end of the survey that they missed the sound in the video.

In this respect, companies should also consider background music as well as sound effects, when designing virtual stores (also see Table 2.1 and Table 4.1). Here, companies or brands could also cooperate with streaming service providers such as Spotify, Apple Music or even with Universal Music to create a unique and personalized shopping experience. Visitors could then listen to their very own playlists or their favorite music during their visit to the virtual store. The sense of touch can be generated in the form of vibrations from the controller or other effects triggered by the VR glasses. Even if the social corner is one of the less popular features, the social experience is just as important to Gen Z. The opportunity to talk to others, get to know others and have the feeling of being part of a community is particularly important to Gen Z. Features such as social interaction via voice or video could be integrated into virtual stores, similar to what is known from the gaming industry. In addition, social or VIP membership events could be initiated, e.g., in the form of meetings with influencers or concerts. User-generated content could also be integrated into virtual stores.

In addition to the sensory and social experience, the immersive experience plays a particularly important role in virtual stores. Immersive means that Gen Z has the feeling of actually being in the virtual store. This can be created through a realistic store design using graphics, colors and animations. However, this also includes the real presentation and effect of products. Gen Z wants the products to be displayed as they would be in real life. They also want to get the feeling that they can really touch the products. Features such as the true-to-scale presentation of products and the virtual store in general, as well as exploring them in a 360-degree view, also play a role here. The customized presentation of the virtual store, e.g., adjusting the location, lighting or colors, is not as important to Gen Z. Interaction in the form of trying on and trying out products with the help of virtual try-ons is also less important to them. Nevertheless, they would like to be able to configure products. In addition to product configuration, there are other features that should always be considered and integrated into virtual stores when designing virtual stores such as gaming elements. These are also very popular with Gen Z. For example, scavenger hunts could be integrated, in which visitors have to find a certain number of elements during their virtual store visit and when they have found all the elements, they could be rewarded with a 10% discount code (see Table 2.1). The search function and search history are also particularly important to Gen Z. These should also be taken into account when designing a virtual store. The search history usually requires the creation of an account, but this could easily be implemented in virtual stores in the same way as in e-commerce stores.

In addition, the accounts could be linked to the avatars that customers would use to visit the virtual store. In this way, companies and brands also benefit from the collection of primary data (see Sect. 2.4). Product reviews are also important for Gen Z. These could also be integrated into the virtual store in very different ways, e.g., they could appear when visitors hover over products, or they could be integrated into the individual product detail pages, which visitors are taken to when they click on the product of interest. Features that Gen Z would not like so much and that companies should avoid are (excessive) advertising. This could, for example, be integrated in such a way that it is only perceived indirectly, in the form of displays on the walls of a store or in the form of stands or hanging from the ceiling. Furthermore, virtual sales assistants are preferred over real sales assistants. Virtual sales assistants could, e.g., be AI-based avatars, chatbots or even playable recommendations, e.g., for a product. However, AI sales assistants should primarily be available at the touch of a button to avoid that visitors feel observed or inconvenient in any way.

Table 2.1 in Chap. 2 and Table 4.1 in Chap. 4 provide good overviews of the relevant characteristics and features of virtual stores as well as their sub-features. These can be used by companies or brands to create shopping experiences in virtual stores based on Gen Z's preferences.

7.3 Limitations and Outlook on Future Research

This work is the first to empirically investigate a representative sample of German Gen Z online shoppers to gain insights into the CX and its influence on Gen Z's intention to use virtual stores. However, this work also has some potential for improvement and limitations.

As part of the survey, an attempt was made to give the participants a practical insight into the possible design of virtual stores. For this purpose, a video in the form of a compilation of various virtual stores with different features was shown as an example (see also Appendix D). However, this form of stimulation is still a long way from the actual practical experience of this new shopping channel using VR glasses. An experience is particularly driven by emotions and subjective experiences, i.e., when it comes to evaluating features that could lead to experiences, it is even more valuable if participants have visited virtual stores with VR glasses before. This allows them to assess much better whether a shopping experience will occur and not have to make hypothetical assumptions.

This could also greatly reduce the cognitive load on the respondents, as it could be easier for them to evaluate real experiences than to imagine them. In addition, this could also significantly improve the values of the emotional dimension of the customer experience. For example, a qualitative study to investigate the shopping experience in virtual stores could lead to significantly more valuable findings (e.g., in the form of the first or second study design discussed in Chap. 5). In future studies, a prototype of a virtual store could be designed on the basis of the knowledge gained in this thesis with regard to virtual stores. The participants could then go through this virtual store prototype in advance, as in Lau and Lee (2018), and complete certain tasks, such as configuring a product or going on a scavenger hunt.

Based on the findings of this work, regarding the preferences of Gen Z in virtual stores, products such as clothing, shoes and textiles, electronic goods and household appliances or furniture, furnishings and household goods would be particularly suitable for the design of such a prototype. However, the examples shown in the video may have influenced the respondents' preferences, e.g., groceries and fashion were both shown in the video. Groceries ranked fourth out of nine. 191 people out of 302 could imagine using virtual stores for groceries. In the qualitative research project and other studies, on the other hand, only a clear minority could imagine using virtual stores for groceries. However, the video may also have led to participants being able to better imagine what is possible in order to decide what they would want to use it for. The research project did not show any use cases with groceries and food, but only for fashion and consumer electronics. Conversely, fashion was rejected by the majority in the research project and in the study it was ranked first among the products. Another reason could be the influence of quick commerce, or delivery services such as Picnic, which have already made ordering food and groceries online the norm. As a result, Generation Z can just as easily imagine buying groceries from virtual stores. This again shows the subjectivity and at the same time the need to let consumers try out a virtual store and then evaluate the shopping experience. Furthermore, the results indicate that it is generally difficult for Gen Z to assess what virtual stores need to offer. This may indicate a lack of experience with virtual stores, as only 13.58% of the participants have had any experience with virtual stores. The latter once again underlines the necessity and usefulness of qualitative studies before quantitative studies are carried out. It is also advisable for companies to continuously involve consumers, e.g., by asking them how they found the experience after visiting a virtual store and whether they would like to take part in a survey to improve the experience based on direct customer feedback. In contrast to the present study, a longitudinal study could also be conducted in order to validate the results over several periods of time and increase their significance.

There are also several virtual store features that have a subconscious effect on the consumer, such as music or sounds (Zentes, Swoboda, Morschett, & Schramm-Klein, 2012, p. 322). A qualitative study with a direct experience could make it easier for the participants to assess such features in relation to experiences. Nevertheless, the investigation of the shopping experience remains strongly driven by subjective perceptions on the part of the consumer. Consumers may prefer something different depending on the motive for shopping, for example, or, as already confirmed, their personality. Following on from the findings on limitation through subjectivity, it should be noted that behavior-oriented research is becoming more difficult due to heterogeneous ideas and strongly subjective perceptions of consumers. It is therefore important for companies and brands to continuously involve consumers, especially Gen Z, and to obtain and incorporate feedback directly in the sense of try fast, fail fast, learn fast, repeat.

Section 7.1 already pointed out that other consumer characteristics that were not taken into account in this study could have an influence on the results. These include shopping motives, which could play a major role (see e.g., Zaharia & Hackstetter, 2017 or Martínez-López, Pla-García, Gázquez-Abad, & Rodríguez-Ardura, 2014). This is because the behavior of consumers and the choice of shopping location also depends greatly on their shopping motives, e.g., online different than stationary, but virtually similar to stationary, convenience and experience orientation versus price and time orientation (Gröppel-Klein, 2012, p. 662; Haeusel, 2012, p. 637; Zentes et al., 2017, p. 328). This had been also confirmed by Vrechopoulos et al. (2004, 20, 25) as stated in Sect. 2.3.2. Retail channels are used for different purposes and hence other store design characteristics and features are preferred by the customer, e.g., product information and availability in virtual stores is not as important as in e-commerce stores, while in virtual stores gamification is more important. Hence, shopping motives should definitely be investigated and taken into account in further studies. Virtual stores in particular tend to appeal to hedonistically (rich, interactive and immersive experience) motivated shoppers, while utilitarian (efficiency and transacting simplicity) oriented shoppers would presumably continue to prefer e-commerce stores. Dwivedi et al. (2022, p. 25) also came to this conclusion.

Furthermore, only German online shoppers were surveyed. However, virtual stores could also appeal to stationary shoppers. The analysis showed that virtual stores have many of the features of brick-and-mortar stores. In this context, it would be interesting to find out, whether virtual stores turn consumers, who previously felt that traditional e-commerce stores, did not meet their needs into online shoppers. Can virtual stores also motivate those consumers to shop online who previously shopped mainly in brick-and-mortar stores?

This once again underlines the need to take shopping motives into account. Furthermore, the selection and reduction to online shoppers may be an indication of why the relationship between CX and BI is negative and the explanatory power of behavioral intention and the overall model is so low. Online shoppers are less experience-oriented and more utility and efficiency-oriented. However, since virtual stores are more experience-oriented and this survey was also designed for the shopping experience in virtual stores, the wrong target group may have been surveyed with online shoppers. As it turned out, the shopping experience for online shoppers has a negative influence on the intention to use virtual stores, which was originally assumed to be positive. This can be interpreted to mean that online shoppers perceive the experience in virtual stores as negative and are more likely to use virtual stores if they are utility and efficiency-oriented rather than experience-oriented. Future studies should therefore also include stationary shoppers or focus solely on stationary shoppers.

In line with Razorfish and Vice Media Group (2022), introverts of Gen Z tend to rather use virtual stores than extraverts. However, the influence of CX on the intention to use is higher for extraverts than for introverts. Nevertheless, this suggests that introverts are more likely to be the target group for virtual stores. Future work can further investigate the influence of personality, especially with regard to the intention to use. In addition, the characteristics PERS, GAME and VREX were considered independently of each other in this study. Further studies could also examine these characteristics together using a cluster analysis.

As the overall intention to use was not high, it would also make sense to survey other age groups, such as not only Gen Z, but also Generation X and Z (also known as Millennials). This makes it possible to find out whether the low intention to use is due to the age group. In addition to age, the influence of other demographic criteria should also be taken into account, such as average monthly income. This is because shopping experience-oriented channels such as brick-and-mortar stores have shown that people with higher incomes tend to make more experience-oriented purchases (Gröppel-Klein, 2012, p. 652).

Since the non-probability sampling method quota sampling was used in this work, it cannot be confirmed, whether the non-significant or weak effects occur as a result of idiosyncrasies of the sample selected or these effects truly do not exist (Sarstedt et al., 2018, p. 659). Further studies could use probability sampling methods instead of non-probability sampling.

Further conclusions can be drawn for future studies with regard to the research model established.

Once again, it was found that it is significantly difficult to generically investigate the customer experience due to its complexity. The lack of research projects, not only in relation to shopping experiences in virtual stores, but also in relation to the customer experience construct in general, also plays a significant role. Due to the complexity, the CX construct has already been divided into five dimensions. However, it has been shown that a further subdivision into so-called sub-dimensions, in the form of a second-order construct, appears to be useful (e.g., Schwertfeger, 2012). For example, COD could be further subdivided into the three sub-dimensions usability, personalization, and information availability.

Due to the low R-squared of the behavioral intention to use virtual stores, an alternative model was examined in which the CX was not examined as a higher-or-construct, but rather the direct effect of the dimensions on the BI. This achieved a higher R-squared. In future studies, it is therefore recommended to examine CX either as a higher-order construct with sub-dimensions to the dimensions or the direct effect of the individual dimensions of CX on BI. However, it can also be concluded from the results that BI may not be well suited as a dependent variable for CX. BI as a dependent variable was examined in the form of different intentions, i.e., recommendation, use for information, use for shopping, use for trying out products. Subsequent studies could examine customer share as an output instead of BI, or they could examine BI multidimensionally as Schwertfeger (2012, p. 73) did with customer share. Other dependent variables could be satisfaction or attitude. Although satisfaction was surveyed as part of the additional questions, it is currently still difficult to survey, just like attitudes, as hardly any experience has been gained with virtual stores, possibly in a qualitative study. However, in the future, when more experiences with virtual stores have been made, this could be a good alternative to BI. With regard to the choice of CX dimensions, it became clear that the integration of an immersive dimension is necessary in the context of virtual stores. Although no significant influence was found for either the emotional or the cognitive dimension. This may be due to the wrong choice of features. For instance, the additional questions showed that features such as search history, search function, product reviews and recommendations, instructions or filtering options, which are all in line with the cognitive experience, are definitely important to consumers in virtual stores. The conceptualization and operationalization of the cognitive dimension could therefore be adapted against this background and on the basis of these findings. As already mentioned, no significant influence was found between the emotional dimension and the customer experience. This could be due to respondents having difficulty understanding how they would feel in virtual stores.

Further studies should explicitly ask about feelings, i.e., "I would feel… in virtual stores" and not "I would be… in virtual stores" (e.g., like I. Krasonikolakis et al., 2018, p. 1253).

In this study, the S-O-R framework by Russell and Mehrabian (1977) was only used to explain consumer behavior in virtual stores (Foscht et al., 2017, p. 28). In future studies, it could be integrated into the research model as well (Donovan & Rossiter, 1982; Schwertfeger, 2012, p. 73).

In summary, this thesis makes a significant contribution to research into the customer experience in virtual stores and its influence on the intention to use virtual stores on the part of Generation Z online shoppers. This work contributes significantly to the understanding of virtual stores, especially with regard to their design. Important insights were gained into the preferences of Generation Z with regard to virtual stores, which make it easier for companies and brands in particular to enter the consumer metaverse. Furthermore, important starting points for future research projects were identified. Researchers can build on the findings of this work. In addition, as part of the thesis, not only were eleven different store types of virtual stores identified, but also a number of tools were created, such as the tables on the store characteristics and features of brick-and-mortar, e-commerce and virtual stores, as well as the matching of the C&F of virtual stores with the CX dimensions, not to mention the use case list of existing virtual stores, which can be continuously expanded.

Reference List

Abbott, L. (1955). *Quality and Competition: An Essay in Economic Theory*. New York: Columbia University Press. https://doi.org/10.7312/abbo92492

Adidas AG (2016). The Adidas Oxford Street Store Basement. Retrieved from https://londonflagship-virtualtour.adidasdigital.com/

Adidas AG (2023). Adidas arrives on roblox, bringing the iconic three-stripes to a range of digital products. Press release. Retrieved from https://news.adidas.com/partnerships/adidas-arrives-on-roblox--bringing-the-iconic-three-stripes-to-a-range-of-digital-products/s/358d9708-121f-4e9f-b34d-8186266eea0f

Ahlert, D., & Kenning, P. (2007). *Handelsmarketing: Grundlagen der marktorientierten Führung von Handelsbetrieben*. Berlin, Heidelberg: Springer. https://doi.org/10.1007/978-3-540-69447-2

Ahlert, D., Kenning, P., & Brock, C. (Eds.) (2020a). *Handelsmarketing* (3rd ed.). Berlin, Heidelberg: Springer. https://doi.org/10.1007/978-3-662-61851-6

Ahlert, D., Kenning, P., & Brock, C. (2020b). Die Präsentationspolitik. In D. Ahlert, P. Kenning, & C. Brock (Eds.), *Handelsmarketing* (3rd ed., pp. 295–309). Berlin, Heidelberg: Springer. https://doi.org/10.1007/978-3-662-61851-6_10

Aladwani, A. M., & Palvia, P. C. (2002). Developing and validating an instrument for measuring user-perceived web quality. *Information & Management*, *39*(6), 467–476. https://doi.org/10.1016/S0378-7206(01)00113-6

Alderson, W. (1967). *Marketing Behavior and Executive Action: A Functionalist Approach to Marketing Theory*. Homewood, Illinois: Richard D. Irwin.

Alo Yoga (2022). Alo brings wellness to the metaverse with roblox. Retrieved from https://www.aloyoga.com/blogs/alo-blog/alo-yoga-brings-wellness-to-the-metaverse-with-roblox

Alo Yoga (2023). Alo Immersive Store. Retrieved from https://www.aloyoga.com/pages/immersive-store

Apple Inc. (2023a). Introducing Apple Vision Pro. Retrieved from https://www.youtube.com/watch?v=TX9qSaGXFyg

Apple Inc. (2023b). Use Memoji on your iPhone or iPad Pro. Retrieved from https://support.apple.com/en-us/111115

M. Hake, *Shopping in Virtual Stores*, BestMasters,
https://doi.org/10.1007/978-3-658-48634-1

Apple Inc. (2024a). Apple Vision Pro available in the U.S. on February 2. Retrieved from https://www.apple.com/newsroom/2024/01/apple-vision-pro-available-in-the-us-on-february-2/

Apple Inc. (2024b). Vision Pro. Retrieved from https://www.apple.com/apple-vision-pro/

Applin, S. A. (2020). These virtual stores are a joyful twist on e-commerce. Retrieved from https://www.fastcompany.com/90586505/virtual-stores-cost-plus-world-market-ralph-lauren-matterport-obsess

Arnoldy, S., Witt, S., Lütjen, P., & Kopankiewicz, J. (2022). Retail & consumer goods on the way to the metaverse. Whitepaper. Retrieved from https://www.pwc.de/de/handel-und-konsumguter/pwc-retail-and-consumer-goods-on-the-way-to-the-metaverse.pdf

Auxier, B., & Arbanas, J. (2023). While we wait for the metaverse to materialize, young people are already there. Retrieved from https://www2.deloitte.com/us/en/insights/industry/technology/gen-z-and-millennials-are-metaverse-early-adopters.html

Backhaus, K., Erichson, B., Gensler, S., Weiber, R., & Weiber, T. (2021). *Multivariate Analysemethoden.* Wiesbaden: Springer Fachmedien Wiesbaden. https://doi.org/10.1007/978-3-658-32425-4

Baek, E., Choo, H. J., & Lee, S. H. (2018). Using warmth as the visual design of a store: Intimacy, relational needs, and approach intentions. *Journal of Business Research, 88*, 91–101. https://doi.org/10.1016/j.jbusres.2018.03.013

Bagozzi, R. P. (1980). *Causal models in marketing. Theories in marketing series.* New York, NY, Chichester: Wiley.

Bagozzi, R. P., Yi, Y., & Phillips, L. W. (1991). Assessing Construct Validity in Organizational Research. *Administrative Science Quarterly, 36*(3), 421. https://doi.org/10.2307/2393203

Baker, J. [J.], Grewal, D. [D.], & Parasuraman, A. (1994). The Influence of Store Environment on Quality Inferences and Store Image. *Journal of the Academy of Marketing Science, 22*(4), 328–339. https://doi.org/10.1177/0092070394224002

Baker, J. [Julia], Levy, M., & Grewal, D. [Dhruv] (1992). An Experimental Approach to Making Retail Store Environmental Decisions. *Journal of Retailing, 68*(4), 445–460.

Baker, J. [Julia], Parasuraman, A. P., Grewal, D. [Dhruv], & Voss, G. B. (2002). The Influence of Multiple Store Environment Cues on Perceived Merchandise Value and Patronage Intentions. *Journal of Marketing, 66*(2), 120–141. https://doi.org/10.1509/jmkg.66.2.120.1847

Ball, M. (2020a). The Metaverse: What It Is, Where to Find it, and Who Will Build It. Retrieved from https://www.matthewball.vc/all/themetaverse

Ball, M. (2020b). The Metaverse: What it is, where to find it, and who will build it. Retrieved from https://www.matthewball.vc/all/themetaverse

Ball, M. (2022). *The Metaverse and How It Will Revolutionize Everything.* New York City: Liveright.

Baluch, A., & Main, K. (2023). 38 E-Commerce Statistics Of 2023. Retrieved from https://www.forbes.com/advisor/business/ecommerce-statistics/

Barclay, D. W., Thompson, R., & Higgins, C. (1995). The Partial Least Squares (PLS) Approach to Causal Modeling: Personal Computer Use as an Illustration. *Technology Studies, 2*, 285–309.

Barnes, S. J., & Vidgen, R. (2002). An Integrative Approach to the Assessment of E-Commerce Quality. *Journal of Electronic Commerce Research, 3*, 114–127.

Barrera, K. G., & Shah, D. (2023). Marketing in the Metaverse: Conceptual understanding, framework, and research agenda. *Journal of Business Research*. Advance online publication. https://doi.org/10.1016/j.jbusres.2022.113420

Becker, J.-M., Klein, K., & Wetzels, M. (2012). Hierarchical Latent Variable Models in PLS-SEM: Guidelines for Using Reflective-Formative Type Models. *Long Range Planning*, *45*(5–6), 359–394. https://doi.org/10.1016/j.lrp.2012.10.001

Beilharz, F. (2024). Alles über die Generation Z (Gen Z). Retrieved from https://felixbeilharz.de/generation-z-fakten/

Berekoven, L. (1995). *Erfolgreiches Einzelhandelsmarketing: Grundlagen und Entscheidungshilfen* (2nd ed.). München: Beck.

Bergkvist, L., & Rossiter, J. R. (2007). The Predictive Validity of Multiple-Item versus Single-Item Measures of the Same Constructs. *Journal of Marketing Research*, *44*(2), 175–184. https://doi.org/10.1509/jmkr.44.2.175

Berry, L. L., Carbone, L. P., & Haeckel, S. H. (2002). Managing the Total Customer Experience. *MIT Sloan Management Review*, *43*(3), 85–89.

Biocca, F., & Delaney, B. (1995). Immersive virtual reality technology. In F. Biocca & M. R. Levy (Eds.), *Communication in the Age of Virtual Reality* (pp. 57–124). New York: Lawrence Erlbaum Associates, Inc.

Bishop, C. (2024). What is customer satisfaction score? (+ how to measure CSAT). Retrieved from https://www.zendesk.de/blog/customer-satisfaction-score/

Bitkom e.V. (2023). Die Zukunft der Consumer Technology – 2023. Retrieved from https://www.bitkom.org/sites/main/files/2023-08/bitkom-studie-die-zukunft-der-consumer-technology-2023.pdf

Bloomingdale's (2022). Bloomingdale's 150th Anniversary: Immersive Experience. Retrieved from https://www.bloomingdales.com/c/anniversary/immersive-shopping/

Boehm, K., Esser, R., & Seidel, A. E. (2022). Media Consumer Survey 2022. Retrieved from https://www2.deloitte.com/content/dam/Deloitte/de/Documents/technology-media-telecommunications/TMT_Media-Consumer-Survey-2022-Metaverse.pdf

Boer, T. de, Momani, F., & Federowski, R. (2022). Quick commerce—a lasting revolution? How omnichannel retailers are rising to the challenges of q-commerce. Retrieved from https://www.rolandberger.com/en/Insights/Publications/Quick-commerce-a-lasting-revolution.html

Bollen, K. A. (1989). *Structural Equations with Latent Variables*. New York: Wiley. https://doi.org/10.1002/9781118619179

Brakus, J. J., Schmitt, B. H., & Zarantonello, L. (2009). Brand Experience: What is It? How is it Measured? Does it Affect Loyalty? *Journal of Marketing*, *73*(3), 52–68. https://doi.org/10.1509/jmkg.73.3.05

Brauer, S. (2023). *Crate and Barrel NYC Flatiron Flagship*. LinkedIn. Retrieved from https://www.linkedin.com/posts/sebastian-brauer-0a4209196_last-week-we-opened-the-doors-to-our-new-ugcPost-7133110383631892480-Oxtv?utm_source=share&utm_medium=member_ios

Bressau, D., & Zaharia, S. (2022). *Meta-Commerce: Einflussfaktoren auf die Konsumentenakzeptanz* (Master's Thesis). Hochschule Niederrhein, Krefeld.

Bruhn, M., & Hadwich, K. (Eds.) (2012). *Customer Experience: Forum Dienstleistungsmanagement*. Wiesbaden: Springer Gabler. https://doi.org/10.1007/978-3-8349-4001-8

Bruhn, M., & Mayer-Vorfelder, M. (2011). *Kundenerfahrung als Forschungsgegenstand im Marketing: Konzeptionalisierung, Operationalisierung und empirische Befunde* (Research report). Universität Basel, Basel. Retrieved from https://wwz.unibas.ch/fileadmin/user_upload/wwz/99_WWZ_Forum/Forschungsberichte/D-128_Kundenerfahrung_Bruhn_Mayer.pdf

Brun, I., Rajaobelina, L., Ricard, L., & Berthiaume, B. (2017). Impact of customer experience on loyalty: a multichannel examination. *The Service Industries Journal, 37*(5–6), 317–340. https://doi.org/10.1080/02642069.2017.1322959

Bundesverband Digitale Wirtschaft (2023). Metaverse Info Sheet. Retrieved from https://www.bvdw.org/wp-content/uploads/2024/01/Infosheet_Metaverse_EN.pdf

Burberry (2022). Burberry Regent Street Experience. Retrieved from https://burberry.appliedinnovationexchange.com/

Burgos, M. (2023). 'Gucci visions' maps out the maison's 102 years of history in florence and in the metaverse. Retrieved from https://www.designboom.com/art/gucci-visions-102-years-history-metaverse-physical-exhibitions-florence-06-25-2023/

ByondXR (2022). Top Trends in Virtual Store Design & Creation. Retrieved from https://www.byondxr.com/blog/top-trends-in-virtual-store-design-creation/

ByondXR (2023). Spatial Computing: The Newest Technology Reshaping the Retail Industry. Retrieved from https://www.byondxr.com/blog/spatial-computing-the-newest-technology-reshaping-the-retail-industry/

Byrnes, R. (2022). Want to demystify the metaverse hype? Think of it as an internet evolution. Retrieved from https://www.accenture.com/us-en/blogs/accenture-research/want-to-demystify-the-metaverse-hype-think-of-it-as-an-internet-evolution

Cambridge academic content dictionary: With more than 2.000 content-area words ; from algebra to zoology ; CD-ROM dictionary and thesaurus in one (1. ed., 2nd pr) (2009). Cambridge: Cambridge Univ. Press.

Campbell-Gross, H. (2022). Metaverse retail: How it will change commerce and what to do about it. Retrieved from https://www.bazaarvoice.com/blog/metaverse-retail/

Capgemini Research Institute (2022). Total immersion: How immersive experiences and the Metaverse benefit customer experience and operations. Retrieved from https://www.capgemini.com/de-de/insights/research/studie-immersive-experience-metaverse/

Chang, H.-J., Eckman, M., & Yan, R.-N. (2011). Application of the Stimulus-Organism-Response model to the retail environment: the role of hedonic motivation in impulse buying behavior. *The International Review of Retail, Distribution and Consumer Research, 21*(3), 233–249. https://doi.org/10.1080/09593969.2011.578798

Chazan, G. (2020). Germany set for hard lockdown as coronavirus surges. Retrieved from https://www.ft.com/content/99327e7b-4d58-40c4-9957-dd8fd92a6da7

Cheah, J.-H., Roldán, J. L., Ciavolino, E., Ting, H., & Ramayah, T. (2021). Sampling weight adjustments in partial least squares structural equation modeling: guidelines and illustrations. *Total Quality Management & Business Excellence, 32*(13–14), 1594–1613. https://doi.org/10.1080/14783363.2020.1754125

Chen, J. V., Ha, Q.-A., & Vu, M. T. (2022). The Influences of Virtual Reality Shopping Characteristics on Consumers' Impulse Buying Behavior. *International Journal of Human–Computer Interaction*, 1–19. https://doi.org/10.1080/10447318.2022.2098566

Chen, L.-D., & Tan, J. (2004). Technology Adaptation in E-commerce. *European Management Journal, 22*(1), 74–86. https://doi.org/10.1016/j.emj.2003.11.014

Chen, Z., & Dubinsky, A. J. (2003). A conceptual model of perceived customer value in e-commerce: A preliminary investigation. *Psychology & Marketing, 20*(4), 323–347. https://doi.org/10.1002/mar.10076

Childers, T. L., Carr, C. L., Peck, J., & Carson, S. (2001). Hedonic and utilitarian motivations for online retail shopping behavior. *Journal of Retailing, 77*(4), 511–535. https://doi.org/10.1016/S0022-4359(01)00056-2

Chin, W. W. (1998). The partial least squares approach for structural equation modeling. In G. A. Marcoulides (Ed.), *Quantitative methodology series. Modern methods for business research* (pp. 295–358). Mahwah, NJ: Lawrence Erlbaum.

Chin, W. W., & Dibbern, J. (2010). An Introduction to a Permutation Based Procedure for Multi-Group PLS Analysis: Results of Tests of Differences on Simulated Data and a Cross Cultural Analysis of the Sourcing of Information System Services Between Germany and the USA. In V. Esposito Vinzi, W. W. Chin, J. Henseler, & H. Wang (Eds.), *Handbook of Partial Least Squares* (pp. 171–193). Berlin, Heidelberg: Springer Berlin Heidelberg. https://doi.org/10.1007/978-3-540-32827-8_8

Chittaro, L., & Ration, R. (2000). Adding Adaptive Features to Virtual Reality Interfaces for E-Commerce. In G. Goos, J. Hartmanis, J. van Leeuwen, P. Brusilovsky, O. Stock, & C. Strapparava (Eds.), *Adaptive Hypermedia and Adaptive Web-Based Systems: International Conference, AH 2000, Trento, Italy, August 28–30, 2000 Proceedings* (Vol. 1892, pp. 86–97). Berlin, Heidelberg: Springer Berlin Heidelberg. https://doi.org/10.1007/3-540-44595-1_9

Cleff, T. (2019). *Applied statistics and multivariate data analysis for business and economics: A modern approach using SPSS, Stata, and Excel.* Cham, Switzerland: Springer. https://doi.org/10.1007/978-3-030-17767-6

Cline, E. (2011). *Ready Player One.* Crown.

Clover, J. (2024). Apple Has Sold Approximately 200,000 Vision Pro Headsets. Retrieved from https://www.macrumors.com/2024/01/29/apple-vision-pro-headset-sales/

Cochran, W. G. (1977). *Sampling Techniques.* New York: John Wiley & Sons.

Cohen, J. (1988). *Statistical Power Analysis for the Behavioral Sciences* (2nd ed.). New York: y Lawrence Erlbaum Associates.

Cohen, J. (1992). Statistical Power Analysis. *Current Directions in Psychological Science, 1*(3), 98–101. https://doi.org/10.1111/1467-8721.ep10768783

Crate & Barrel (2025). Flatiron Flagship. Retrieved from https://virtualstore.crateandbarrel.com/flagship/

Darbinyan, R. (2022). Virtual Shopping In The Metaverse: What Is It And How Will AI Make It Work. Retrieved from https://www.forbes.com/sites/forbestechcouncil/2022/03/16/virtual-shopping-in-the-metaverse-what-is-it-and-how-will-ai-make-it-work/?sh=7c506bc75f27

Das, G., & Varshneya, G. (2017). Consumer emotions: Determinants and outcomes in a shop ping mall. *Journal of Retailing and Consumer Services, 38*, 177–185. https://doi.org/10.1016/j.jretconser.2017.06.008

Davis, A., Murphy, J., Owens, D., Khazanchi, D., & Zigurs, I. (2009). Avatars, People, and Virtual Worlds: Foundations for Research in Metaverses. *Journal of the Association for Information Systems, 10*(2), 90–117. https://doi.org/10.17705/1jais.00183

De Keyser, A., Lemon, K. N., Klaus, P., & Keiningham, T. L. (2015). *A Framework for Understanding and Managing the Customer Experience* (Working Paper).

Demodern (2017a). IKEA Virtual Reality Showroom. Retrieved from https://demodern.com/projects/ikea-vr-showroom

Demodern (2017b). Mazda Virtual Reality Auto Konfigurator. Retrieved from https://demodern.de/projekte/mazda-popup-vr-experience

Diamantopoulos, A. (2006). The error term in formative measurement models: interpretation and modeling implications. *Journal of Modelling in Management*, *1*(1), 7–17. https://doi.org/10.1108/17465660610667775

Diamantopoulos, A., Sarstedt, M., Fuchs, C., Wilczynski, P., & Kaiser, S. (2012). Guidelines for choosing between multi-item and single-item scales for construct measurement: a predictive validity perspective. *Journal of the Academy of Marketing Science*, *40*(3), 434–449. https://doi.org/10.1007/s11747-011-0300-3

Diamantopoulos, A., & Winklhofer, H. M. (2001). Index Construction with Formative Indicators: An Alternative to Scale Development. *Journal of Marketing Research*, *38*(2), 269–277. https://doi.org/10.1509/jmkr.38.2.269.18845

Dingwall, K. (2016). Adidas launches 360 degree shopping experience. Retrieved from https://de.fashionnetwork.com/news/Adidas-launches-360-degree-shopping-experience,767111.html

Djaiz, L. K., & Zaharia, S. (2022). *Akzeptanz von Gamification-Ansätzen im deutschen Online-Handel*. Hochschule Niederrhein, Krefeld.

Dogadkina, O. (2022). Transformed By The Metaverse, The Virtual Retail Experience Grows More Immersive And Engaging Than Ever Before. Retrieved from https://www.forbes.com/sites/forbestechcouncil/2022/07/26/transformed-by-the-metaverse-the-virtual-retail-experience-grows-more-immersive-and-engaging-than-ever-before/

Dogecoin (2024). Dogecoin: the people's cryptocurrency. Retrieved from https://dogecoin.com/

Donovan, R., & Rossiter, J. R. (1982). Store Atmosphere: An Environmental Psychology Approach. *Journal of Retailing*, *58*(1), 34–57.

The Drum Awards (2023). EY metaverse lab: helping clients identify, implement and scale Metaverse opportunities. Retrieved from https://thedrumawards.com/live/en/page/results#/metaverse/ey-metaverse-lab-helping-clients-identify-implement-and-scale-metaverse-opportunities

DuBoff, R. (2021). Bridging the Omnichannel Gap with Virtual Stores. Retrieved from https://medium.com/@rduboff/is-the-virtual-store-the-future-of-shopping-e2ce3389c2c4

Dunn, A. M., Heggestad, E. D., Shanock, L. R., & Theilgard, N. (2018). Intra-individual Response Variability as an Indicator of Insufficient Effort Responding: Comparison to Other Indicators and Relationships with Individual Differences. *Journal of Business and Psychology*, *33*(1), 105–121. https://doi.org/10.1007/s10869-016-9479-0

Dwivedi, Y. K., Hughes, L., Baabdullah, A. M., Ribeiro-Navarrete, S., Giannakis, M., Al-Debei, M. M., Wamba, S. F. (2022). Metaverse beyond the hype: Multidisciplinary perspectives on emerging challenges, opportunities, and agenda for research, practice and policy. *International Journal of Information Management*, *66*, 1–55. https://doi.org/10.1016/j.ijinfomgt.2022.102542

Dypiangco, S. (2023). The Future of Brand Monetization on Roblox is E-commerce. Retrieved from https://www.metaversemarcom.io/post/the-future-of-brand-monetization-on-roblox-is-e-commerce

Dyson Limited (2021). Dyson Demo VR: A new way to experience Dyson technology. Retrieved from https://www.dyson.com/campaigns/dyson-demo-vr/dyson-demo-vr-page

ECC Cologne, & Salesforce.com (2022). Trend Check Handel Vol. 3: Konsumententrends in Krisenzeiten. Retrieved from https://www.ifhkoeln.de/produkt/trend-check-handel/

ECC Koeln (2022). ECC Club Studie: Metaverse—Unendliche Weiten für den Handel? ECC Club Studie 2022. Retrieved from https://www.ifhkoeln.de/produkt/ecc-club-studie-2022-metaverse/

ECC Koeln, & Salesforce.com (2022). Trend Check Handel Vol. 1: Die aktuellen Krisen und ihre Folgen. Retrieved from https://www.ifhkoeln.de/produkt/trend-check-handel/

The Economist (2022). In "The Metaverse", Matthew Ball explains where the idea came from: And where it might be going. Retrieved from https://www.economist.com/culture/2022/07/27/in-the-metaverse-matthew-ball-explains-where-the-idea-came-from

Emperia (2021a). Cyberdog: Virtual store projects. Retrieved from https://emperiavr.com/project/cyberdog/

Emperia (2021b). Harrods x Burberry. Retrieved from https://emperiavr.com/project/harrods-x-burberry/

Emperia (2022a). Bloomingdale's 150th Anniversary Holiday Store. Retrieved from https://emperiavr.com/project/bloomingdales-holiday-store/#demo

Emperia (2022b). Holiday shopping in the metaverse: virtual stores. Retrieved from https://emperiavr.com/2022/10/03/holiday-shopping-in-the-metaverse-virtual-stores/

Emperia (2022c). Lacoste. Virtual Store. Retrieved from https://emperiavr.com/project/lacoste/

Emperia (2022d). Ralph Lauren Virtual Store. Bloomingdale's 150th Anniversary Bloomingdale's 150th Anniversary Holiday Store. Retrieved from https://emperiavr.com/project/ralph-lauren/#demo

Emperia (2023a). Bicester Village. Retrieved from https://emperiavr.com/project/bicester-village/#demo

Emperia (2023b). L'Occitane Christmas. Retrieved from https://emperiavr.com/project/loccitane-christmas/#demo

Emperia (2023c). Lululemon. Retrieved from https://emperiavr.com/project/lululemon/#demo

Emperia (2023d). Virtual Store Projects: Bloomingdale's Holidays. Retrieved from https://emperiavr.com/project/bloomingdales-christmas/

Emperia (2023e). Virtual Stores Projects: Tommy Hilfiger. Retrieved from https://emperiavr.com/project/tommy-hilfiger/

Emperia (2024). Immerse customers in your brand experience with Apple Vision Pro. Retrieved from https://emperiavr.com/apple-vision-pro/

Enders, C. K. (2010). *Applied missing data analysis. Methodology in the social sciences*. New York: Guilford Press.

Ericsson, K. A., & Simon, H. A. (1980). Verbal reports as data. *Psychological Review, 87*(3), 215–251. https://doi.org/10.1037/0033-295X.87.3.215

Eroglu, S. A., Machleit, K. A., & Davis, L. M. (2001). Atmospheric qualities of online retailing. *Journal of Business Research, 54*(2), 177–184. https://doi.org/10.1016/S0148-2963(99)00087-9

Falke KGaA (2023). Falke Virtual Experience. Retrieved from https://www.falke-virtual-experience.com/index.html#tp0

Fang, H., Zhang, J., Şensoy, M., & Magnenat-Thalmann, N. (2014). Reputation mechanism for e-commerce in virtual reality environments. *Electronic Commerce Research and Applications, 13*(6), 409–422. https://doi.org/10.1016/j.elerap.2014.08.002

Faul, F., Erdfelder, E., Buchner, A., & Lang, A.-G. (2009). Statistical power analyses using G*Power 3.1: Tests for correlation and regression analyses. *Behavior Research Methods, 41*(4), 1149–1160. https://doi.org/10.3758/BRM.41.4.1149

Fendi (2022). Fendi 57th Street Flagship Store New York City. Retrieved from https://fendi.obsessvr.com/57thstreetflagship-virtualstore/#/

Fendi (2024). New York 57th Street. Retrieved from https://www.fendi.com/ii-en/store-locator/united-states/595-madison-avenue

Fernando, J., Boyle, M. J., & Rathburn, P. (2023). FAANG Stocks: Definition and Companies Involved. Retrieved from https://www.investopedia.com/terms/f/faang-stocks.asp

Fishbein, M., & Ajzen, I. (1975). *Belief, attitude, intention and behavior: An introduction to theory and research. Addison-Wesley series in social psychology*. Reading, Mass.: Addison-Wesley. Retrieved from https://people.umass.edu/aizen/f&a1975.html

Fließ, S., Hogreve, J., & Nonnenmacher, D. (2005). Die emotionale Wirkung von Schaufenstern auf das Kaufverhalten. *Transfer*. (3), 26–31. Retrieved from https://www.researchgate.net/profile/Sabine-Fliess/publication/257637156_Die_emotionale_Wirkung_von_Schaufenstern_auf_das_Kaufverhalten/links/5620deeb08ae93a5c9251d39/Die-emotionale-Wirkung-von-Schaufenstern-auf-das-Kaufverhalten.pdf

Flora, L. (2023). Elizabeth Arden uses generative AI for new virtual store launch. Retrieved from https://www.glossy.co/beauty/elizabeth-arden-uses-generative-ai-for-new-virtual-store-launch/

Fonrouge, G. (2023). Retailers are gamifying shopping with virtual storefronts to boost engagement, loyalty. Retrieved from https://www.cnbc.com/2023/06/09/j-crew-launches-virtual-beach-house-storefront-for-40th-anniversary.html

Fornell, C., & Bookstein, F. L. (1982). Two Structural Equation Models: LISREL and PLS Applied to Consumer Exit-Voice Theory. *Journal of Marketing Research, 19*(4), 440. https://doi.org/10.2307/3151718

Forrester Research, Inc. (2014). Amazon Leads In Forrester's First UK Customer Experience Index. Retrieved from https://www.forrester.com/blogs/amazon-leads-in-forresters-first-uk-customer-experience-index/

Forum.smartpls.com (2022). High Significance but Low R2,f2 and q2—is this normal? Retrieved from https://forum.smartpls.com/viewtopic.php?t=3701

Foscht, T., Swoboda, B., & Schramm-Klein, H. (2017). *Käuferverhalten: Grundlagen—Perspektiven—Anwendungen* (6th ed.). Wiesbaden: Springer Fachmedien. https://doi.org/10.1007/978-3-658-17465-1

Freter, H. (2008). *Markt- und Kundensegmentierung: Kundenorientierte Markterfassung und -bearbeitung* (2nd ed.). *Kohlhammer Edition Marketing*. Stuttgart: Kohlhammer.

Gal, D., & Rucker, D. D. (2011). Answering the Unasked Question: Response Substitution in Consumer Surveys. *Journal of Marketing Research, 48*(1), 185–195. https://doi.org/10.1509/jmkr.48.1.185

Gandzeichuk, I. (2022). The Future Of Virtual Shopping Malls: What will a virtual shopping mall look like? Retrieved from https://www.forbes.com/sites/forbestechcouncil/2022/02/25/the-future-of-virtual-shopping-malls/

Gentile, C., Spiller, N., & Noci, G. (2007). How to Sustain the Customer Experience: An Overview of Experience Components that Co-create Value With the Customer. *European Management Journal*, *25*(5), 395–410. https://doi.org/10.1016/j.emj.2007.08.005

Gesellschaft für integrierte Kommunikationsforschung (2022). Best for Planning (b4p). Retrieved from https://gik.media/best-4-planning/

Gibson, W. (1994). *Neuromancer: Roman* (10th ed.). *Heyne-Bücher 01, Heyne allgemeine Reihe: Nr. 8449*. München: Heyne.

Givenchy (2022). Willkommen im Givenchy Beauty House. Retrieved from https://www.givenchybeauty.com/de/de/maison/givenchy-beauty-house-roblox.html?srsltid=AfmBOoolCOrVfVcC1ky1EwoOf_PoAbpVQGmuSjEpU4IVcJKmqcCY1nU2

Goel, L., & Prokopec, S. (2009). If you build it will they come?—An empirical investigation of consumer perceptions and strategy in virtual worlds. *Electronic Commerce Research*, *9*(1–2), 115–134. https://doi.org/10.1007/s10660-009-9031-7

Goodhue, Lewis, & Thompson (2012). Does PLS Have Advantages for Small Sample Size or Non-Normal Data? *MIS Quarterly*, *36*(3), 981–1001. https://doi.org/10.2307/41703490

Grand View Research (2021). B2C E-commerce Market Size, Share & Trends Analysis Report. Retrieved from https://www.grandviewresearch.com/industry-analysis/b2c-e-commerce-market

Grand View Research (2023a). E-commerce Industry Data Book: B2B E-commerce and B2C E-commerce Market Size, Share, Trends Report E-commerce Industry Data Book. Retrieved from https://www.grandviewresearch.com/sector-report/e-commerce-industry-data-book

Grand View Research (2023b). Metaverse Market Size, Share & Trends Analysis Report 2030. Retrieved from https://www.grandviewresearch.com/industry-analysis/metaverse-market-report

Grayston, D. (1974). MUSIC WHILE YOU WORK. *Industrial Management*, *74*(6), 38–39. https://doi.org/10.1108/eb056423

Gregor, S. (2006). The Nature of Theory in Information Systems. *MIS Quarterly*, *30*(3), 611–642. Retrieved from http://www.jstor.org/stable/25148742.

Grewal, D. [Dhruv], Baker, J. [Julie], Levy, M., & Voss, G. B. (2003). The effects of wait expectations and store atmosphere evaluations on patronage intentions in service-intensive retail stores. *Journal of Retailing*, *79*(4), 259–268. https://doi.org/10.1016/j.jretai.2003.09.006

Gröppel-Klein, A. (1991). *Erlebnisstrategien im Einzelhandel: Analyse der Zielgruppen, der Ladengestaltung und der Warenpräsentation zur Vermittlung von Einkaufserlebnissen*. Zugl.: Paderborn, Univ., Diss., 1990. *Konsum und Verhalten: Vol. 29*. Heidelberg: Physica-Verl.

Gröppel-Klein, A. (2012). Point-of-Sale-Marketing. In J. Zentes, B. Swoboda, D. Morschett, & H. Schramm-Klein (Eds.), *Handbuch Handel. Strategien—Perspektiven—Internationaler Wettbewerb* (2nd ed., pp. 645–669). Wiesbaden: Springer Gabler.

GS1 Germany (2018). Category Management im Omni-Channel Retailing. Retrieved from https://www.gs1-germany.de/gs1-standards/umsetzung/fachpublikationen/detailansicht/75365/

Gucci (2021). Gucci Garden auf Roblox. Retrieved from https://www.gucci.com/ch/de/st/stories/article/gucci-gaming-roblox?srsltid=AfmBOorpb2unErMHj_ashnp_DYgm4LgjTMmT8BWEyqL2VD6ps3BulMW8

Gucci (2022). Welcome to Gucci Town. Retrieved from https://www.gucci.com/us/en/st/stories/article/gucci-town-on-roblox?srsltid=AfmBOoqL3mapJzywx-NdxQZgjUAOVjw7rkDuipnDcSc0KAp6W5Kq5Mrl

Gucci (2023). Gucci Visions. Retrieved from https://guccipalazzo.gucci.com/#/en/

Gucci (2024). Gucci Cosmos Land. Retrieved from https://www.gucci.com/de/de/st/stories/article/cosmos-london-sandbox?srsltid=AfmBOorySyDivE8dGyrd8GengDdRQHzK6KTz8wLM7WFYN4ODMi0XUM_k

Gudergan, S. P., Ringle, C. M., Wende, S., & Will, A. (2008). Confirmatory tetrad analysis in PLS path modeling. *Journal of Business Research, 61*(12), 1238–1249. https://doi.org/10.1016/j.jbusres.2008.01.012

Guibert, S. (2023). The Metaverse: Opportunities for business operations. Drive immersive, augmented experiences across your organization. Retrieved from https://prod.ucwe.capgemini.com/wp-content/uploads/2023/03/The-Metaverse.-Opportunities-for-Business-Operations.pdf

Gupta, S. [Sudheer], & Vajic, M. (2000). The Contextual and Dialectical Nature of Experiences. In J. Fitzsimmons & M. Fitzsimmons (Eds.), *New Service Development: Creating Memorable Experiences* (pp. 33–51). 2455 Teller Road, Thousand Oaks California 91320 United States: SAGE Publications, Inc. https://doi.org/10.4135/9781452205564.n2

Gurman, M. (2024). Apple's Vision Pro Is Latest Bid to Prove Consumers Can Embrace Headsets. Retrieved from https://www.bloomberg.com/news/articles/2024-01-31/apple-s-vision-pro-is-latest-bid-to-prove-consumers-can-embrace-headsets

Gutkuhn, J. (2022). Erster virtueller Showroom von H&M. Retrieved from https://www.deptagency.com/de-de/insight/hm-kooperiert-mit-dept-und-journee-fur-den-launch-des-ersten-eigenen-virtuellen-showrooms/

Haas, E. (2022). Book Review: The Metaverse and How it will Revolutionize Everything by Matthew Ball. Retrieved from https://www.sps.nyu.edu/homepage/metaverse/metaverse-blog/book-review-the-metaverse-and-how-it-will-revolutionize-everything-by-matthew-ball.html

Hackl, C. (2021). Defining the Metaverse today. Retrieved from https://www.forbes.com/sites/cathyhackl/2021/05/02/defining-the-metaverse-today/

Hackl, C. (2022). Metaverse Commerce: Understanding The New Virtual To Physical And Physical To Virtual Commerce Models. Retrieved from https://www.forbes.com/sites/cathyhackl/2022/07/05/metaverse-commerce-understanding-the-new-virtual-to-physical-and-physical-to-virtual-commerce-models/?sh=4be443175632

Hackl, C. (2023). *Into the Metaverse*. Great Britain: Bloomsbury Publishing Plc.

Haeusel, H.-G. (2012). Ladengestaltung: Wie man emotionale PoS-Welten inszeniert. In J. Zentes, B. Swoboda, D. Morschett, & H. Schramm-Klein (Eds.), *Handbuch Handel: Strategien—Perspektiven—Internationaler Wettbewerb* (2nd ed., pp. 631–644). Wiesbaden: Springer Gabler.

Hair, J. F. [Joe F.], Ringle, C. M., & Sarstedt, M. (2011). PLS-SEM: Indeed a Silver Bullet. *Journal of Marketing Theory and Practice, 19*(2), 139–152. https://doi.org/10.2753/MTP1069-6679190202

Hair, J., Black, W., Babin, B., & Anderson, R. (2010). *Multivariate Data Analysis: A Global Perspective* (7th ed.). New Jersey: Pearson.

Hair, J. F., Hult, G. T. M., Ringle, C. M., & Sarstedt, M. (2022). *A Primer on Partial Least Squares Structural Equation Modeling (PLS-SEM)* (3rd ed.). Thousand Oaks: Sage.

Hair, J. F., Hult, G. M., Ringle, C. M., Sarstedt, M., Richter, N. F., & Hauff, S. (2017). *Partial Least Squares Strukturgleichungsmodellierung: Eine anwendungsorientierte Einführung*. München: Verlag Franz Vahlen.

Hair, J. F., & Sarstedt, M. (2019). Factors versus Composites: Guidelines for Choosing the Right Structural Equation Modeling Method. *Project Management Journal, 50*(6), 619–624. https://doi.org/10.1177/8756972819882132

Hair, J. F., Sarstedt, M., Ringle, C. M., & Gudergan, S. (2024). *Advanced issues in partial least squares structural equation modeling* (2nd ed.). Thousand Oaks, California: Sage.

Hair, J. F., Sarstedt, M., Ringle, C. M., & Mena, J. A. (2012). An assessment of the use of partial least squares structural equation modeling in marketing research. *Journal of the Academy of Marketing Science, 40*(3), 414–433. https://doi.org/10.1007/s11747-011-0261-6

Hair, J. F., Jr., Hult, G. T. M., Ringle, C. M., Sarstedt, M., Danks, N. P. [Nicholas P.], & Ray, S. [Soumaya] (2021). *Partial Least Squares Structural Equation Modeling (PLS-SEM) Using R: A Workbook*. Cham: Springer International Publishing. https://doi.org/10.1007/978-3-030-80519-7

Hake, M., Coeper, C., Otschik, T., Schuhmann, J., & Zaharia, S. (2023). *Determinants of the Acceptance of Meta-Commerce: A qualitative study* (Research Project). Hochschule Niederrhein, Krefeld.

Hanson, J. (2021). Meet Obsess, The Company Powering An Immersive E-Commerce Revolution For Holiday And Beyond. Retrieved from https://www.forbes.com/sites/janehanson/2021/11/24/meet-obsess-the-company-powering-an-immersive-e-commerce-revolution-for-holiday-and-beyond/

Havlena, W. J., & Holbrook, M. B. (1986). The Varieties of Consumption Experience: Comparing Two Typologies of Emotion in Consumer Behavior. *Journal of Consumer Research, 13*(3), 394. https://doi.org/10.1086/209078

HCI International 2024 (2024). VAMR 2024: 16th International Conference On Virtual, Augmented And Mixed Reality. Retrieved from https://2024.hci.international/cfp/CfP_VAMR_2024.pdf

Heinemann, G. (2022). *Der neue Online-Handel: Geschäftsmodelle, Geschäftssysteme und Benchmarks im E-Commerce* (13th ed.). Wiesbaden: Springer Fachmedien Wiesbaden. https://doi.org/10.1007/978-3-658-36665-0

Henseler, J., Ringle, C. M., & Sarstedt, M. (2015). A new criterion for assessing discriminant validity in variance-based structural equation modeling. *Journal of the Academy of Marketing Science, 43*(1), 115–135. https://doi.org/10.1007/s11747-014-0403-8

Henseler, J., Ringle, C. M., & Sinkovics, R. R. (2009). The use of partial least squares path modeling in international marketing. In R. R. Sinkovics & P. N. Ghauri (Eds.), *New Challenges to International Marketing* (Vol. 20, pp. 277–319). Emerald Group Publishing Limited. https://doi.org/10.1108/S1474-7979(2009)0000020014

Hirschman, E. C., & Holbrook, M. B. (1982). Hedonic Consumption: Emerging Concepts, Methods and Propositions. *Journal of Marketing, 46*(3), 92–101. https://doi.org/10.1177/002224298204600314

Hoaglin, D. C., & Iglewicz, B. (1987). Fine-Tuning Some Resistant Rules for Outlier Labeling. *Journal of the American Statistical Association, 82*(400), 1147–1149. https://doi.org/10.2307/2289392

Hofacker, L., & Hübner, P. (2022). Metaverse im Handel. EHI Whitepaper. Retrieved from https://www.ehi.org/produkt/whitepaper-metaverse-im-handel/

Hoffman, D. L., & Novak, T. P. (2018). Consumer and Object Experience in the Internet of Things: An Assemblage Theory Approach. *Journal of Consumer Research, 44*(6), 1178–1204. https://doi.org/10.1093/jcr/ucx105

Homburg, C. (2017). *Marketingmanagement: Strategie—Instrumente—Umsetzung—Unternehmensführung* (6th ed.). Wiesbaden: Springer Fachmedien Wiesbaden. https://doi.org/10.1007/978-3-658-13656-7

Homburg, C. (2020). *Marketingmanagement: Strategie—Instrumente—Umsetzung—Unternehmensführung* (7th ed.). Wiesbaden: Springer Fachmedien Wiesbaden. https://doi.org/10.1007/978-3-658-29636-0

Homburg, C., & Giering (1996), A. Konzeptualisierung und Operationalisierung komplexer Konstrukte: Ein Leitfaden für die Marketingforschung. *Journal of Research and Management, 18*(1), 5–24.

Hugo Boss (2023). Boss enters metaverse fashion week with an immersive, ai-inspired showroom experience. Press Release. Retrieved from https://group.hugoboss.com/en/newsroom/news/news-detail/boss-enters-metaverse-fashion-week-with-an-immersive-ai-inspired-showroom-experience

Hulland, J. (1999). Use of partial least squares (PLS) in strategic management research: a review of four recent studies. *Strategic Management Journal, 20*(2), 195–204. https://doi.org/10.1002/(SICI)1097-0266(199902)20:2<195::AID-SMJ13>3.0.CO;2-7

Hulland, J., Baumgartner, H., & Smith, K. M. (2018). Marketing survey research best practices: evidence and recommendations from a review of JAMS articles. *Journal of the Academy of Marketing Science, 46*(1), 92–108. https://doi.org/10.1007/s11747-017-0532-y

Hwang, H., Sarstedt, M., Cho, G., Choo, H., & Ringle, C. M. (2023). A primer on integrated generalized structured component analysis. *European Business Review, 35*(3), 261–284. https://doi.org/10.1108/ebr-11-2022-0224

Hwang, H., & Takane, Y. (2004). Generalized structured component analysis. *Psychometrika, 69*(1), 81–99. https://doi.org/10.1007/BF02295841

Iacobucci, D., & Churchill, G. A. (2018). *Marketing research: Methodological foundations* (12th ed.). Nashville, TN: Earlie Lite Books.

Igbaria, M., Guimaraes, T., & Davis, G. B. (1995). Testing the Determinants of Microcomputer Usage via a Structural Equation Model. *Journal of Management Information Systems, 11*(4), 87–114. https://doi.org/10.1080/07421222.1995.11518061

IMDb (2024a). Ready Player One. Retrieved from https://www.imdb.com/title/tt1677720/

IMDb (2024b). Steven Spielberg. Retrieved from https://www.imdb.com/name/nm0000229/bio/?ref_=nm_ov_bio_sm

Interaction Design Foundation (2016a). Skeuomorphism: What is Skeuomorphism? Retrieved from https://www.interaction-design.org/literature/topics/skeuomorphism

Interaction Design Foundation (2016b). What is Ease of Use? Retrieved from https://www.interaction-design.org/literature/topics/ease-of-use

Interbrand (2023). Interbrand launches 2023 Breakthrough Brands Report revealing the emerging brands disrupting the global market. Retrieved from https://interbrand.com/newsroom/interbrand-launches-2023-breakthrough-brands-report-revealing-the-emerging-brands-disrupting-the-global-market/

Janssen, J., & Laatz, W. (2017). *Statistische Datenanalyse mit SPSS*. Berlin, Heidelberg: Springer Berlin Heidelberg. https://doi.org/10.1007/978-3-662-53477-9

Jarvis, C. B., MacKenzie, S. B., & Podsakoff, P. M. (2003). A Critical Review of Construct Indicators and Measurement Model Misspecification in Marketing and Consumer Research. *Journal of Consumer Research, 30*(2), 199–218. https://doi.org/10.1086/376806

Javornik, A. (2016). Augmented reality: Research agenda for studying the impact of its media characteristics on consumer behaviour. *Journal of Retailing and Consumer Services, 30*, 252–261. https://doi.org/10.1016/j.jretconser.2016.02.004

JD Sports (2020). Use Nike Virtual View to try the Need It Now Icon Clash collection before you buy. Retrieved from https://blog.jdsports.com/nike-need-it-now-icon-collection/

Jin, B., Kim, G., Moore, M., & Rothenberg, L. (2021). Consumer store experience through virtual reality: its effect on emotional states and perceived store attractiveness. *Fashion and Textiles, 19*(8), 1–21. https://doi.org/10.1186/s40691-021-00256-7

Kang, H. J., Shin, J., & Ponto, K. (2020). How 3D Virtual Reality Stores Can Shape Consumer Purchase Decisions: The Roles of Informativeness and Playfulness. *Journal of Interactive Marketing, 49*(1), 70–85. https://doi.org/10.1016/j.intmar.2019.07.002

Kemmer, J., Schweiger, S., & Taubert, J. (2023). Studie zu den Anforderungen und Erwartungen der Generation Z an den Einzelhandel. Retrieved from https://publica-rest.fraunhofer.de/server/api/core/bitstreams/6e301bcb-d98f-4497-859e-4ac3f8962ffc/content

Khan, R. (2022). Metaverse—Revolutionizing How Consumers Shop. Retrieved from https://www.forbes.com/sites/roomykhan/2022/07/12/metaverserevolutionizing-how-consumers-shop/

Kim, J.-H., Kim, M., Park, M., & Yoo, J. (2023). Immersive interactive technologies and virtual shopping experiences: Differences in consumer perceptions between augmented reality (AR) and virtual reality (VR). *Telematics and Informatics, 77*, 1–15. https://doi.org/10.1016/j.tele.2022.101936

Kirst, N. (2022). Erlebniswelt Retail: Douglas wird opulent. Retrieved from https://page-online.de/kreation/erlebniswelt-retail-douglas-wird-opulent/

Kock, N., & Hadaya, P. (2018). Minimum sample size estimation in PLS-SEM: The inverse square root and gamma-exponential methods. *Information Systems Journal, 28*(1), 227–261. https://doi.org/10.1111/isj.12131

Kollmann, T. (2019). *E-Business: Grundlagen elektronischer Geschäftsprozesse in der Digitalen Wirtschaft* (7th ed.). Wiesbaden: Springer Fachmedien. https://doi.org/10.1007/978-3-658-26143-6

Krasonikolakis, I., Vrechopoulos, A., & Pouloudi, A. (2014). Store selection criteria and sales prediction in virtual worlds. Information & Management, 51 (6), pp. 641–652.

Krasonikolakis, I., Vrechopoulos, A., Pouloudi, A., & Dimitriadis, S. (2018). Store layout effects on consumer behavior in 3D online stores. *European Journal of Marketing, 52*(5/6), 1223–1256. https://doi.org/10.1108/EJM-03-2015-0183

Krasonikolakis, I. G., & Vrechopoulos, A. (2009). Setting The Research Agenda For Store Atmosphere Studies In Virtual Reality Retailing: An Interdisciplinary Approach. *MCIS 2009 Proceedings, 115*. Retrieved from http://aisel.aisnet.org/mcis2009/115

Krasonikolakis, I. G., Vrechopoulos, A., & Pouloudi, A. (2011). Defining, Applying and Customizing Store Atmosphere in Virtual Reality Commerce. *International Journal of E-Services and Mobile Applications, 3*(2), 59–72. https://doi.org/10.4018/jesma.2011040104

Kreis, H., Wildner, R., & Kuß, A. (2021). *Marktforschung: Datenerhebung und Datenanalyse* (7th ed.). Wiesbaden: Springer Fachmedien Wiesbaden. https://doi.org/10.1007/978-3-658-32459-9

Kroeber-Riel, W., Weinberg, P., & Gröppel-Klein, A. (2009). *Konsumentenverhalten* (9th ed.). *Vahlens Handbücher der Wirtschafts- und Sozialwissenschaften*. München: Verlag Franz Vahlen.

Lacoste (2023). Lacoste Virtual Holiday Store. Retrieved from https://www.lacoste.com/us/virtual-store.html

Lam, L. W. (2012). Impact of competitiveness on salespeople's commitment and performance. *Journal of Business Research, 65*(9), 1328–1334. https://doi.org/10.1016/j.jbusres.2011.10.026

Larson, K. (2021). E-Commerce Leader Obsess Takes Virtual Shopping To The Next Level With Latest Funding Round. Retrieved from https://www.forbes.com/sites/kristinlarson/2021/06/29/e-commerce-leader-obsess-takes-virtual-shopping-to-the-next-level-with-latest-funding-round/

Lassak, F. (1995). Zum Online-Shopping in die virtuelle Stadt: Start die Agentur Multiversum Media Lab, Hamburg, baut eine Stadt im Internet. *Werben Und Verkaufen (W&V)*. (14), 36.

Latan, H., Hair, J. F. Jr., Noonan, R., & Sabol, M. (2023). Path Modeling: Basic Concepts and Recent Methodological Enhancements. In H. Latan, J. F. Hair, & R. Noonan (Eds.), *Partial Least Squares Path Modeling: Basic Concepts, Methodological Issues and Applications* (2nd ed., pp. 3–22). Cham: Springer International Publishing.

Lau, K. W., & Lee, P. Y. (2018). Shopping in virtual reality: a study on consumers' shopping experience in a stereoscopic virtual reality. *Virtual Reality, 23*(3), 255–268. https://doi.org/10.1007/s10055-018-0362-3

Lee, A. (2022). Exclusive: Crocs Dishes On Its Fuzz-lined Vision of Virtual Holiday Shopping. Retrieved from https://wwd.com/business-news/technology/exclusive-crocs-virtual-holiday-store-obsess-1235414948/

Lee, K. C., & Chung, N. (2008). Empirical analysis of consumer reaction to the virtual reality shopping mall. *Computers in Human Behavior, 24*(1), 88–104. https://doi.org/10.1016/j.chb.2007.01.018

Lee, L.-H., Braud, T., Zhou, P., Wang, L., Xu, D., Lin, Z., . . . Hui, P. (2021). All One Needs to Know about Metaverse: A Complete Survey on Technological Singularity, Virtual Ecosystem, and Research Agenda. *ArXiv, 14*(8), 1–66.

Leipe, J. (2023). Aldimania im Metaverse: Aldi Süd überrascht mit neuer Kollektion für den Sommer. Retrieved from https://www.aldi-sued.de/de/newsroom/alle-pressemitteilungen/marke-und-produkte/2023/ALDImania-im-Metaverse-ALDI-SUED-ueberrascht-mit-neuer-Kollektion-fuer-den-Sommer.html

Lemon, K. N., & Verhoef, P. C. (2016). Understanding Customer Experience Throughout the Customer Journey. *Journal of Marketing, 80*(6), 69–96. Retrieved from https://doi.org/10.1509/jm.15.0420

Li, H., Daugherty, T., & Biocca, F. (2001). Characteristics of Virtual Experience in Electronic Commerce: A Protocol Analysis. *Journal of Interactive Marketing, 15*(3), 13–30. https://doi.org/10.1002/dir.1013

Lietz, P. (2010). Research into Questionnaire Design: A Summary of the Literature. *International Journal of Market Research, 52*(2), 249–272. https://doi.org/10.2501/S147078530920120X

Linden Research, Inc. (2023). Second Life. Retrieved from https://secondlife.com/

Lockwood, L. (2023). Bloomingdale's Ties In With "Wonka" for "Best Holiday Ever" Promotion. Retrieved from https://wwd.com/business-news/retail/bloomingdales-partners-with-wonka-for-best-holiday-ever-promotion-1235909131/

Lohmöller, J.-B. (1989). *Latent Variable Path Modeling with Partial Least Squares*. Heidelberg: Physica-Verlag HD. https://doi.org/10.1007/978-3-642-52512-4

Lombard, M., & Ditton, T. (1997). At the Heart of It All: The Concept of Presence. *Journal of Computer-Mediated Communication, 3*(2). https://doi.org/10.1111/j.1083-6101.1997.tb00072.x

Lorenz-Spreen, P., Mønsted, B. M., Hövel, P., & Lehmann, S. [Sune] (2019). Accelerating dynamics of collective attention. *Nature Communications, 10*(1), 1–9. https://doi.org/10.1038/s41467-019-09311-w

Lucas, J. W. (2003). Theory-Testing, Generalization, and the Problem of External Validity. *Sociological Theory, 21*(3), 236–253. https://doi.org/10.1111/1467-9558.00187

Ludmir, C. (2024). A First Look Into Brands' Shopping Experiences on Apple's Vision Pro. Retrieved from https://www.forbes.com/sites/claraludmir/2024/02/06/a-first-look-into-brands-shopping-experiences-on-apples-vision-pro/

Lynch, J. G. (1999). Theory and External Validity. *Journal of the Academy of Marketing Science, 27*(3), 367–376. https://doi.org/10.1177/0092070399273007

Lynch, J. J. G. (1982). On the External Validity of Experiments in Consumer Research. *Journal of Consumer Research, 9*(3), 225. https://doi.org/10.1086/208919

Maas, R. (2019). *Generation Z für Personaler und Führungskräfte: Ergebnisse der Generation-Thinking-Studie*. München: Carl Hanser Verlag GmbH & Co. KG. https://doi.org/10.3139/9783446462397

Mango (2024). Mango strengthens its commitment to innovation by entering Roblox: Nota Prensa. Retrieved from https://www.mangofashiongroup.com/en/w/mango-afianza-su apuesta-por-la-innovaci%C3%B3n-con-su-entrada-en-roblox?p_l_back_url=%2Fen%2Fpress-releases

Mantzios, M. (2023). Dark Mode vs. Light Mode: The UX debate settled. Retrieved from https://www.fastcompany.com/90961802/dark-mode-vs-light-mode-ux-debate-settled

Marcoulides, G. A., & Chin, W. W. (2013). You Write, but Others Read: Common Methodological Misunderstandings in PLS and Related Methods. In H. Abdi, W. W. Chin, V. Esposito Vinzi, G. Russolillo, & L. Trinchera (Eds.), *New Perspectives in Partial Least Squares and Related Methods* (Vol. 56, pp. 31–64). New York, NY: Springer New York. https://doi.org/10.1007/978-1-4614-8283-3_2

Marin-Lopez, X. (2023). Obsess launches self-service virtual store builder for brands. Retrieved from Obsess launches self-service virtual store builder for brands

Marr, B. (2022). The 10 Best Examples Of The Metaverse Everyone Should Know About. Retrieved from https://www.forbes.com/sites/bernardmarr/2022/05/16/the-10-best-examples-of-the-metaverse-everyone-should-know-about/

Martínez-López, F. J., Pla-García, C., Gázquez-Abad, J. C., & Rodríguez-Ardura, I. (2014). Utilitarian motivations in online consumption: Dimensional structure and scales. *Electronic Commerce Research and Applications, 13*(3), 188–204. https://doi.org/10.1016/j.elerap.2014.02.002

Matovina, S., Johns, E., Ward, M., & Dalton, P. (2016). World's First Virtual Reality Department Store. Retrieved from https://www.ebayinc.com/stories/press-room/au/worlds-first-virtual-reality-department-store/

Mattila, A. S., & Wirtz, J. (2001). Congruency of scent and music as a driver of in-store evaluations and behavior. *Journal of Retailing, 77*(2), 273–289. https://doi.org/10.1016/S0022-4359(01)00042-2

McDowell, M. (2020). What to know about virtual stores. Retrieved from https://www.voguebusiness.com/technology/what-to-know-about-virtual-stores

McKinsey & Company (2022a). Studie: Das Metaverse kann bis 2030 einen Wert von bis zu 5 Billionen Dollar erreichen. Pressemitteilung. Retrieved from https://www.mckinsey.de/~/media/mckinsey/locations/europe and middle east/deutschland/news/presse/2022/2022–06–21 metaverse/220621 pm metaverse.pdf

McKinsey & Company (2022b). Value creation in the metaverse: The real buisness of the virtual world.

McMillen, J. (2023). Virtual Store Fronts Are Expanding: 'Avamalls' Could Be Next. Retrieved from https://www.forbes.com/sites/jennmcmillen/2023/06/26/virtual-store-fronts-are-expanding-avamalls-could-be-next/?sh=2867befd1f4e

Meffert, H., Burmann, C., Kirchgeorg, M., & Eisenbeiß, M. (2024). *Marketing: Grundlagen marktorientierter Unternehmensführung Konzepte—Instrumente—Praxisbeispiele.* Wiesbaden: Springer Fachmedien Wiesbaden. https://doi.org/10.1007/978-3-658-41755-0

Meta Platforms, Inc. (2021a). Connect 2021: Our vision for the metaverse. Reality Labs. Retrieved from https://tech.facebook.com/reality-labs/2021/10/connect-2021-our-vision-for-the-metaverse/

Meta Platforms, Inc. (2021b). Dyson VR Demo. Retrieved from https://www.meta.com/en-gb/experiences/6327037827369470/

Meta Platforms, Inc. (2023a). New Meta Avatar Outfits From Naomi Osaka. Retrieved from https://about.fb.com/news/2023/05/meta-avatar-outfits-naomi-osaka/

Meta Platforms, Inc. (2023b). What is the Metaverse? Retrieved from https://about.meta.com/what-is-the-metaverse/

Meta Platforms, Inc. (2024). Express yourself with Meta avatars. Retrieved from https://www.meta.com/de/en/avatars/

Meyer, C., & Schwager, A. (2007). Understanding Customer Experience. *Harvard Business Review, 85*(2), 116–126, 157.

Milgram, P., & Kishino, F. (1994). A Taxonomy of Mixed Reality Visual Displays. *IEICE Trans. Information Systems, E77-D*(12), 1321–1329.

Milgram, P., Takemura, H., Utsumi, A., & Kishino, F. (1994). Augmented Reality: A class of displays on the reality-virtuality continuum. *Proceedings of SPIE, 2351*, 282–292. https://doi.org/10.1117/12.197321

Milliman, R. E. (1982). Using Background Music to Affect the Behavior of Supermarket Shoppers. *Journal of Marketing*, *46*(3), 86. https://doi.org/10.2307/1251706

Minsky, M. (1980). Telepresence. *OMNI Magazine*, pp. 44–52. Retrieved from https://web.media.mit.edu/~minsky/papers/Telepresence.html

MIT Technology Review Insights, & Siemens (2023). The emergent industrial metaverse: An interface between the real and digital worlds will transform how we work, live, and interact. Retrieved from https://www.siemens.com/global/en/company/digital-transformation/industrial-metaverse/the-emergent-industrial-metaverse.html?gclid=EAIaIQobChMIzaDvoa_-ggMV6paDBx2NvwwbEAAYAiAAEgIJSfD_BwE&acz=1&gad_source=1

Morris, T. (2022). Just what's happening with the metaverse? Retrieved from https://blog.gwi.com/chart-of-the-week/metaverse-predictions/

Moser, C. A., & Stuart, A. (1953). An Experimental Study of Quota Sampling. *Journal of the Royal Statistical Society. Series a (General)*, *116*(4), 349. https://doi.org/10.2307/2343021

Mull, J. (2023). 4 ways to leverage social proof in marketing. Retrieved from https://www.forbes.com/sites/forbesbusinessdevelopmentcouncil/2023/06/30/4-ways-to-leverage-social-proof-in-marketing/

Munir, A., Kear, A., Abdul, A., & J., B. (2018). The Effect of Music on Shoppers' Shopping Behaviour in Virtual Reality Retail Stores: Mediation Analysis. *International Journal of Advanced Computer Science and Applications*, *9*(1). https://doi.org/10.14569/IJACSA.2018.090118

MVFW (2023). Decentraland Metaverse Fashion Week 2023. Retrieved from https://mvfw.org/

The Myer-Briggs Company (2024). MBTI® personality types: The 16 Myers-Briggs Type Indicator® (MBTI®) personality types. Retrieved from https://eu.themyersbriggs.com/en/tools/MBTI/MBTI-personality-Types

Namogoo (2022). Top influencers weigh in: E-Commerce trends to watch in 2023. Blog. Retrieved from https://www.namogoo.com/blog/top-influencers-weigh-in-ecommerce-trends-to-watch-in-2023/

Nasermoadeli, A., Ling, K. C., & Maghnati, F. (2013). Evaluating the Impacts of Customer Experience on Purchase Intention. *International Journal of Business and Management*, *8*(6), 128–138. https://doi.org/10.5539/ijbm.v8n6p128

Nie, Norman H., Bent, Dale H., Hull, C. Hadlai (2022). IBM SPSS Statistics (Version 29.0.0) [Computer software]. IBM; IBM. Retrieved from https://www.ibm.com/support/pages/downloading-ibm-spss-statistics-29

NIKE, Inc. (2020). Nike Virtual View: Need it Now. Retrieved from https://nikevirtualview.com/needitnow/index.html

NIKE, Inc. (2021). Nikeland auf Roblox: Das Nike Footballverse wartet auf dich. Retrieved from https://www.nike.com/de/kinder/nikeland-roblox

NIKE, Inc. (2023). Nike Virtual Studios and EA SPORTS Will Bring.SWOOSH Virtual Creations to EA SPORTS Experiences. Retrieved from https://about.nike.com/en/newsroom/releases/nike-virtual-studios-dot-swoosh-ea-sports-partnership

Nokia, & Ipsos (2022). Gen Z and the metaverse: A multi-market study on how Gen Z currently experience the metaverse and the role they want to play in its future.

Novak, T. P., Hoffman, D. L., & Yung, Y.-F. (2000). Measuring the Customer Experience in Online Environments: A Structural Modeling Approach. *Marketing Science*, *19*(1), 22–42. https://doi.org/10.1287/mksc.19.1.22.15184

Obsess (2020). Virtual Store Spotlight: The Ralph Lauren Virtual Experience. Retrieved from https://obsessar.com/blog-ralph-lauren-virtual-stores/

Obsess (2021a). How to create a shoppable virtual tour of your retail store. Retrieved from https://obsessar.com/blog-retail-store-shoppable-virtual-tour/

Obsess (2021b). The metaverse is the new mall. Retrieved from https://obsessar.com/blog-the-metaverse-is-the-new-mall/

Obsess (2021c). What is a Virtual Store? Retrieved from https://obsessar.com/blog-what-is-a-virtual-store/

Obsess (2022a). Four ways to cut costs with virtual stores. Retrieved from https://obsessar.com/blog-cut-costs-with-virtual-stores/

Obsess (2022b). How the metaverse can help the retail industry with sustainability. Retrieved from https://obsessar.com/blog-metaverse-can-help-sustainable-shopping/

Obsess (2022c). The latest in footwear: The Crocs virtual jibbitz experience. Retrieved from https://obsessar.com/blog-crocs-virtual-jibbitz-experience/

Obsess (2023a). Amplify the reach of physical retail through shoppable virtual stores. Retrieved from https://obsessar.com/virtualized-retail-stores/

Obsess (2023b). Integrate your e-commerce site with a virtual store. Retrieved from https://obsessar.com/feature-ecommerce-integration/

Obsess (2023c). Introducing: Branded Avatars, a first-of-its-kind custom avatar technology by Obsess. Retrieved from https://obsessar.com/blog-branded-avatars/

Obsess (2023d). Ready-to-use virtual store templates. Retrieved from https://obsessar.com/ready-to-use-virtual-store-templates/

Obsess (2023e). Top 5 Features That Drive Engagement in Virtual. Retrieved from https://obsessar.com/blog-top-features-that-drive-engagement/

Obsess (2023f). Virtual Store Spotlight: Crate & Barrel Flagship for Furniture and Homeware. Retrieved from https://obsessar.com/blog-crate-and-barrel-home-virtual-store/

Obsess (2023g). Virtual Store Spotlight: Holiday World of J.Crew. Retrieved from https://obsessar.com/blog-jcrew-virtual-experience/

Obsess (2023h). Virtual Store Spotlight: The Ralpf Lauren Virtual Experience. Retrieved from https://obsessar.com/blog-ralph-lauren-virtual-stores/

Obsess (2024a). Insights into immersive experiences in retail, based on a 2023 survey. Retrieved from https://obsessar.com/blog-immersive-experiences-in-retail-insights/

Obsess (2024b). J.Crew partners with Obsess to launch the first-ever virtual closet for Apple Vision Pro. Retrieved from https://obsessar.com/j-crew-for-apple-vision-pro/

Obsess (2024c). Obsess launches 4 of the first-ever shopping apps for apple vision pro. Retrieved from https://obsessar.com/obsess-launches-4-of-the-first-ever-shopping-apps-for-apple-vision-pro/

Obsess (2024d). Salon Tycoon in amikaverse: Powered by Obsess. Retrieved from https://www.youtube.com/watch?reload=9&v=N0GRzuJVVwM

Oehlrich, M. (2022). *Wissenschaftliches Arbeiten und Schreiben: Schritt für Schritt zur Bachelor- und Master-Thesis in den Wirtschaftswissenschaften* (3rd ed.). *Lehrbuch*. Wiesbaden, Heidelberg: Springer Gabler. https://doi.org/10.1007/978-3-658-34791-8

Palmer, A. (2010). Customer experience management: a critical review of an emerging idea. *Journal of Services Marketing, 24*(3), 196–208. https://doi.org/10.1108/08876041011040604

Palmer, M. T. (1995). Interpersonal communication and virtual reality: Mediating interpersonal relationships. In F. Biocca & M. R. Levy (Eds.), *Communication in the Age of Virtual Reality* (pp. 277–299). New York: Lawrence Erlbaum Associates, Inc.

Pan, J. (2023). Retail everywhere. Retrieved from https://jonpan.medium.com/retail-everywhere-74a42b97c56a

Pantano, E., & Servidio, R. (2012). Modeling innovative points of sales through virtual and immersive technologies. *Journal of Retailing and Consumer Services, 19*(3), 279–286. https://doi.org/10.1016/j.jretconser.2012.02.002

Papagiannidis, S., See-To, E., & Bourlakis, M. (2014). Virtual test-driving: The impact of simulated products on purchase intention. *Journal of Retailing and Consumer Services, 21*(5), 877–887. https://doi.org/10.1016/j.jretconser.2014.02.010

Park, S.-M., & Kim, Y.-G. (2022). A Metaverse: Taxonomy, Components, Applications, and Open Challenges. *IEEE Access, 10*, 4209–4251. https://doi.org/10.1109/ACCESS.2021.3140175

Perri, L. (2022a). What's New in the 2022 Gartner Hype Cycle for Emerging Technologies. Retrieved from https://www.gartner.com/en/articles/what-s-new-in-the-2022-gartner-hype-cycle-for-emerging-technologies

Perri, L. (2022b). Die 10 wichtigsten strategischen Prognosen von Gartner für 2023 und darüber hinaus. Retrieved from https://www.gartner.de/de/artikel/die-10-wichtigsten-strategischen-prognosen-von-gartner-fuer-2023-und-darueber-hinaus

Perri, L. (2024). 30 Emerging Technologies That Will Guide Your Business Decisions. Retrieved from https://www.gartner.com/en/articles/30-emerging-technologies-that-will-guide-your-business-decisions

Petereit, D. (2024). Webdesign: Diese Trends für 2024 musst du kennen. Retrieved from https://t3n.de/news/webdesign-trends-2024-kennen-1597796/

Petro, G. (2022). Gen Z Set To Lead Retailers Into The Metaverse. Retrieved from https://www.forbes.com/sites/gregpetro/2022/05/14/gen-z-set-to-lead-retailers-into-the-metaverse/

Pfeiffer, J. (2023). Von E-Commerce zu Virtual Commerce: Was Einkaufserlebnisse in virtuellen Welten so spannend macht. *Nürnberg Institut Für Marktentscheidungen E. V., 15*(2), 10–17. Retrieved from https://www.nim.org/fileadmin/user_upload/2023_NIM_MIR_Virtuelle_Konsumerlebnisse_DE.pdf

Pfeiffer, T. (2023). Der Homunkulus im Metaverse: Ist Virtual Reality bereit für unsere sieben Sinne? *NIM Marketing Intelligence Review, 15*(2), 36–41. Retrieved from https://www.nim.org/fileadmin/user_upload/2023_NIM_MIR_Virtuelle_Konsumerlebnisse_DE.pdf

PFSweb, Inc. (2021). Overcome the physical disconnect: How retailers can maintain customer loyalty in an omnichannel world. Retrieved from https://marketing.pfscommerce.com/overcoming-the-physical-disconnect

Pine, B. J., & Gilmore, J. H. (1998). Welcome to the experience economy. *Harvard Business Review, 76*(4), 97–105. Retrieved from https://hbr.org/1998/07/welcome-to-the-experience-economy

Porter, S., Harrison, J., Ang, A., Golik, R., & Gupta, S. [Sandeep] (2022). What's possible for the gaming industry in the next dimension? Gaming Industry Survey 2022. EY. Retrieved from https://www.ey.com/en_us/tmt/what-s-possible-for-the-gaming-industry-in-the-next-dimension/chapter-3-insights-on-the-metaverse-and-the-future-of-gaming

Presser, S. [S.], Couper, M. P., Lessler, J. T., Martin, E., Martin, J., Rothgeb, J. M., & Singer, E. (2004). Methods for Testing and Evaluating Survey Questions. *Public Opinion Quarterly*, *68*(1), 109–130. https://doi.org/10.1093/poq/nfh008

Prüfer, P., & Rexroth, M. (2005). *Kognitive Interviews* (GESIS How-to-Reihe no. 15). Zentrum für Umfragen, Methoden und Analysen, Mannheim. Retrieved from https://nbn-resolving.org/urn:nbn:de:0168-ssoar-201470

R Core Team (2021). R: A Language and Environment for Statistical Computing. R Foundation for Statistical Computing. Retrieved from https://www.R-project.org

Ralph Lauren (2023a). The 888 House. Retrieved from https://ralphlaurenvirtualstores.com/888-house/#/en_US

Ralph Lauren (2023b). Ralph Lauren Debuts The RL 888 Handbag With Dynamic Campaign. Retrieved from https://corporate.ralphlauren.com/on/demandware.static/-/Sites-RalphLauren_Corporate-Library/default/dwbd61efa8/assets/images/PRESS_RELEASES/230822_RL888.pdf

Ray, S. [Soumya], & Danks, N. (2020). SEMinR. Retrieved from https://cran.r-project.org/web/packages/seminr/vignettes/SEMinR.html

Ray, S. [Soumya], Danks, N. P. [Nicholas Patrick], & Calero Valdez, A. (2022). seminr: Building and Estimating Structural Equation Models. Retrieved from https://cran.r-project.org/web/packages/seminr/index.html

Razorfish, & Vice Media Group (2022). The Metaverse: What gaming today teaches us about the metaverse tomorrow. Retrieved from https://www.razorfish.com/articles/perspectives/razorfish-vmg-metaverse-research/

Ready Player Me (2022). Look great anywhere with Tommy Hilfiger's Parallel collection. Retrieved from https://readyplayer.me/case-studies/look-great-anywhere-with-tommy-hilfiger-parallel-collection

Ready Player Me (2023a). Case Study: BMW's Immersive Experiences With 3D Avatars. Retrieved from https://readyplayer.me/case-studies/bmws-immersive-experiences-with-3d-avatars

Ready Player Me (2023b). What is Ready Player Me. Retrieved from https://docs.readyplayer.me/ready-player-me/what-is-ready-player-me

Ready Player Me (2024). Create your avatar and use it across thousands of games. Retrieved from https://readyplayer.me/players

Regt, A. de, & Barnes, S. J. (2019). V-Commerce in Retail: Nature and Potential Impact. In M. C. tom Dieck & T. Jung (Eds.), *Augmented Reality and Virtual Reality* (pp. 17–25). Cham: Springer International Publishing. https://doi.org/10.1007/978-3-030-06246-0_2

Repp, M., Horvat, D., Michel, A. F., & Maier, J. (2023, February 28). *Wenn der Avatar shoppen geht: Kaufen und Verkaufen im Metaverse*. Panel. dfv Conference Group, e-tailment, & Meta Platforms, Inc. Metaverse Now, Berlin. Retrieved from https://dfvcg-events.de/metaverse/

Revilla, M., & Höhne, J. K. (2020). How long do respondents think online surveys should be? New evidence from two online panels in Germany. *International Journal of Market Research*, *62*(5), 538–545. https://doi.org/10.1177/1470785320943049

Ringle, C. M., Wende, S., & Becker, J.-M. (2024a). Fit Measures in SmartPLS. Retrieved from https://www.smartpls.com/documentation/algorithms-and-techniques/model-fit/

Ringle, C. M., Wende, S., & Becker, J.-M. (2024b). SmartPLS 4 [Computer software]. Monheim am Rhein: SmartPLS GmbH: SmartPLS GmbH. Retrieved from https://www.smartpls.com

Roblox Corporation (2023). 2023 Digital Expression, Fashion & beauty Trend: How Gen Z Express Themselves in Immersive Spaces.

Roblox Corporation (2024a). Alo Sanctuary. Retrieved from https://www.roblox.com/games/8523408215/Alo-Sanctuary

Roblox Corporation (2024b). Q4 2023 Supplemental Materials. Retrieved from https://s27.q4cdn.com/984876518/files/doc_financials/2023/q4/Q4-23-Supplemental-Materials.pdf

Roblox Corporation, & Ralph Lauren (2021). The Winter Escape. Retrieved from https://www.roblox.com/games/7608438089/The-Winter-Escape

Rohleder, B. (2021). E-Commerce-Trends 2021. Retrieved from https://www.bitkom.org/sites/default/files/2021-11/bitkom-charts-pk-e-commerce-trends-2021-18-11-21.pdf

Rohleder, B. (2022). E-Commerce 2022. Retrieved from https://www.bitkom.org/sites/main/files/2022-11/Bitkom_Charts_ECommerce2022_final.pdf

Rose, S., Clark, M., Samouel, P., & Hair, N. (2012). Online Customer Experience in e-Retailing: An empirical model of Antecedents and Outcomes. *Journal of Retailing*, *88*(2), 308–322. https://doi.org/10.1016/j.jretai.2012.03.001

Rose, S., Hair, N., & Clark, M. (2011). Online Customer Experience: A Review of the Business-to-Consumer Online Purchase Context. *International Journal of Management Reviews*, *13*(1), 24–39. https://doi.org/10.1111/j.1468-2370.2010.00280.x

Rossiter, J. R. (2002). The C-OAR-SE procedure for scale development in marketing. *International Journal of Research in Marketing*, *19*(4), 305–335.

Russell, J. A., & Mehrabian, A. (1977). Evidence for a three-factor theory of emotions. *Journal of Research in Personality*, *11*(3), 273–294. https://doi.org/10.1016/0092-6566(77)90037-X

Ruusunen, N., Hallikainen, H., & Laukkanen, T. (2023). Does imagination compensate for the need for touch in 360-virtual shopping? *International Journal of Information Management*, *70*, 1–11. https://doi.org/10.1016/j.ijinfomgt.2023.102622

SAP (2024). Build 3D virtual stores with the market-leading experiential shopping platform. Retrieved from https://store.sap.com/dcp/en/product/display-2001014493_live_v1/virtual-store-platform

Sarstedt, M., Bengart, P., Shaltoni, A. M., & Lehmann, S. [Sebastian] (2018). The use of sampling methods in advertising research: a gap between theory and practice. *International Journal of Advertising*, *37*(4), 650–663. https://doi.org/10.1080/02650487.2017.1348329

Sarstedt, M., Hair, J. F., Cheah, J.-H., Becker, J.-M., & Ringle, C. M. (2019). How to Specify, Estimate, and Validate Higher-Order Constructs in PLS-SEM. *Australasian Marketing Journal*, *27*(3), 197–211. https://doi.org/10.1016/j.ausmj.2019.05.003

Sarstedt, M., & Mooi, E. (Eds.) (2019). *A Concise Guide to Market Research: The Process, Data, and Methods Using IBM SPSS Statistics* (3rd ed.). Berlin, Heidelberg: Springer Berlin Heidelberg. https://doi.org/10.1007/978-3-662-56707-4

Sarstedt, M., Ringle, C. M., & Hair, J. F. (2022). Partial Least Squares Structural Equation Modeling. In C. Homburg, M. Klarmann, & A. Vomberg (Eds.), *Handbook of Market Research* (pp. 588–613). Cham: Springer International Publishing.

Schamberger, T., Schuberth, F., Henseler, J., & Dijkstra, T. K. (2020). Robust partial least squares path modeling. *Behaviormetrika, 47*(1), 307–334. https://doi.org/10.1007/s41237-019-00088-2

Schmitt, B. (1999). Experiential Marketing. *Journal of Marketing Management, 15*(1–3), 53–67. https://doi.org/10.1362/026725799784870496

Schmitt, B. (2009). Customer Experience Management. In M. Bruhn, F.-R. Esch, & T. Langner (Eds.), *Handbuch Kommunikation: Grundlagen—Innovative Ansätze—Praktische Umsetzungen* (1st ed., pp. 697–711). Wiesbaden: Gabler.

Schmitt, B. (2011). Experience Marketing: Concepts, Frameworks and Consumer Insights. *Foundations and Trends® in Marketing, 5*(2), 55–112. https://doi.org/10.1561/1700000027

Schnack, A., Wright, M. J., & Elms, J. (2021). Investigating the impact of shopper personality on behaviour in immersive Virtual Reality store environments. *Journal of Retailing and Consumer Services, 61*, 1–11. https://doi.org/10.1016/j.jretconser.2021.102581

Schuemie, M. J., van der Straaten, P., Krijn, M., & van der Mast, C. A. (2001). Research on presence in virtual reality: A survey. *Cyberpsychology & Behavior, 4*(2), 183–201. https://doi.org/10.1089/109493101300117884

Schuman, H., & Presser, S. [Stanley] (1979). The Open and Closed Question. *American Sociological Review, 44*(5), 692. https://doi.org/10.2307/2094521

Schwertfeger, M. (2012). *Einkaufserlebnisse im Handel: Theoretische Konzeption und empirische Analyse.* Wiesbaden: Springer Fachmedien. https://doi.org/10.1007/978-3-658-00511-5

Scott, K. (2022). *Neal Stephenson, Award-winning science fiction author: Behind The Tech with Kevin Scott.* Retrieved from https://open.spotify.com/episode/28shMVkcuFvjsy8YR2kfjI?si=frJHQOP1TfKXNdmQ00i2NA

Shah, V., & Aina, J. (2023). Shop: What might shopping be like in the Metaverse? Retrieved from https://about.meta.com/what-is-the-metaverse/

Shen, B., Tan, W., Guo, J., Zhao, L., & Qin, P. (2021). How to Promote User Purchase in Metaverse? A Systematic Literature Review on Consumer Behavior Research and Virtual Commerce Application Design. *Applied Sciences, 11*(23). https://doi.org/10.3390/app112311087

Sheppard, B. H., Hartwick, J., & Warshaw, P. R. (1988). The Theory of Reasoned Action: A Meta-Analysis of Past Research with Recommendations for Modifications and Future Research. *Journal of Consumer Research, 15*(3), 325. https://doi.org/10.1086/209170

Sheth, J. N., Mittal, B., & Newman, B. I. (1999). *Customer behavior: Consumer behavior and beyond. The Dryden Press series in marketing.* Fort Worth, Philadelphia, San Diego, New York, Orlando, Austin, San Antonio, Toronto, Montreal, London, Sydney, Tokyo: The Dryden Press.

Shmueli, G. (2010). To Explain or to Predict? *Statistical Science, 25*(3). https://doi.org/10.1214/10-STS330

Shmueli, G., Ray, S. [Soumya], Velasquez Estrada, J. M., & Chatla, S. B. (2016). The elephant in the room: Predictive performance of PLS models. *Journal of Business Research, 69*(10), 4552–4564. https://doi.org/10.1016/j.jbusres.2016.03.049

Singh, N. (2023). Virtual Stores: The ultimate endpoint for 3D assets. In The Interline (Ed.), *The Digital Product Creation Report (DPC) Report* (pp. 85–87). Retrieved from https://www.theinterline.com/2023/12/13/digital-product-creation-report-2023-available-now/

Skarbez, R., Smith, M., & Whitton, M. C. (2021). Revisiting Milgram and Kishino's Reality-Virtuality Continuum. *Frontiers in Virtual Reality*, *2*. https://doi.org/10.3389/frvir.2021.647997

Solis, B. (2024). 2024: A Spatial Computing Odyssey Charts A Course To A Metaverse. Retrieved from https://www.forbes.com/sites/briansolis/2024/02/13/2024-a-spatial-computing-odyssey-charts-a-course-to-a-metaverse/

Sommer, R., Wynes, M., & Brinkley, G. (1992). Social Facilitation Effects in Shopping Behavior. *Environment and Behavior*, *24*(3), 285–297. https://doi.org/10.1177/0013916592243001

Songuer, D. (2022). Fieldnotes from the Metaverse. Retrieved from https://medium.com/fieldnotes-from-the-metaverse/fieldnotes-from-the-metaverse-neuromancer-and-snow-crash-caab3d782fb9

Sousa, R., & Voss, C. A. (2006). Service Quality in Multichannel Services Employing Virtual Channels. *Journal of Service Research*, *8*(4), 356–371. https://doi.org/10.1177/1094670506286324

Spatial (2023). MVFW: Tommy Hilfiger Monolith. Retrieved from https://www.spatial.io/s/MVFW-Tommy-Hilfiger-Monolith-642217d890a2f49f474391e4?share=6703924856899178836

Steadman, I. (2012). Tesco brings 'virtual grocery stores' to the UK. Retrieved from https://www.wired.co.uk/article/tesco-virtual-store

Stephenson, N. (1992). *Snow crash: Roman. Goldmann Blanvalet: Vol. 23686*. München: Goldmann.

Stephenson, N. (2022). *Snow Crash* (2nd ed.). New York City: Penguin Books.

Steuer, J. (1992). Defining Virtual Reality: Dimensions Determining Telepresence. *Journal of Communication*, *42*(4), 73–93. https://doi.org/10.1111/j.1460-2466.1992.tb00812.x

Suh, A., & Prophet, J. (2018). The state of immersive technology research: A literature analysis. *Computers in Human Behavior*, *86*, 77–90. https://doi.org/10.1016/j.chb.2018.04.019

Tate, A. (2022). Parallel by Tommy Hilfiger. Retrieved from https://blog.inf.ed.ac.uk/atate/2022/08/21/parallel-by-tommy-hilfiger/

Taylor Nation LLC (2023). Shop the Tree. Retrieved from https://storeuk.taylorswift.com/pages/shop-the-tree

Thomaset, K. (2023). So gelingt Marketing auf Roblox. *T3n Magazin*. (74), 116–119.

Trier, M., & Steiger, A. (2023). Kundenzufriedenheit im Virtual Reality Commerce—Erfolgreiche Interaktion in virtuellen Welten. *Wirtschaftsinformatik & Management*, *15*(3), 203–212. https://doi.org/10.1365/s35764-023-00470-6

Turner, D. P. (2020). Sampling Methods in Research Design. *Headache*, *60*(1), 8–12. https://doi.org/10.1111/head.13707

UK Safer Internet Centre (2022). What is Skin Gambling in Gaming? Retrieved from https://saferinternet.org.uk/blog/what-is-skin-gambling-in-gaming

Vans, & Roblox Corporation (2021). Vans World. Retrieved from https://www.vans.de/roblox-vans-world.html?srsltid=AfmBOoqLQQtUb2elpupCkG77d_zytzPHJ547dW8uxmk70qpFv5uD43Ht

Venkatesh, Morris, & Davis (2003). User Acceptance of Information Technology: Toward a Unified View. *MIS Quarterly*, *27*(3), 425. https://doi.org/10.2307/30036540

Venkatesh, Thong, & Xu (2012). Consumer Acceptance and Use of Information Technology: Extending the Unified Theory of Acceptance and Use of Technology. *MIS Quarterly*, *36*(1), 157. https://doi.org/10.2307/41410412

Verhoef, P. C., Lemon, K. N., Parasuraman, A. P., & Roggeveen, A. L. (2009). Customer Experience Creation: Determinants, Dynamics, and Management Strategies. *Journal of Retailing*, *85*(1), 31–41. https://doi.org/10.1016/j.jretai.2008.11.001

Virtuloc, s. (2022). Yamaha Virtual Showroom. Retrieved from https://www.youtube.com/watch?v=IVVXKvKqn4Q

Vomberg, A., & Klarmann, M. (2022). Crafting Survey Research: A Systematic Process for Conducting Survey Research. In C. Homburg, M. Klarmann, & A. Vomberg (Eds.), *Handbook of Market Research* (pp. 67–120). Cham: Springer International Publishing.

Vrechopoulos, A. P., O'Keefe, R. M., Doukidis, G. I., & Siomkos, G. J. (2004). Virtual store layout: an experimental comparison in the context of grocery retail. *Journal of Retailing*, *80*(1), 13–22. https://doi.org/10.1016/j.jretai.2004.01.006

Wakefield, K. L., & Baker, J. [Julie] (1998). Excitement at the mall: Determinants and effects on shopping response. *Journal of Retailing*, *74*(4), 515–539. https://doi.org/10.1016/S0022-4359(99)80106-7

Warshaw, P. R., & Davis, F. D. (1985). Disentangling behavioral intention and behavioral expectation. *Journal of Experimental Social Psychology*, *21*(3), 213–228. https://doi.org/10.1016/0022-1031(85)90017-4

Wedel, M., Bigné, E., & Zhang, J. (2020). Virtual and augmented reality: Advancing research in consumer marketing. *International Journal of Research in Marketing*, *37*(3), 443–465. https://doi.org/10.1016/j.ijresmar.2020.04.004

Weiber, R., & Sarstedt, M. (2021). *Strukturgleichungsmodellierung: Eine anwendungsorientierte Einführung in die Kausalanalyse mit Hilfe von AMOS, SmartPLS und SPSS* (3rd ed.). Wiesbaden: Springer Fachmedien Wiesbaden. https://doi.org/10.1007/978-3-658-32660-9

Weijters, B., Cabooter, E., & Schillewaert, N. (2010). The effect of rating scale format on response styles: The number of response categories and response category labels. *International Journal of Research in Marketing*, *27*(3), 236–247. https://doi.org/10.1016/j.ijresmar.2010.02.004

Weinberg, P. (1992). *Erlebnismarketing*. München: Vahlen.

Weiß, E.-M. (2023). Metaverse-VP Shah über Avatare, Interoperabilität und die Zukunft des Internets. Retrieved from https://www.heise.de/hintergrund/Metaverse-VP-Shah-ueber-Avatare-Interoperabilitaet-und-die-Zukunft-des-Internets-9213707.html

White Baker, E., Hubona, G. S., & Srite, M. (2019). Does "Being There" Matter? The Impact of Web-Based and Virtual World's Shopping Experiences on Consumer Purchase Attitudes. *Information & Management*, *56*(7). https://doi.org/10.1016/j.im.2019.02.008

Whiting, K. (2023). Consumer, enterprise or industrial? The 3 main ways we are using the 'metaverse' explained. Retrieved from https://www.weforum.org/agenda/2023/02/metaverse-use-cases-industrial-consumer-enterprise/

Whyte, J. (2002). *Virtual Reality and the Built Environment*. Routledge. https://doi.org/10.4324/9780080520667

Wiggers, K. (2023). Emperia is helping brands like Bloomingdales build shopping experiences in VR. Retrieved from https://techcrunch.com/2023/01/25/emperia-is-helping-brands-build-shopping-experiences-in-vr

Willemsen, B. (2023). Gartner Top 10 Strategic Technology Trends for 2024. Retrieved from https://www.gartner.com/en/articles/gartner-top-10-strategic-technology-trends-for-2024

Wilson, B. (2010). Using PLS to Investigate Interaction Effects Between Higher Order Branding Constructs. In V. Esposito Vinzi, W. W. Chin, J. Henseler, & H. Wang (Eds.), *Handbook of Partial Least Squares* (pp. 621–652). Berlin, Heidelberg: Springer Berlin Heidelberg. https://doi.org/10.1007/978-3-540-32827-8_28

Wold, H. (1966). Estimation of Principal Components and Related Models by Iterative Least Squares. In P. R. Krishnajah (Ed.), *Multivariate Analysis* (pp. 391–420). New York: Academic Press.

Wootton, C. (2023, November 15). *Growing our Brands Business*. Roblox Corporation. Investor Day 2023, Webcast. Retrieved from https://youtu.be/pcsUexdj-tU

World Economic Forum, & Accenture (2023). Demystifying the Consumer Metaverse. Retrieved from https://www3.weforum.org/docs/WEF_Demystifying_the_Consumer_Metaverse.pdf

Xi, N., & Hamari, J. (2021). Shopping in virtual reality: A literature review and future agenda. *Journal of Business Research, 134*, 37–58. https://doi.org/10.1016/j.jbusres.2021.04.075

Yim, M. Y.-C., Chu, S.-C., & Sauer, P. L. (2017). Is Augmented Reality Technology an Effective Tool for E-commerce? An Interactivity and Vividness Perspective. *Journal of Interactive Marketing, 39*, 89–103. https://doi.org/10.1016/j.intmar.2017.04.001

Zaharia, S., & Hackstetter, T. (2017). Segmentierung von Onlinekäufern auf Basis ihrer Einkaufsmotive. In *Dialogmarketing Perspektiven 2016/2017* (pp. 45–72). Wiesbaden: Springer Fachmedien Wiesbaden. https://doi.org/10.1007/978-3-658-16835-3_3

Zaharia, S., & Schmitz, M. (2019). Customer Experience in Online-Retailing: An Analysis of the Main Segments in German Online-Retailing. International Conference on Applied Human Factors and Ergonomics.

Zalando SE (2023). Zalando brings a virtual fitting room pilot to millions of customers. Retrieved from https://corporate.zalando.com/en/technology/zalando-brings-virtual-fitting-room-pilot-millions-customers

Zentes, J., Morschett, D., & Schramm-Klein, H. (2017). *Strategic Retail Management: Text and International Cases* (3rd ed.). Wiesbaden: Springer Fachmedien Wiesbaden. https://doi.org/10.1007/978-3-658-10183-1

Zentes, J., Swoboda, B., & Foscht, T. (2012). *Handelsmanagement* (3rd ed.). Vahlen. https://doi.org/10.15358/9783800644254

Zentes, J., Swoboda, B., Morschett, D., & Schramm-Klein, H. (Eds.) (2012). *Handbuch Handel: Strategien—Perspektiven—Internationaler Wettbewerb* (2nd ed.). Wiesbaden: Springer Gabler. https://doi.org/10.1007/978-3-8349-3847-3

Zitron, E. (2023). RIP Metaverse. Retrieved from https://www.businessinsider.com/metaverse-dead obituary-facebook-mark-zuckerberg-tech-fad-ai-chatgpt-2023-5

Zuckerberg, M. (2021). Founder's Letter, 2021. Retrieved from https://about.fb.com/news/2021/10/founders-letter/

The manufacturer's authorised representative in the EU is Springer Nature Customer Service Centre GmbH, Europaplatz 3, 69115 Heidelberg, Germany. If you have any concerns regarding our products, please contact ProductSafety@springernature.com

Printed and bound by CPI Group (UK) Ltd, Croydon, CR0 4YY

01/10/2026

02225951-0003